THE D

MODERN SOCIETY

ONE WEEK LOAN

Other titles available from The Policy Press include:

Beyond the threshold: The measurement and analysis of social exclusion edited by Graham Room ISBN 1 86134 003 6 £13.95

The Gypsy and the State: The ethnic cleansing of British society (2nd edn) by Derek Hawes ISBN 1 86134 011 7 £14.95

Social insurance in Europe edited by Jochen Clasen ISBN 1 86134 054 0 £16.95

Partnership against poverty and exclusion? Local regeneration strategies and excluded communities in the UK by Mike Geddes ISBN 1 86134 071 0 £12.95

Setting adequacy standards: How governments define minimum incomes by John Veit-Wilson ISBN 1 86134 072 9 £11.95

[All the above titles are available from
Biblios Publishers' Distribution Services Ltd, Star Road, Partridge Green, West Sussex RH13 8LD, UK
Telephone +44 (0)1403 710971, Fax +44 (0)1403 711143]

THE DYNAMICS OF
MODERN SOCIETY

Poverty, policy and welfare

Edited by Lutz Leisering and Robert Walker

First published in Great Britain in 1998 by

The Policy Press
University of Bristol
Rodney Lodge
Grange Road
Bristol BS8 4EA

Telephone +44 (0)117 973 8797
Fax +44 (0) 117 973 7308
e-mail: tpp@bristol.ac.uk
Website: http://www.bristol.ac.uk/Publications/TPP

British Library Cataloguing in Publication Data
A catalogue record for this book is available from the British Library

ISBN 1 86134 059 1

Lutz Leisering is Reader in Sociology and Social Policy at the University of Bremen. **Robert Walker** is Director of the Social Security Unit, Centre for Research in Social Policy, Loughborough University.

Front cover: Photograph supplied by Mark Simmons, Bristol.
Cover design: Qube, Bristol.

Printed in Great Britain by Ashford Press, Southampton.

Contents

Acknowledgements

The roots of this volume lie in David Ellwood's path-breaking analysis of poverty and welfare spells in the US during the 1980s. Having met David in the late 1980s the British editor brought these ideas to Britain and Stephan Leibfried did likewise in Germany. By the early 1990s the British and the German research teams (the latter co-directed by the German editor) had published monographs (Walker with Ashworth, 1994; Leibfried/Leisering et al, 1995), and forged links with each other: the idea of drawing together leading European and American scholars pursuing the new approach to society and poverty was born.

There are many people and organisations to thank: the Anglo-German Foundation for the Study of Industrial Society, for funding the initial seminar at Bremen, North Germany, from which this volume emerged; and to the following for the generous support they gave to this seminar: Dr Cunningham and Dr Martin, the Hans-Böckler-Foundation of the German Trade Union Congress (DGB); Dr Mezger, and the Deutsche Forschungs-gemeinschaft (German Research Council) given as part of its research programme on life course studies (Sfb 186) at the University of Bremen, headed by Walter Heinz. We also thank Stephan Leibfried who initiated the cooperation between the editors and their research teams at Bremen and Loughborough, the authors and their discussants, Lynn Hanna who helped with redrafting, and last, but by no means least, Rosie Woolley, Sharon Walker, Lisa Bäuml, Dörte Simon and Olaf Jürgens who prepared the manuscript. All the above should share the credit for the completion of this volume while the two editors alone bear responsibility for any remaining shortcomings.

Notes on contributors

Jutta Allmendinger is a professor at the Institute of Sociology, University of Munich.

Karl Ashworth is a research fellow in the Centre for Research in Social Policy, Loughborough University.

Petra Buhr is a research fellow at the Special Research Centre 186, University of Bremen.

David Ellwood is Malcolm Wiener Professor of Public Policy and Academic Dean, John F. Kennedy School of Government, Harvard University.

Jonathan Gershuny is Director of the ESRC Research Centre on Micro-Social Change at the University of Essex.

Bjørn Gustafsson is a professor at the University of Göteburg.

Daniel Hill is a research scientist at the Institute for Survey Research at the University of Michigan, Ann Arbor.

Martha Hill is a research scientist at the Institute for Survey Research at the University of Michigan, Ann Arbor.

Thomas Hinz is a lecturer at the Institute of Sociology, University of Munich.

Sarah Jarvis is a research fellow at the ESRC Research Centre on Micro-Social Change at the University of Essex.

Stephen Jenkins is Research Professor at the ESRC Research Centre on Micro-Social Change at the University of Essex.

Peter Krause is a research scientist at the German Institute of Economic Research in Berlin.

Lutz Leisering is a reader in Sociology and a research scientist at the Special Research Centre 186, University of Bremen.

Stephen McKay is a research fellow in the Centre for Research in Social Policy at the Loughborough University.

Andreas Motel is a research fellow at the Institute of Sociology, Free University of Berlin.

Andrew Shaw was a research fellow in the Centre for Research in Social Policy, Loughborough University and is now a research executive for Social and Community Planning Research.

Wolfgang Voges is a research scientist at the Centre for Social Policy Research, University of Bremen.

Michael Wagner is a professor at the Institute of Sociology, University of Cologne.

Robert Walker is Director of the Social Security Unit, Centre for Research in Social Policy, Loughborough University and Professor of Social Policy Research.

Andreas Weber is a research fellow at the Centre for Social Policy Research at the University of Bremen.

List of tables and figures

Tables

Figures

Preface

Societies are having to adapt at an increasing pace to powerful external and internal pressures. The globalisation of the economy, with the growing influence of international corporations and supranational political organisations, is imposing limits on the freedom of national states. Within economically advanced Western economies, the current concomitants of globalisation are higher unemployment, limited job tenure, increased inequality and financial insecurity for large parts of the population.

At the same time, new lifestyles are emerging which emphasise consumption rather than production and often entail novel, more transitory and individualistic forms of family life. These developments can, in turn, devalue the sense of community, restrict allegiances between generations and challenge the capacity of conventional redistributive policies.

Fortuitously, at a time when social and economic forces are making instability a way of life, researchers have developed new modes of enquiry that take account of the dynamic nature of people's lives. Approaches to 'thinking dynamically' have triggered the beginning of an intellectual revolution, one that blends insights from across the social sciences, merges quantitative and qualitative methodologies, combines macro and micro views of society and exploits the power of international comparison.

The mission of these researchers is to describe, explain and understand the radical shifts in individual behaviour, and in the roles of social institutions, that are characteristic of a modern, post-industrial society. Their incentive is the need to make policy that will be effective in a rapidly changing world. Past theories, essentially static in form, are challenged by new ways of thinking. These are in turn supported empirically by panel surveys, which allow people's circumstances to be tracked over time, and by the powerful computer software and statistical techniques used to analyse these. Great questions of our time are disentangled by linking social change to the changing life course patterns of individuals and vice versa.

This collection of essays aims to contribute to this new science of society as well as illustrate its importance for public policy making. It does this by taking an international perspective and focusing primarily on poverty and the receipt of social assistance benefits. Poverty can be likened to the miner's canary of old: through its death a canary revealed the presence of methane long before the miners themselves had become aware of it. Poverty in its turn is extremely sensitive to social change: it increases and changes in form before society has fully faced up to the underlying social change. However, poverty is not a benign social indicator; poor people suffer like the canary and its very existence is a challenge to action.

Studies of class mobility, family processes and the careers of marginalised individuals demonstrate that scholars have long been interested in the dynamics of individual lives. However, the means to study these issues adequately, to link theory with empirical evidence, have only recently become available in Europe with the arrival of panel data and the concepts and techniques necessary to handle them. The first results from research into the micro-dynamics of poverty and social assistance have already revolutionised these fields of study and begun to influence the formulation of policy.

The first information which will enable the dynamics of welfare to be studied from an international comparative perspective is already being collected. However, while comprehensive, dynamic analysis of the European Panel Study (Europanel) is still some years away, this volume includes early results from two ongoing European comparative studies: Karl Ulrich Mayer's Eurocareers Project **(Chapter Five)** and one on social assistance careers led by Stephan Leibfried and Lutz Leisering **(Chapter Fourteen)**. Linking evidence from this type of sources to current theories of late modernity, we particularly draw on the work of German and British sociologists, notably Ulrich Beck and Anthony Giddens.

The volume is divided into five sections. The chapters in **Part One** briefly review the economic and social developments, sometimes termed 'modernism' or 'late/post modernism', that have created the need for a new social science **(Chapter One)**, introduce the key concepts that underlie the dynamic approach **(Chapters Two and Three)**, and show how dynamic analysis has already

influenced the process of welfare reform in the United States
(**Chapter Four**).

Part Two is devoted to life course dynamics. **Chapter Five**
explores the ways in which the life course is moulded differently
by the unique institutions providing training and education in
Britain, Germany and Sweden. **Chapter Six** investigates the
influence of parental circumstances as determinants of social and
economic success in early adulthood in the USA, the only country
with an annual panel survey stretching as far back as 1968.
Chapter Seven focuses on the dynamics of lone parenthood in
Britain while **Chapter Eight** considers income dynamics in old age
in Germany.

The two chapters which make up **Part Three** on poverty
dynamics examine the situation in Britain and Germany
respectively. **Chapter Nine** documents the pattern of flows in and
out of poverty and considers the implications of these new
findings for traditional theories of the nature and causes of
poverty. **Chapter Ten** provides a parallel analysis but one which
straddles the unification of Germany. It shows that from 1993
onwards after the unification boom, unemployment and poverty
increased. Nevertheless, a transitory boost to labour market and
income maintenance policies at an unprecedented scale succeeded
in smoothing the transition.

Part Four focuses on the traditional response to poverty, the
provision of social security and, especially, means-tested social
assistance. The first two chapters examine the effect of major
political and economic shocks: **Chapter Eleven** considers the
impact on German social assistance of the collapse of communism
in Eastern Europe and of the influx of refugees from various parts
of the world, while **Chapter Twelve** examines the consequences of
the major economic recession of the early 1990s on the British
social welfare system. The next two chapters examine the
dynamics of social assistance in more detail. **Chapter Thirteen**
focuses on the routes off benefit that people in Britain take and the
barriers that stand in their way. **Chapter Fourteen** contrasts
provisions in Germany and Sweden, explores the reasons for
differences and considers some of the implications.

The final section, **Part Five**, draws together the main themes
that bind the volume together: that the dynamic approach is both
a theory and a method; that it changes the conceptualisation of
social phenomena and social problems; that it offers new

understanding and insight; that it predicates different policy agendas; and that it provides an essential strategy for interpreting and responding to the challenges created by modernity.

Part One

Changing concepts

Part One

one

New realities: the dynamics of modernity

Lutz Leisering and Robert Walker

> Modern institutions differ from all preceding
> forms of social order in respect of their
> dynamism. (Giddens, 1991, p 1)

Dynamism is the distinctive feature of modernity. The nature and
rate of change distinguishes modern societies from those which
went before. Our more or less successful attempts to cope with
the changes in our own lives, and in the institutions that surround
and define us, help to make us what we are.

This central theme is developed in this opening chapter by
considering first the nature of the changes affecting individuals
and social institutions and secondly, the emergence of the
'individual', the 'self' and the 'life course' as new social entities.
These ideas are then further explored with reference to the
changed understanding of poverty.

The emphasis given to poverty in this volume should not be
surprising. The modern welfare state is an institutional response
to social problems of modernity, and to poverty in particular.
Different welfare regimes can be classified in terms of the priority
they give to relieving or eradicating poverty. Nations are
repeatedly ranked and evaluated with respect to their current
poverty rates. Poverty often provides an early warning of the
effects of fundamental social change.

Dynamics of modernity – society and individual

Since the Enlightenment, ideas of progress, growth and improvement have been central to the collective ideology of advanced societies. While traditional societies also witnessed dramatic changes and transformations, the dynamism of modern society resides in novel institutions that display an intrinsic propensity to continual and unlimited change. It is this propensity, and not change as such, that we refer to as dynamism. Many years ago Karl Marx and Max Weber described the momentum of functional rationalities operating in the market economy, in large-scale bureaucracies, in science and technology and in other social spheres. This is part of the process of societal differentiation. Anthony Giddens identifies three motors generating the dynamics of modern societies (1991, pp 16-21): the emergence of large social structures that gain momentum beyond the actions of individuals; the modern principle of constantly revising knowledge and practices, and the processes of globalisation that open up new horizons in space and time.[1]

The emergence of large structures and global processes does not mean that the individual has become a *quantité négligeable*. On the contrary, the unfolding of societal dynamics that we are currently experiencing relies on the specific dynamics of individual lives. As Giddens notes (1991, p 32), "for the first time in human history, 'self' and 'society' are interrelated in a global milieu". In traditional societies the key link between societal change and individual action was the succession of generations. Each generation passed on its sociocultural heritage to the next. Innovations occurred but changes within the lifetime of one generation were normally limited. In today's society individuals have to undergo and effect more changes in their own lifetimes than their predecessors. This is the meaning of 'lifelong learning'. It follows that the succession of generations is speeding up. 'Social generations' conceived in terms of shared ideas and habits (Mannheim, 1952 [German 1928]) succeed each other at a faster rate.

Individual mobility is crucial to modernity. It is a functional prerequisite of changes in social structures such as the transition from agricultural to industrial production and to a service society. Mobility is also a powerful means by which people drive forward their ambitions in life. Irrespective of the factual mobility that occurs, the idea of mobility is fundamental to the legitimisation of

Western societies. The promise of mobility allows 'open societies' to maintain a system of firmly established structural inequalities. The optimism about macro-dynamics, the belief in societal progress, translates on the micro-level into the belief in individual progress.

Robert Erikson and John Goldthorpe (1992, p 5) have specified three components in the self-interpretation of open societies. The first is mobility, with more upward than downward movements. The second is the belief that mobility is widespread and that social positions are acquired by achievement rather than being ascribed so are open to all citizens. Finally, there is the promise that both mobility and the openness of access will increase with socioeconomic development, thereby progressively tearing down the barriers of class. Certainly, the pace of life has accelerated in many ways during the postwar decades. People are experiencing faster changes in jobs, occupations and qualifications, income, knowledge, spouses and in many other walks of life.

However, the picture of a wholesale increase in life dynamics is misleading. Various cross-currents operate. Traffic flow in some big cities is getting slower; administrative and court procedures are tending to become more cumbersome and lengthy; some growth processes are reaching built-in limits, for example, the upgrading of educational achievement and the attainment of what Fred Hirsch (1977) has called 'positional goods'. There are also cross-currents on the level of macro-dynamics. One example is that in European countries the demographic renewal of the population has reached an all-time low due to falling birth rates. The result is that smaller new generations have to carry a bigger share of social change than their ancestors (cf Kaufmann, 1975). However, most importantly, the class barriers to social mobility have remained more or less unchanged. While there has been more upward than downward mobility, resulting in a general upgrading of the stratification structure, the openness or fluidity of the social hierarchy has not increased – the structure is in a state of 'constant flux' (Erikson and Goldthorpe, 1992). If the degree of individual socioeconomic mobility is measured in relative terms (thereby discounting the mobility resulting from a general upgrading of the occupational structure), it can be said to have remained fairly constant over time (Erikson and Goldthorpe, 1992, pp 367f). The rate of relative mobility varies little between Western countries.

The liberal belief in socioeconomic progress, currently being revitalised under the name of 'globalisation', requires quali-fication. The open society has only partially fulfilled its promise. There are countervailing forces, with elites seeking to secure their power and privilege, which create processes of social closure. However, the promise of equal opportunity and increased mobility persists. The general trend towards the upgrading of jobs and higher incomes, reflected in rising *absolute* mobility rates, lends empirical support to this idea. It is absolute, rather than relative mobility which shapes the experience and expectations of individuals. Mass consumption, with rapid changes in fashions of consumption, may well add to the impression of rising mobility. However, the promise of equal opportunity as a means of legitimising inequality can only be sustained by powerful 'national mythologies' (Erikson and Goldthorpe, 1992, p 372, cf p 23 and p 368). It must also be acknowledged that societies place differing emphasis on the idea of mobility. The USA epitomises the culture of mobility and yet there is little evidence that mobility rates there are much higher than in other countries.

As an alternative to the idea of increasing mobility, Erikson and Goldthorpe discuss models of cyclical and directionless dynamics as expounded in works by Sorokin, Lipset and Zetterberg and Featherman, Jones and Hauser. One version suggests that socioeconomic development may comprise a series of thresholds, structural disconformities that generate a regime characterised by high rates of mobility, followed by periods during which mobility remains constant or even falls due to counter-vailing forces of social closure. There is evidence that in some countries the early phase of industrialisation was associated with such a threshold, and many believe that we are encountering a similar developmental threshold now. However, the effects of the significantly enhanced dynamics evident in markets, technologies, knowledge and social organisation on the dynamics of individual lives are not yet clear.

Individualism, life course and the state

The individual is not just an adjunct of abstract social structures. The rise of the modern individual is part and parcel of the rise of modern society. Modernity implies the institutionalisation of the '*individual*', the '*self*' and the '*life course*' as new social entities. In pre-modern times a person belonged entirely to one social setting: a local community, in which several social functions were fused. In modern times, processes of 'functional differentiation' described by Parsons (1966) and Luhmann (1977) and 'social disembedding' as depicted by Giddens (1991) have dissociated social relationships from local contexts. In this way the individual has emerged as a separate social unit that must coordinate activities in diverse social spheres that are differentiated by function. With increasing globalisation, the pressure imposed on individuals by functional systems mounts still further. These external pressures are paralleled by the quest for new forms of self-expression, life planning and lifestyles intrinsic to the modern individual.

The notion of a free individual, of an autonomous agent guided by reason, is a liberal idea of the 18th and 19th centuries, still alive in the 20th century. However, there is more to this idea than the notion of the free market. Even American sociologists have emphasised that the institutional requisites of individualism extend beyond economic freedom. Parsons identifies the Educational Revolution, together with the Industrial Revolution and the Democratic Revolution, as the main sources of 'institutionalised individualism' (Parsons and Platt, 1974, p 1; cf Meyer, 1986a). Janowitz (1976) sees the welfare state as a stage in the development of a liberal democracy which aims to self-perfect the individual through therapy and social treatment. Inherent in this idea is the notion of the individual subject to continual self-redefinition and redefinition by others. Meyer (1986b), for one, conceives the 'self' as a cultural project of personal growth and development, produced and disseminated by Western development agencies, teachers and psychologists across the world.

Along parallel lines, the Swiss-German sociologist Martin Kohli (1986) has argued that increasingly people in the 19th and 20th century live their lives not from a day-to-day perspective but with an eye on their entire life span. Increased life expectancy, social security systems that allow long-term life planning, and cultural images of individual development have forged 'the life course' as a new social institution that constitutes modern individuality. This modern self does not have the substantive identity that is assumed in the traditional philosophical concept of the autonomous subject.   Rather self-identity is continually constructed by the individuals by way of reflexive ordering of their biographies (Chapter 3, Giddens, 1991, pp 53, 80, 145ff; Brose and Hildenbrand, 1988). The self is part of the modern principle of constantly revising knowledge and practices referred to as 'reflexivity' by Giddens (cf fn 1).

This volume focuses on the impact of the state and public policy on life course dynamics. The modern individual and the modern state, far from being adversaries, now mutually reinforce each other. The individual as an autonomous agent is the result of processes of social inclusion and of widening participation, secured by law and state policies. The welfare state is the third stage in the evolution of citizenship as delineated by Marshall (1950) in his model of the emergence of civil, political and social rights.   Rights of citizenship pertain to individuals, not to aggregate entities such as social groups or nations. Social rights, in particular, define individual entitlements to goods and services. While economic policies aim at raising aggregate outcomes, such as gross net product or export rates that are expected to have an influence on individual welfare, social policies are immediately targeted on individual lives. More specifically, the welfare state is a key force in creating the life course, that is in shaping the *temporal order of individual lives*.

While in public debate the welfare state is often associated with a move towards equality and vertical redistribution between rich and poor, in practice horizontal redistribution during the *life cycle* prevails (Falkingham and Hills, 1995). This was so in the formative years of the welfare state: children and the elderly were the first client groups to be singled out by public policies and hence constituted the first 'welfare classes' (Kaufmann and Leisering, 1984; Leisering, 1992, Chapter 1).   Intertemporal redistribution became a principle of Bismarckean German social insurance and was explicit in Beveridge's approach to reforming social security in Britain in the 1940s (Glennerster, 1995, pp 13f). Today, an interest in the life cycle has been rekindled by concern about the consequences of increased life expectancy and imminent changes in the age structure of the population.

However, the expansion of the welfare state and the pluralisation of lifestyles mean that social policies are no longer limited to redistribution across the life cycle (Mayer and Müller 1986). The concept of the 'life cycle', relating to age and the family cycle, is quasi-biological and static and may have outlived its usefulness. A more recent term, the 'life course', denotes a temporal order of life shaped by institutions and public policies and propelled by continual biographical decisions made by the individual. Present-day social policy is *'life-course policy'* (Leibfried/Leisering et al, 1995, Chapter 1).[2]

Education and old age insurance, for example, contribute to the social definition of childhood, youth and old age, thereby *structuring* the life course with the three standard phases of youth, adulthood and old age. Social policy systems also establish relationships between the different phases and stages of life and hence *integrate* the life course. Education in youth enhances life chances in adulthood. Likewise, senior citizen pensions allow adults in their working life to be certain about their retirement prospects. Systems of risk management such as unemployment insurance, social assistance and accident insurance, bridge life's financial discontinuities at whatever stage they occur. Welfare states differ with regard to the emphasis they put on each of these three domains. In the USA, public policy gives priority to education, whereas the German welfare state, for example, centres on a comprehensive scheme of old age insurance. Risk management is stronger in the UK and in Germany than in the USA.

In addition to the policies of structuration and integration, there is a hidden social policy agenda geared to shaping the life course according to *normative models* relating to class and gender. Schools and universities not only convey knowledge but also distinctive norms of behaviour, lifestyle and habits. This 'hidden curriculum' in education, most pronounced in Germany and the UK, reinforces differences of class (in Germany by a tripartite high school system) and gender. Earnings-related old-age pensions reinforce a 'normal life course' based on a full employment history of the male breadwinner. By grading the level of benefits according to distance from the labour market, the systems of risk management act as work incentives. These different social policy outcomes – normally the focus of separate fields of research and hence not usually viewed as a whole – together help to construct and define the life course. The three dimensions of the impact of the welfare state on the life course – structuration, integration, normative modelling – are depicted in Figure 1.1, referring to the three main areas of social policy: education, senior citizen pensions, and risk management. Structuration, integration, and normative modelling can be envisaged as nested 'belts' of the institutionalisation of the life course by the welfare state.

Figure 1.1: Life course and the welfare state

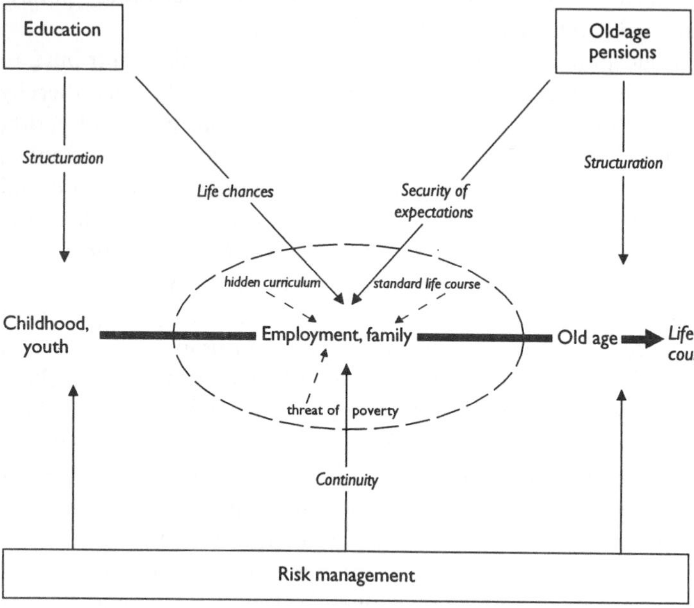

Source: adapted from Leisering (1995a)

Policy makers face a double challenge: the increased dynamics affecting the large institutions and social structures are paralleled by radical changes in individual lifestyles. Each impacts on the other: individual life course patterns need to adapt to new structures of social organisation, while social institutions and public policies need to be redesigned to meet the exigencies of new ways of living. As a result, new intellectual questions and new challenges for policy emerge. Do new macro-dynamics lead to increased individual mobility? Or is there a discongruity between rising mobility experienced by the upper strata of society and life chances of those in the lower strata being frozen or even deteriorating (Massey, 1996)? Or, again, are we facing a divergence between different spheres of life, with lifestyles and consumption patterns rapidly changing while the class structure of society remains more or less constant? Do the new life-course dynamics enhance the quality of life or do they simply lead to social dislocation?

The experience during the last 20 years is that developments are seldom universally disruptive or beneficial and that the traditional tendency for social theorists to juxtapose dichotomous alternatives does not do full justice to the complexity of modern life. Growing unemployment and reductions in social spending have, for example, been paralleled by the growing economic security of the elderly (resulting from increased assets, private and occupational pensions and the enhanced pension entitlements acquired by women). The challenge for policy makers is to predict which developments are potentially most destructive and which are more or less benign, and to act early enough to protect and support those most likely to be detrimentally affected.

Poverty dynamics

Poverty is the illegitimate lower end of the structure of inequality (Marshall, 1972). It is not just one of many social problems but an indicator, a mirror or a seismograph, reflecting a whole range of ongoing social changes. No change in social life, no rise and no fall comes about without leaving a sediment among the poor (Simmel, 1908). Politically, poverty marks the moral bottom line that should not be crossed. To avoid, or at least to alleviate poverty, is the common denominator of most welfare states, although the 1996 welfare reform in the USA shows even this communality is not immune to change. Anglo-Saxon countries – adopting the so-called poverty approach – have made the relief of poverty their overriding goal. Others have sought to go further to secure the living standards of the middle class against periods of risk; the German social insurance state or the reformed Swedish model of the 1990s are obvious examples of this approach. Paradoxically, the more that welfare state provisions in a country go beyond combating poverty, the more poverty comes to be considered a product of the state. In such circumstances poverty, measured, for example, by the number of claimants of social assistance, points to gaps and deficiencies in the first line social security systems.

Liberal theories assume that mobility in capitalist societies overall is upward, whereas Marxists predict a general downward movement, resulting in proletarianisation, increasing misery (*Verelendung*) and, in recent times, deskilling and dequalification. While the Marxist model is not well supported by empirical evidence (Erikson and Goldthorpe, 1992, p 369f), the service proletariat, consisting mostly of women, has been growing (Esping-Andersen, 1993). This development may become increasingly important in continental European countries due to the growth of low paid service jobs and the downward pressure on wage levels exerted by economic globalisation. Reflecting these changes, new concepts of social structuring have gained prominence in the 1980s and 1990s: social polarisation; the underclass, and social exclusion (see for example Room, 1995). These notions replaced conventional class categories by a simple dichotomous model of social structure such as included-excluded and by concepts of marginality which comprised social and ethnic criteria as well as economic ones. The term 'underclass' originated in the USA, spreading to Europe in the 1990s, while the term 'social exclusion' featured first in France and is now widely used in the European debate, especially in EU policies and research programmes.

Inherent in the concepts of underclass and social exclusion is the presumption that some individuals and groups experience an irreversible downward career which locks them into poverty, unemployment or deprivation for very long periods. In this, the political left is inadvertently aligned with right-wing critics who lament the 'dependency' of welfare claimants.[3] The latter argue that the recipients of state aid are trapped by the logic of the financial disincentives to work created by state provision and rendered increasingly helpless. With the financial imperative to work removed, unemployment and inactivity erode the moral character of the poor, further lessening their chances of finding work, ratcheting up levels of unemployment.

There is no consensus about the nature and causes of the 'new poverty' which became apparent in the 1980s and 1990s. Ulrich Beck (1992) is one the few sociologists who has sought to explore the novel character of today's poverty within the framework of a general theory of post-industrial society that rises above the ingrained political views of the left and the right. Beck accepts the consensus view that economic growth and the expansion of the welfare state have largely extinguished the old, 'industrial' poverty: living standards have been upgraded for all citizens – the tide lifting all boats – while relative positions have remained unaltered. However, in his view there is a new post-industrial poverty which is different from, though no less disturbing, than the old poverty. In his book *Risk society: Towards a new modernity* (1992, German 1986), Beck was probably the first European theorist to sketch a new, dynamic picture of poverty[4] which has subsequently been confirmed by empirical research in Germany and the UK, reflected in later chapters in this volume. In a post-industrial society, according to Beck, poverty and unemployment are 'temporalised' and 'democratised'. 'Temporalisation' *(Verzeitlichung)* means that poverty is a phase in people's lives, be it short term, long term or recurrent rather than a state or a class. This reflects the growing discontinuity of individual life courses. 'Democratisation' *(Demokratisierung)* means that poverty is no longer confined to members of the lower classes but reaches well into the middle classes if only as a temporary experience. Social risks are shared by many members of society – the new ecological and technological risks of (late) modernity affect everybody (cf Leisering 1995b).

The dynamic approach to poverty is not new. It was pioneered by one of the founders of empirical poverty research, B. Seebohm Rowntree, who expounded a life-cycle theory of poverty (1901, pp 169-72). In his view, labourers were not continuously poor throughout their lives but only during particular stages when earnings were low or the demands of subsistence high.

> The life of a labourer is marked by five alternating periods of want and comparative plenty.... A labourer is thus in poverty, and therefore underfed – (a) In childhood – when his constitution is being built up. (b) In early middle life – when he should be in his prime. (c) In old age. The accompanying diagram may serve to illustrate this: [*see Figure 1.2*] We thus see that the 7,230 persons shown by this inquiry to be in a state of 'primary poverty', *represent merely that section who happened to be in one of these poverty periods at the time the inquiry was made.* Many of these will, in course of time, pass on into a period of comparative prosperity; this will take place as soon as the children, now dependent, begin to earn. But their places below

the poverty line will be taken by others who are at present living in that prosperous period previous to, or shortly after, marriage. Again, many now classed as above the poverty line were below it until the children began to earn. The proportion of the community who at one period or other of their lives suffer from poverty to the point of physical privation is therefore much greater, and the injurious effects of such a condition are much more widespread than would appear from a consideration of the number who can be shown to be below the poverty line at any given moment. (Rowntree, 1901, pp 169-72)

Figure 1.2: Poverty in the life cycle

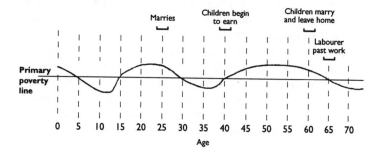

Source: Rowntree (1901, p 171) (redrawn)

Present-day life courses differ from the simple life cycle model of Rowntree. The welfare state has smoothed the life cycle and the growing complexity of social institutions and individual life plans has produced a variety of life course patterns and new risks.

Even before the arrival of formal dynamic poverty research during the 1980s in the USA (the 1990s in Europe), social scientists had begun to ask questions that foreshadowed later work. However, these pioneers were understandably prone to make mistakes as they learned to handle unfamiliar concepts. First, there were those, influenced by the *labelling approach* of interactionist sociology, who focused on processes of marginalisation and downward careers. Institutions of social control, such as social work, police or psychiatry, were seen as forces that reinforced or even created downward spiralling careers in delinquency, homelessness or mental illness. Secondly, proponents of the *'cycle of deprivation'* described a process of cumulative psycho-social decay that was not necessarily linked to social institutions. The most famous example of this genre is the pioneering analysis of the individual consequences of long-term unemployment by Jahoda et al (1971, German first edition 1933). The third important antecedent of formal analysis of dynamic poverty focused on the *intergenerational transfer* of poverty and deprivation, although even now appropriate data is difficult to obtain. Oscar Lewis (1959), for example, spoke of a culture of poverty in which the lifestyles and norms adopted by the poor of one generation restrict the opportunities and achievements of their offspring to such an extent that they were also condemned to a life of poverty. While the importance of empirical foundation for theories of intergenerational transfer should not be overestimated (cf Rutter and Madge, 1976; Atkinson, 1989; Buhr, 1991), they continue to play a role in the public policy debate.

All three of the above approaches assume that poverty is generally long term, providing a one-way ticket to ever greater misfortune. Sweeping social criticism or even political fatalism was not an unnatural response to such dramatic pictures of misery. However, these early approaches were constrained by partial theories and by limited methods and data. The focus was on routes into rather than out of poverty. Only those people currently in poverty were sampled; those who had managed to overcome poverty were excluded. These studies also mostly centred on specific groups not representative of the poor, such as the homeless or the inhabitants of ghettos. Poverty remained undifferentiated and the poor were seen as victims rather than as agents.

More recent research, which has benefited from the conceptual analytic tools described in the next chapter, has revealed that the nature and origins of poverty are much more complex than initially thought. While social criticism remains an appropriate response to the new findings, political fatalism most certainly is not.

Notes

[1] Giddens speaks of these three factors respectively as the emergence of 'abstract systems', institutionalised 'reflexivity' and the 'separation of time and space'. *Abstract systems*, that is symbolic tokens or media, above all money, and expert systems disembed human action from the particularities of locality, acquiring a momentum beyond the restrictions of concrete social relations. *Reflexivity* refers to the constant revision of knowledge and practices. The Enlightenment idea of the perfection of the human being through gradual accumulation of secure knowledge gives way to doubt as a principle of life. While in traditional societies time was bound to locality, modernity is based on a unified, global concept and measurement of time thereby *separating time and space*. New horizons both in time and space are opened up for social action and social relations. Past and future emerge as frames of making history.

[2] See also the review by Brückner (1995). Giddens develops a related concept of *life politics* juxtaposed with conventional ('social-democratic') 'emancipatory politics'. While the latter centres around vertical redistribution of economic resources, the former aims at lifestyles and self-actualisation. Our concept of *life-course policy* covers both. Giddens' concept is defined in terms of ends while we focus on the institutions designed to meet these ends.

[3] For an illuminating critique of this discourse in the USA see Bane and Ellwood (1994, Chapter 3).

[4] Ralph Dahrendorf (1988, revised German edition 1992) and Anthony Giddens (1994) also address issues of poverty and underclass in the framework of a general theory of present-day society, although they are not led to a dynamic conception of poverty. Unfortunately, the chapter on poverty and unemployment in Beck (1986) is not included in the English translation (Beck, 1992).

two

New tools: towards a dynamic science of modern society

Robert Walker and Lutz Leisering

To investigate and fully understand the changes in society, encapsulated in the concept of modernity, requires new ways of thinking and alternative modes of enquiry. Perhaps as a symbiotic part of the process of modernisation itself, an intellectual revolution is underway that emphasises the dynamics of modern life and places it at the heart of the scientific project. Hitherto social science has sought to describe society in terms of structures and states that have more than a modicum of permanence. The sciences of social change and of social mobility, important though they have always been, have had many of the characteristics of sub-disciplines: areas of enquiry with their own language that have largely been left to specialists. By contrast, within dynamic approaches to the study of society, states and structures are conceived to be either the more or less long-lasting products of ongoing social processes or even, on occasion, illusions that owe their existence to researchers being forced by data limitations to study 'stills' from the 'movie of real life'.

There is not space to do full justice to the emerging dynamic science of society. However, it is appropriate to introduce some of the concepts and technical tools used by the authors of later chapters. The discussion will make frequent reference to poverty: the new dynamic approach has already challenged preconceptions concerning the nature of poverty and the role of social assistance in preventing and alleviating it (Walker with Ashworth, 1994; Walker, 1997a; Leibfried/Leisering et al, 1995).

Conceptual tools

States, trajectories and domains

Hindus expect to pass through five stages, āśramas, during the course of their lives.[1] Each stage brings different challenges and responsibilities, new pleasures and a new way of living. Each stage is a process of development which is by way of preparation for the next. The transitions between stages are times of rapid change and uncertainty, often marked by celebration: the marshalling of moral, practical and symbolic support that helps to propel the person along the life cycle.

The experience of Hindus is shared by us all to varying degrees as we pass through life's stages on the journey from birth to death. It also makes key concepts in a dynamic approach to the study of social science real: social state, transitions and trajectories. Within a dynamic approach to the study of society, individuals are conceptualised as following trajectories comprising a sequence of states and transitions. However, in contrast to Hinduism, there is no expectation that the sequences that individuals follow will be either fixed or linear: people can find themselves in similar states to those that they have experienced before and may regress as well as progress in material and other ways. For this reason the US term 'life course' is typically used in preference to the British term 'life cycle' which, like the Hindu asramas, implies a fixed sequence.

Whereas, āśramas apply to the whole life experience, it is often convenient to define various trajectories in different domains of life which an individual follows simultaneously. All of us, for example, can be thought to be engaged on a trajectory defined with respect to the labour market. This will comprise such states as full-time and part-time employment, unemployment, and economic inactivity. School children and others who have not yet worked, may arbitrarily be omitted in studies of labour market trajectories but, in other respects, it may be appropriate to include them, likewise the retired or permanently incapacitated.

Trajectories within different domains often intersect, with important implications for the individual and others. For example, much welfare provision is designed as a response to the intersections of family life and labour market trajectories: family dissolution often has implications for employment prospects, while unemployment is known to be associated with an increased risk of relationship breakdown. As both of these examples show, the trajectories of different individuals also intersect with consequences for all concerned.

Duration

If traditional social science has been concerned with the individual in a social context, the new dynamic social science adds a third component, time, which is operationalised as duration.[2] Each social state has a duration which is often the focus of interest and can be used as part of the definition of the state. For example, whereas poverty has traditionally been defined as the state when resources fall short of needs, the dynamic perspective would additionally focus on the length of time for which a person remains in poverty (Walker with Ashworth, 1994). Analysts might well argue that long periods of poverty are intrinsically different from short ones, that the experience, its antecedents and consequences are sufficiently unique for the two social states to be differentiated and categorised as separate social phenomena (Walker, 1997b).

In much dynamic analysis the unit of analysis is a spell. Spells are composite, multi-level units of analysis comprising a subject of study, such as an individual or social institution, a social state and its duration. For example, research on poverty dynamics often focuses not on poor people as such but on spells of poverty. In such circumstances the research questions will span ones to do with how many people are poor to ones that concern the number and average length of spells and the time lapsing between them.

From the wider perspective, it is worth noting that the number of individuals currently occupying a state is a function of the flow of people in and out of the state and the average duration of their stay. For example, if the flow of people into unemployment remains constant but the number leaving decreases, the number of people in that state increases and the average time spent unemployed must lengthen.

Censorship

It is often impossible to measure directly every dimension of a composite unit of analysis, not even one as basic as duration. The analyst has to be content to use models of the underlying temporal concept. This is because the duration of the unit of analysis often exceeds the period for which it is observed. For example, it is historians rather than social scientists who are able to take a life as the unit of analysis since most of the latter are primarily concerned with people who are still alive today; they cannot, for instance, directly investigate the empirical reality of the five life stages experienced by Hindus alive today. Similarly, the policy analyst cannot directly measure the time that the poor will spend in poverty, nor the average time for which current claimants will have received benefit when finally they leave. Research funds and the lifetimes of researchers are also limited.

Most data available to social scientists is therefore 'censored'. The examples above were chosen to illustrate what is termed right-hand censorship: when the termination of a state is not known or cannot be directly observed. Left-hand censorship, when the beginning of a social state is unknown, also occurs frequently and can be even more problematic than right-hand censorship, although there are tools to handle both.

The extent of censorship is a function of the ratio between the true duration of the unit of observation, such as a spell, and the actual period of time for which the unit is observed. The longer the period of observation relative to the duration of the unit of observation, the less attention needs to be given to the censorship involved.

Incidence, prevalence and continuity

Extending the period of observation is likely to increase both the number of units (eg, spells) counted and the number of people whose trajectories include the social state under investigation. This can have important substantive and policy implications. It may mean, for example, that the number of people who will ever need to rely on social assistance will be many times the current caseload. However, the precise relationship between the number of people who are in a given state at a particular time (incidence), and the number who will experience that state over a given period (prevalence) is quite complex.

This may be illustrated with respect to poverty. The prevalence of poverty is determined by the total duration of poverty within a population, the length of spells, the degree to which the spells are recurrent and the time for which the system or institution is observed. A lower bound is set by the situation in which poverty is experienced entirely by one sub-population comprising people who are permanently poor. In this case, the incidence and prevalence are the same. The upper bound coincides with circumstances in which poverty is a once in a life-time event, with each spell lasting for the shortest possible period that the global sum of poverty allows. In this case, incidence and prevalence diverge: low incidence is accompanied by high prev-alence. The type of poverty that prevails in situations of low as opposed to high prevalence are markedly different: permanent in the first case and very transient in the second.

Plotting the prevalence of poverty against the length of the observation period also reveals much about the characteristics of poverty suffered by the population being studied (Figure 2.1). If

Figure 2.1: Prevalence of poverty and length of observation period

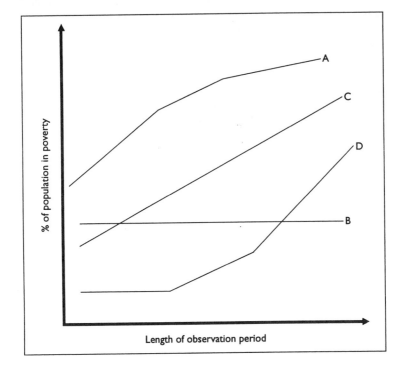

the line rises steeply and linearly (line C), the poverty is likely to be experienced in short spells by different people. A horizontal line suggests that poverty tends to be permanent (B), whereas a convex curve indicates that spells are comparatively short but that poverty is concentrated within a sub-population who suffer recurrent spells (A). A concave curve suggests that spells are distributed widely within the population but are of similar length (D).

Figure 2.1 reminds us that the distribution of a phenomenon within a population is intimately connected with its distribution over time. The two distributions are linked by the concepts of duration and continuity: duration is the time that a person spends in a particular state or for which the phenomenon persists; and continuity is the extent to which the state continues over time or is experienced as repeated episodes or spells. The distribution of a phenomenon over time and across a population can determine the social experience and meaning of the phenomenon in question.

With reference to poverty, this means that low prevalence describes a situation in which poverty is borne by a few people who experience it permanently. They are likely to be cut off economically and socially from the wider community and to be demoralised by the low prospect of ever sharing in the good life. Those in the same society who are not poor have little prospect of becoming so and are unlikely to be moved by the plight of the less fortunate. These conditions are ideal for the development of social exclusion or an underclass and the enforcement of economic apartheid. In a society characterised by high prevalence, poverty will be a common and shared experience, albeit as a short-lived phenomenon, that may trigger a collective response to the problem. However, the lack of concentration of poverty may also undermine the capability of the poor for collective action, whereas an underclass lends itself more easily to self-organisation and to powerful dramatisation by the advocates of the poor.

In other situations, the risk of suffering poverty will be more variable and everybody's prospects less certain. The poor will reasonably be able to hope for an end to their poverty, although the chance that they could experience another spell will be real. Those not poor know that they could become so and various forms of poverty, defined in terms of the number, duration and spacing of spells, are likely to coexist.

Fractals, state dependency and heterogeneity

Dynamic social science focuses on the consequences of different durations and the factors that cause duration, the time that a person spends in a state, to vary. Addressing the factors behind it can be particularly challenging.

A common finding is that the longer a person occupies a social state, the lower his or her chances of leaving it. In the context of poverty and the receipt of social assistance, right-wing commentators have taken this finding as evidence of dependency, the process by which people's attitudes and behaviour change over time in response to living on benefit and which, in turn, makes it increasingly difficult for them to leave. It is argued that claimants may no longer bother to look for work, or may have lost the habit of work that appeals to prospective employers.

However, others have challenged the importance of this so-called 'state dependency'. Walker and Ashworth, in Chapter Twelve, for example, emphasise what might be labelled the greenhouse effect. Glass in a greenhouse enables all wavelengths of light to pass through from the Sun, but traps the longwave radiation emitted from the ground. Likewise, a broad range of people claim social assistance but only those with particular characteristics, notably good qualifications and recent work experience, are able to leave benefit quickly. The observable decline in the probability of leaving benefit is largely the result of a selection process: those able to do so leave early, while those unable to do so accumulate in the system. This process is termed the 'heterogeneity effect'. However, a further problem is that there is usually some unobserved heterogeneity, that is hetero-geneity that cannot be explained by the variables included in the analysis.

Attempts to establish the consequences on future trajectories of long durations in a state are plagued by similar problems. The fact, for example, that people who have suffered one spell of poverty are more likely to experience poverty again is not definitive evidence that poverty begets more poverty.

The thesis of state dependence suggests that individuals can change during the time that they occupy a particular social state, perhaps simply as a result of being in the state. This implies that individuals may follow trajectories within what might initially be assumed to be stable social states. In the same way that extending the observation period is likely to increase the numbers passing through any social state, so increasing the resolution of the time window is likely to reveal more instability and social mobility. This is the so-called fractal effect (Ashworth and Walker, 1995). For example, in an analysis of economic activity during the course of a year it may be appropriate to discount the fact that a person worked on a single day and to treat them as long-term un-employed. There are other occasions when it is necessary to adopt a higher resolution of time. For example, in Britain one day of employment could result in the person being denied social assistance for anywhere between one and 26 weeks.

Macro, micro and causality

The major advance likely to be achieved through adopting a dynamic perspective is the development of causal theory that links individual dynamics with the dynamics of institutions and social structures. In Chapter Three, Gershuny draws attention to the importance of individual history in explaining the way we are. To demonstrate causality, it is necessary, if not sufficient, to show that the cause precedes the effect.

Perhaps the most important area for theoretical development lies in contextualising the impact of events that would appear to trigger a change of social state. Such evidence as there is makes clear that the occurrence of a particular event will act as a trigger in some circumstances but not in others. Any explanation of, for example, the nature and extent of poverty, has not only to take account of the probability that any particular event occurs, but also the probability that it will trigger a transition into poverty. The factors that discriminate between the occurrence of events and their effects as triggers are likely to depend upon the personal capabilities of individuals, and the structural circumstances in which they find themselves or may have experienced in the past. Knowing the histories of the individuals, their trajectories in appropriate domains, and the institutions and sequence of events that have impacted on their lives, should make it possible to disentangle the effects of personal and structural factors. The same analytic sequence also opens the possibility of constructing theoretical structures that span micro and macro explanations. Gershuny, in Chapter Three, outlines a recursive model of action in which what individuals have done determines what they do next; this in turn determines what they become and their next course of action. Each action or event in these sequences generally involves the individual interacting with a wider social environment which both affects, and is affected by, the event. The events in individuals' lives gain salience through interaction with social institutions that are themselves moulded by the actions of individuals. This is the most basic model of the relation between structure and action, or between macro and micro, a problem that has haunted modern social science ever since its beginnings.

Technical tools

This section considers the resources that make dynamic research possible, namely longitudinal data and the analytic techniques to handle it.

Panel surveys

The most important resource is undoubtedly the panel survey in which the same individuals are asked at regular intervals the same sequence of questions about their circumstances, attitudes and behaviour. Such data enables change to be directly observed and trajectories mapped. It also means that information about what will subsequently become prior circumstances will be collected at the time, and not gathered retrospectively when the lens of history and the distortion of hindsight intervene. Panel data also allows antecedents to be specified, consequences identified and situations in which an event operates as a trigger and when it does not, to be identified. General household panel surveys have been established in most European countries (see Chapters Nine, Ten and Twelve), modelled on the US-American Michigan Panel Study of Income Dynamics (PSID, see Chapter Six).

While valuable, panel surveys are no panacea; nor do they serve as alternatives to the generation of dynamic theory. They are expensive which means that they are likely to remain the exception rather than the rule. Sample sizes will continue to be precariously small and the coverage of topics will veer towards breadth rather than depth to generate a constituency of users large enough to justify the cost.

There are also specific problems. Depletion of sample size is inevitable because contact is lost with some respondents and others pull out. Even the high response rates that can usually be achieved from the third wave of interviews onwards still mean that, after a decade or so, only a minority of the initial sample will remain. Important though attrition can be, experience suggests that the degree of bias that results is rarely fatal and can be improved by judicious weighting. However, there are other difficulties. Often it is necessary to collect information about events that occur between interviews and this can create a disjuncture in the data series that occurs at the time of the interview. This is because people remember more recent events more accurately than earlier ones. Such 'seam effects' can have a marked effect on the outcome of modelling (see below) and are not easy to overcome. Another difficulty is that panel surveys are conducted in real time. This means that if the events of interest are rare or the processes take a long time to have a measurable effect, the lapse between the start of the project and the completion of the analysis will inevitably take years.

Finally, there is a generic difficulty that applies to all sources of longitudinal data. Whereas cross-sectional surveys often take the household or family as the unit of analysis, this is impractical in panel studies since households change so rapidly that they cannot sensibly be followed over time. Shifting the emphasis from household to individual may not be an inappropriate response if one aspect of modernity is an increase in individualism. However, it requires some conceptual retooling when applied in studies of poverty or social assistance receipt since the traditional, if contested assumption (Middleton et al, 1997), is that resources are shared within households or claimant units.

Life history surveys

The cost of panel surveys and the inevitable delay in assembling findings means that there is a premium in finding other sources of longitudinal data. One approach that scores on cost and speed of response is the application of life history techniques in a one-off survey (see Chapters Seven and Eight). This involves compiling histories of events with dates by means of careful questioning. Typically, this is done domain by domain, beginning with the current situation and taking the respondent backwards in time. Often interviews can take in excess of two hours and may suffer comparatively low response rates as a result.

Among other problems with life history surveys are the biases introduced by the fact that respondents' recall of more distant events is less accurate than of current ones. One consequence of this is 'telescoping': respondents often forget short-lived changes of social state with the further result that estimates of duration are frequently correlated with time (Barnes et al, 1997). Typically, life history samples are cross-sectional in form which means that they are necessarily biased towards survivors, since people who have already died or else moved out of the system will not be included. This may have the effect of emphasising stability at the expense of change. Chapter Thirteen reports a novel attempt to overcome this difficulty using a longitudinal sample.

One other difficulty is the requirement for large sample sizes. Unless the sample is of a cohort of people of the same age, the observation period offered by the survey will be variable and determined by the age of respondents. This means that while the sample is likely to generate a large number of events that occurred when people were young, events occurring later in life will be comparatively rare since few people in the survey will be old enough already to have experienced them (Figure 2.2).

Figure 2.2: Illustrative design of life history data collection

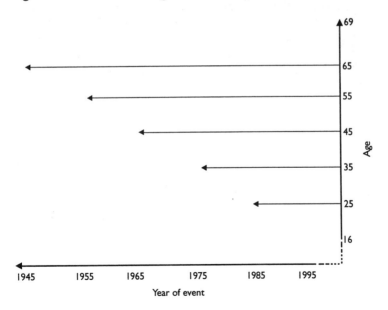

Qualitative panels and biographies

If life history surveys facilitate the construction of individual trajectories, qualitative studies allow biographies or narratives, explanatory accounts of the trajectories, to be created. In the context of dynamic analysis, qualitative research can take many forms. Retrospective studies are analogous to life history surveys in building up a picture of the past from the perspective of the present (biographies), while prospective qualitative research can be compared with panel surveys in that they involve collecting information on repeated occasions (qualitative panels). Qualitative methods can be used, as in traditional cross-sectional work, to prepare for, illuminate and qualify quantitative studies. They may be especially valuable in this regard given the necessary complexity of much dynamic analysis. They may also be used to explore directly the interactions between individuals and the institutions that comprise their social environment. For example, repeated interviewing of social assistance claimants and of the officials with which they interact can be used to investigate behavioural adaptations to bureaucratic procedures and to explore the reality of the concept of welfare dependency (Leibfried/ Leisering et al, 1995). Similar studies with children and their parents may throw light on socialisation processes with respect to, for example, employment and consumption (Lister et al, 1997).

The biographical method, often linked to interactionalist sociology, aims to unravel the subjective dimension of time, the perceptions, self-interpretation and orientations that people develop vis-à-vis their lives. Some writers, such as Martin Kohli, distinguish between the 'life course' – the 'objective' events and transitions that define trajectories which are measured in quantitative terms – and biographies – the subjective side of people's lives to be investigated qualitatively. Exciting possibilities arise from mixed designs that involve repeated interviews in which respondents are invited to look backwards and forwards in time. Data collection is recursive. Information is collected on intentions and expectations which are compared in subsequent interviews with actual events, behaviour and outcomes. The unique flexibility of qualitative research means that respondents can be invited to account for discrepancies between, for example, expectations and outcomes. People following similar trajectories can be brought together to explore shared experiences and to explain and better understand differences (Unell et al, 1994).

Qualitative research is never easy and demands enormous creativity from its practitioners, demands that are added to by the requirements of a dynamic perspective.   Repeated interviews generate enormous quantities of information and, while computer assisted analysis is an important aid, there remain severe practical limits to the volume of material that can be analysed in depth. Sample attrition can be a major problem in the context of a small number of respondents, although the qualitative research process often engenders a strong commitment among research subjects. There are frequently ethical issues relating to the intensive nature of the research and severe problems of confidentiality when the research involves studying more than one participant in any one interaction.   The research process, often deliberately designed to encourage self-reflection, may also itself change respondents' understanding, expectations and trajectories.

Administrative data

Another source of longitudinal data is that drawn from administrative records (see Chapters Eleven and Fourteen).   Such data overcomes the problem of recall inherent in life history surveys and can often generate very large samples (sometimes entire populations).   On the other hand, the analyst generally has no control over the scope, nature and quality of the information gathered by the administration, which is typically collected as the by-product of policy implementation.   Very often the researcher has to make do with a limited number of pieces of information about a large number of people.   This information is phrased in categories produced by the administration for its own purposes and can sometimes be expensive to collect when computerised data is not available.   It is rare for administrative data to cover more than one domain of a person's life.   For example, while information on means-tested benefits is quite broad in scope, it is still generally impossible to use social assistance records to track people after they have left benefit.

Simulation

A final strategy is to dispense with true longitudinal data altogether and simulate life histories from cross-sectional samples. Quasi-cohort analysis constructs synthetic cohorts from a series of cross-sectional studies.   For example, comparisons might be made between people aged 20 in a sample conducted in year Y, those aged 21 in a similar survey conducted in year Y+1 and with people aged 22 in year Y+3. Different individuals are interviewed in each year so there is no possibility of identifying antecedent events. Also, analyses are made at a cohort rather than an individual level. Nevertheless, such techniques have been used to develop interesting hypotheses about lifetime trajectories and the contrasting experiences of successive cohorts.

Dynamic population models are rather more sophisticated than quasi-cohort analysis (Falkingham and Hills, 1995). Such models seek to generate a comprehensive set of life histories by determining the attributes of individuals in year Y+1 on the basis of their attributes in year Y. Actual information is only available for one year, the year of the survey, but each individual is 'aged' throughout an entire lifetime using streams of randomly generated numbers combined with Monte Carlo selection techniques and empirically derived transition probabilities. Dynamic cohort models depart from any single real sample and create model individuals on the basis of behavioural equations and transition probabilities. For example, a person's educational status at any point in time would be determined on the basis of assumptions about age, sex, parental class and education received up until that time. In this way it is possible to simulate entire life histories, albeit on the basis that all the characteristics of the population, the relationships between them and the policy regime remain unaltered throughout everybody's life. This latter proviso is both a strength and a weakness. It means that the long-term effects of existing policies can be modelled by holding everything else constant, but it also means that the population generated is not a true representation of the actual population at any point in time.

Event history analysis

As important as the data, are the techniques to analyse them. The most important set of approaches are known collectively as 'event history analysis' after the nature of the data that can be analysed (Vermunt, 1996; Blossfeld and Rohwer, 1995). Such data, derived by the quantitative methods described above, will generally contain information on the number of specific events, their sequence and the time at which they occurred. The principal aim of the analysis is usually to explain why certain persons are more likely to experience such events than others.

While it is not appropriate to discuss event history models in detail, it is worth drawing attention to the close correspondence between the concepts covered earlier and the technical tools. The first step in any event history analysis is to define the states of interest, be it poverty, family type or whatever. At any point in time a particular individual can only occupy one state. An 'event' is the transition from one state to another: poverty to non-poverty; single to cohabitation and so on. 'Duration' is the time spent within a particular state, that is the time between events. Finally, there are the concepts of the risk set and the risk period. The former is the group of people who are at risk of experiencing a particular event while the risk period is the length of time for which a person is exposed to the risk.

Using these concepts, event history analysis can be described as the analysis of the rate of occurrence of an event during the risk period or the analysis of the duration of the non-occurrence of an event (Yamaguchi, 1991). The risk of the event occurring within a short period is then regressed on a set of covariates, some or all of the variants may themselves vary over time. The analysis allows for the possibility of censorship: at the end of the observation period it is known that an event has not occurred but not whether and when it subsequently does so.

Event history models – sometimes termed hazard models because the dependent variable is the rate at which a hazard (event) occurs – can be categorised in terms of the nature of the dependent variable and the way in which time is treated. Different models allow the dependent variable to be either discrete, one state or another (such as those used in Chapters Eleven, Thirteen and Fourteen), or continuous. Among event history models for discrete dependent variables, some assume that the event may occur at any point in time (continuous-time models) while others assume that changes only occur at particular times (discrete-time models). The former can be further divided into those in which it is assumed that the time dependence of the process being studied takes a particular form (parametric continuous-time models) and those in which the form of the dependency is unspecified (semi-parametric continuous-time models [Cox, 1972]).

The quality of the modelling is affected by the quality of the data. Missing data, often caused by variations in survey and item responses from wave to wave, is an endemic problem for which there are only partial solutions. Censorship is a form of missing data and, while it is often inevitable, even event history models need to assume that the censorship is independent of the process being studied.

Problems of measurement error are exacerbated because of the requirement in longitudinal research for repeated measures. Events, for example, are typically defined with reference to the difference between two measurements, both of which will be subject to error. Depending on the model used, it may be necessary to transform a continuous variable into a discrete one. For example, income poverty will be defined with regard to a particular point on a continuous distribution of the income-to-needs ratio which itself involves measurement of both income and needs. Without adjustment, event history models are particularly sensitive to the problem of unobserved heterogeneity: that is to the omission of variables that affect the risk of an event occurring (Vermunt, 1996).

Nevertheless, despite the practical difficulties and the conceptual complexity, event history techniques have revolutionised the analysis of longitudinal data (Mayer and Huinink, 1990). They are invaluable tools for developing and testing dynamic theory.

Summary

The dynamics that characterise modernism are made understandable by reference to temporal concepts such as those introduced in this chapter. By good fortune, the concepts find their parallel in a set of analytic techniques that enable descriptive and explanatory theory to be informed by empirical data. This is the project on which contributors to this volume are engaged and which our readers are invited to join.

Notes

[1] The stages are: childhood (usually counted as a pre-dharma stage); brahmacarin (student); grihasta (household); vanaprastha (forest dweller or hermit) and sannyasa (renouncement). See Hoskins (1971) for details.

2 See Niklas Luhmann's (1990) distinction of matter, social, and time as dimensions of sociological analysis.

three

Thinking dynamically: sociology and narrative data

Jonathan Gershuny

I meet a man in a bar. He asks me how I got to be a sociologist: I tell him about what I studied, and how each successive job I've had led on to the next one.

I ask my son what he's done today. "Went to school." "No." I say, "Tell me properly." So he tells me properly the sequence of things he's done from the time he woke up.

Narrative data

These two types of narrative accounts of past behaviour, long-term and short-term, have a number of characteristics in common. Both consist of sequences of events placed in order, which can be placed approximately in time, by narrators who, having experienced the events themselves, are competent to answer such questions. Having been asked these types of questions countless times before, we all have to some degree become skilled narrators. We all know our own stories and become practised at telling them.

Social statisticians now often collect quite large and nationally-representative samples of such narratives. The longer-term ones are variously called work histories (if they deal with employment issues), life histories if they include other types of events (marital or fertility, for example). The shorter-term narratives are simply the diaries used in time budget analysis. Both the event histories and the time diaries are organised in the same way, either as a fixed interval 'calendar' of states, conditions or activities or as a more open 'repeating structure' of events, each with a start date/time, one or more activity characteristics, and then either a duration or a finish time (although this third feature may be redundant if the start of the next event marks the termination of the present one). Both types of narrative can be analysed using the same types of descriptive and modelling procedures.

Narratives are an important source of sociological information and will have a key place in the development of a new type of account of change in social structure. Longitudinal data is already quite widely used in studies of social mobility. However, this chapter will involve a more general application, which goes beyond conventional mobility studies (for example, Erikson and Goldthorpe, 1992). Of considerable interest are statistical estimates of the chances that parents will reproduce children who follow their own class or status position. However, such analyses are typically based on rather sparse information (parents' occupation, child's educational attainment, first and current job). In a life history dataset we typically have much more information, continuous and detailed, throughout the life course, on family status, on each episode of education and on employment or unemployment. With such evidence, we can study not just the simple probabilities of moving between states, but the processes which move people between successive events and conditions.

Sociologists have a long-standing problem in understanding the relationship between social structure and individual behaviour. People's actions are both constrained and enabled by social structures. However, social structures are themselves made up of aggregations of individual behaviour. How then can there be social change? How can social beings *act* so as to *alter* that very system of constraints and opportunities *within which they act*? This is what is referred to as 'the problem of agency'. The solution outlined in this chapter is hardly different from the one set out by Giddens in his *The constitution of society* (1984). The central point of what follows is that the new types of narrative data provide an essential part of the *empirical* basis for understanding the relationship between individuals' behaviour and social change.

Nested within the problem of agency, is another rather similar problem best summed up by an old joke attributed to the American economist James Duesenberry: "Economists discuss how people make choices", he tells us, "and sociologists explain why people don't have any choices to make". The sad truth behind the bad joke is a matched pair of disciplinary failures. Economists' accounts do often sound, at least to outsiders, as if they believed that economic behaviour consists entirely of choices, while sociologists' accounts often sound as if people were entirely constrained by expectations attached to roles and statuses. To use the language introduced in this context by Granovetter (1985; referring in turn to Wrong, 1961), we have here, respectively, an undersocialised line of explanation, and an oversocialised one. What is needed is a disciplinary compromise, a middle path, which will give appropriate weight to the structures of constraints and opportunities which derive from our social positions, and to the changes and choices that we must all make from time to time throughout our lives.

This chapter briefly sets out a recursive model of the relationship between people's social structural characteristics and their behaviour. The model views action as embedded in a personal history which provides both a material origin for the individual's personal characteristics, and a context within which choices may be called for. To illustrate the argument, two simple examples of the recursive process will be discussed, using a particular type of narrative data drawn from household panel surveys.

Recursive model of action

The *events* of life narratives *constitute people's individual characteristics.* We have done various things in the past, and some of these serve to establish precisely 'who we are'. We interact in particular ways with the social and material circumstances which surround us to produce new events for the narrative. The ways in which we do this are influenced in part by 'who we are' and in part by the characteristics of the actors and institutions in our environment. In turn, these new events may perhaps change 'who we are'. In short (and using the concept of 'determination' in the weak sense of 'constrains and enables'): we are what we have done; what we are determines what we do next; what we do next determines what we become. And so on. This is a model of *recursive determination*.

Micro-sociological narrative sequence

Each of our lives constitutes a number of different types of narratives – such as marital, employment, fertility – all slotted together. These make up a set of nested cycles, a sort of coiled coil, in which the events of each day slot into weeks, and the weeks into years. Each person lies at the end of an enormously extended sequence of events, say, 25 or 50 distinct activities in a day, which means a sequence of hundreds of thousands of events already accumulated by an adult.

Almost all of these events are inconsequential. Nothing that happens can be made to unhappen, but the inconsequential events happen and are forgotten, like shouts in the street. However, some events have specific causal significance for subsequent events.[1] Such events, or sequences or repetitions of events, are distinct in that they change the *status* or *characteristics* of the person who experiences them.

We can set out a number of examples of the different ways that this happens – a number of different ways in which the past events in the personal narrative can have or acquire salience for the future (some of these characteristics relate to production activities, some to consumption, some to family or demographic events):

- A particular event may directly affect status either for a functional, or for some contingent social, reason (for example, conceiving a child, winning a lottery, losing a limb, falling in love or getting married). We might think of these as *'singular significant events'* which happen in a 'one-off' fashion and their consequences may be mitigated by other events (for example, a divorce), but in general such events have a continuing effect on subsequent behaviour.

- Repeated activities may cumulatively lead to the acquisition of certain types of functional skills or capacities or other characteristics (including norms, expectations and values). These *'cumulatively significant events'* may, for example, be childhood socialisation producing consumption skills or preferences, as in the Bourdieu (1984) account of the child taken to the opera who 'naturally' acquires the tastes of an opera-goer. They may be the case of workers who acquire a skill empirically, by repeated, initially untrained and relatively ineffective activity. In this category also are the 'events' of school-based or other formal education in which we cumulate capacities or qualifications.

- There are *processes of interaction among different accumulating characteristics* that can turn otherwise insignificant events into significant ones. To take an example from the discussion of 'the marital conversation' (Benjamin, 1995), a wife may learn negotiating skills in the workplace which she then deploys in family arguments. A shout in the kitchen, under these circumstances, may have direct consequences for the subsequent division of domestic tasks within the household, and hence – in a way which shall be outlined in a moment – have major long-term implications for her career attainment.

The consequential events and processes are those which serve to place the individual in the social structure. They establish *salient social-structural characteristics* – those attributes which influence the range of possible future actions.

Some events, normally indistinguishable from the incon-sequential, acquire significance simply because they set in train a sequence which includes consequential events.   Just as in the macrosphere we have circumstances in which horseshoe nails lose battles, or butterflies raise hurricanes, so in the microsphere of the life course, reading a book may transform an employment history, or a chance meeting may lead to a marriage. Where these events are truly 'chaotic' (in the mathematicians' sense that an infinitely small variation in their temporal or spatial placement might render them inconsequential) we must treat them (at least in large scale quantitative analysis) as random perturbations (although more intensive 'qualitative' sociological research can reveal their significance).

One of the traditionally important ways of acquiring salient social characteristics, *inheritance*, falls across the three categories given in the example above. In the special case of the inheritance of financial resources, the 'event' vocabulary may seem a little forced – there is the singular event of being born to rich parents. However, in general, inheritance, whether of skills or social connections, is achieved through childhood socialisation, and this does fall naturally into the theoretical language.

We tend to think of an individual's structural characteristics or position in the social structure as being separate from that person's behaviour. In the approach suggested here there can be no such separation. Structure has consequences for behaviour, and behaviour in turn crystallises into structural characteristics, in an endless recursive sequence.

Micro sequence in a more macro context

Narratives are quintessentially micro-social data. To understand the significance of particular events or sequences, we need corresponding macro data. People live in a social environment which includes both other people, and other types of institutions and actors such as families or firms or governments. It is the interaction with this environment which produces new behaviour, new events.

Things can happen to change the salience of events or sequences over historical time. These affect the relationship between an accumulated personal characteristic and the institutional environment with which it interacts. Some examples:

- There may be a change in the *distribution of personal characteristics across the population.* For example, a scarce social accomplishment or an economic skill may be 'salient' to economic behaviour at one point in time, but if a larger proportion of the population subsequently acquires it, it may cease to be so. Functional literacy alone once gave access to a range of employments, but ceased to do so as general literacy levels rose. In this case, *a market phenomenon* modifies the structural significance of particular aspects of the event sequence.

- There may be a change in the *circumstances of institutions.* To continue the previous example, new production technology emerges, which renders a production skill archaic (as in the case where dexterity with an abacus is rendered redundant by the electronic calculator). A change in consumer tastes may mean that the final demand declines, so firms provide fewer jobs. (Again these are market phenomena.) Also in this category may be a change in the relation between cultural or sports providers and consumption skills – for example, where a new design of ski makes it possible for a novice to gain more enjoyment from winter sports.

- There may be a change in the *actions or practices of institutions* in the way they interact with a personal characteristic (this is *a regulatory phenomenon*). For example, as the state changes the marriage laws to permit divorce where previously it did not, so a marriage become less of a constraining event than it was previously. A firm may decide that a particular job requires the possession of some certificate which may or may not be functionally related to the work tasks, so that people who previously could have taken a particular job cannot now do so.

Another way of saying this is that we, as micro-social agents, interact with more macro-societal agents: firms, families, voluntary associations, political parties or governments. These institutions also have their own institutional histories, and have acquired institutional characteristics through recursive processes analogous to our human ones. Individual behaviour emerges from the interplay between salient individual characteristics and relevant institutional characteristics, in a way analogous to the emergence of purchasing behaviour in an economists' model of supply and demand.

Habit and action

The behavioural model suggested here consists mostly of habit, modified at particular rare but important points by choices which might be considered to be in varying degrees rational.

Most people have a personal moment of inertia, which maintains them on a well established trajectory, a given, and for the most part unconsidered, sequence of activities through the day and the year – we get up, wash, eat, go to work, play games, visit friends, and so on. This repetition is the outcome of the process of recursive determination.

However, at particular strategic junctures, we take some form of action to modify the habitual sequence. Sometimes this is forced on us (for example, we are offered a new job or lose one), sometimes we actively choose to consider a consequential decision (we search for a new job), sometimes we make such a choice by accident (we impulsively accept a job offer without thought for its consequences for our family or long-term career). The action we take is a *conscious modification of routine with the aim of achieving some relatively distant object* – a rational choice.

At a minimum, we have the example of the impulsive job change with no more precise intent than to 'do something different'. At a maximum we have a full rational analysis of the time-discounted expected future flow of benefits from the offered job as compared to the present one. Most actions of most people lie somewhere between these two extremes. However, the outcomes of the more considered sorts of actions will tend to correspond in systematic ways to salient structural characteristics, while the less considered actions will be relatively random. In aggregate terms we should expect to find the statistical associations between structural characteristics and behaviour which are characteristic of 'rational choice', accompanied by substantial random 'error' components.

In brief, the model of action is that the historical sequence of events determines an individuals' social-structural characteristics, and establishes habitual activity patterns or 'routines', as well as values and expectations. The values and expectations interact with the individual social-structural characteristics and the character-istics of the institutional and other environment, to produce occasional modifications to the routine through some sort of (limited) rational action. These in turn over time modify the individual's structural characteristics, values and expectations.

Analogies with human capital theory

This model has analogies with both the economic and the sociological varieties of human capital theory. The narrower economic variety (for example, Becker, 1964) deals just with the accumulation of employment-related skills partly through childhood socialisation, partly through education, and partly through empirical 'on the job' experience. The broader socio-logical arguments (for example, Bourdieu, 1984) relate as much to consumption as to production skills, placing emphasis on the impact of accumulated artistic and recreational experiences as well as experiences in the workplace. However, in both cases, the fact that a particular characteristic should constitute 'human capital' is taken as unproblematical.

The advantage of the approach set out here is that it makes explicit that individual characteristics are rendered salient, as enablers or constraints, by the nature of the institutions they interact with. A human characteristic, a skill, that has no counterpart in the institutions that surround it, is not structurally salient. A practised skier can draw no recreational benefit from her prowess if she lives in a rainforest. The discussion of the interrelation of the characteristics to the institutional and other environment means that we do not have to see the advantage deriving from a particular capacity as a given or fixed social fact: 'advantageous characteristics', in this approach, are always to be understood *in relation to the individual's institutional and other context*. The argument provides a broader and more general view of the range of potentially salient characteristics than that offered by the human capital approach: it envisages the same set of processes that are involved in skill acquisition, and also in the formation of habits, beliefs and values, personal 'projects' and expectations for the future, but all of these are seen to interact with macro-level institutions to produce behavioural outcomes.

Perhaps most importantly, from a sociological and social policy viewpoint, this approach can be directly and empirically operationalised. We can move from a clear theoretical statement directly to empirical study – since the evidence that this model calls for is the narrative accounts of the life course and of the day now being collected in many developed countries.

Examples

We will ignore more straightforward examples, such as relating past employment experience to subsequent employment experience (which are closely analogous to the more traditional human capital arguments) and consider instead two relatively unfamiliar examples which show the reciprocal relationship among two rather different event sequences, respectively employment and domestic responsibilities.

Example 1: Allerednic

(Cinderella in reverse, or how the prince marries the princess and turns her into a scullery maid.)

This is an example of how behaviour influences position in the social structure. Figure 3.1 shows the effect of the domestic division of labour (or in this example, domestic responsibilities) on occupational attainment.

It uses the work history evidence from the British Household Panel Study (BHPS) together with evidence about who takes responsibility for domestic tasks. The figure shows the career attainment of husbands in the years subsequent to their marriage (as measured by the Hope–Goldthorpe occupational prestige scores, see Hope and Goldthorpe, 1974), compared to those of two different types of wives – wives who take a traditional gendered view of their domestic responsibilities and wives with a more gender-symmetrical view of household organisation.[2] It shows that those with the more gender-symmetrical work practices have similar patterns of career attainment to their husbands, while those who take work breaks for family care have substantially worse attainment performance (similar results are reported in Dex, 1984). The day-to-day practices of domestic work have a clear impact on women's subsequent occupational prestige and hence, since these are well correlated, their earnings potential.

Figure 3.1: Allerednic story – career attainment of husbands and wives (wives born in 1940s)

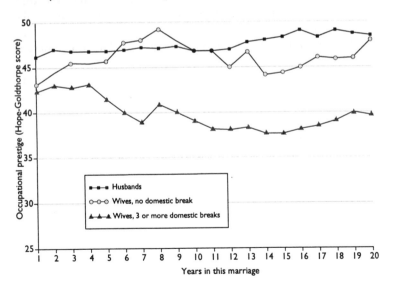

Example 2: Domestic division of labour and women's employment experience

We learn our domestic work habits in infancy: time-budget studies show that girls spend time with their mothers, boys with their fathers. So girls tend to acquire their mothers' domestic work skills, values and habits, and more widely, a particular gender ideology (this sense of the term from Hochschild, 1990); similarly boys fail to learn domestic work skills and develop distinct male gender ideologies. Both take into adult life, as a result, habits and expectations which to a degree reproduce gender specific behaviour across the generations.

However, there are changes in the environment. Today most women have jobs. The day is finite, so if they (and their husbands) maintain the traditional gender ideologies learned from the previous generation, they take on what is known as the 'dual burden' (Meissner et al, 1975). They take their inherited views of gender-segregated domestic work distributions into a set of material circumstances in which this behaviour is inappropriate – since if both husband and wife have paid jobs and yet they maintain the gender differential in housework, the wife has to take on far more work in total than the husband. This manifest inequity constitutes the sort of 'strategic juncture' at which there is pressure to modify the habitual sequence activities.

Table 3.1 shows, for households in the BHPS and the German Socio-Economic Panel (SOEP), different stages in this process of modifying housework practices. The dependent variable in the analysis is the wife's proportion of the total domestic work (an aspect of the daily sequence). Among the causal variables (having control for various other potentially confounding household characteristics) we see the effect of the wife's employment experience.[3] The longer the wife's experience of full-time employment the more equal the division of domestic work. This effect does not come from the work experience itself but from the length of time that the contradiction between the old domestic habits and the new employment situation has had to mature, and the extended process of renegotiation that results.

In the previous example we saw domestic work affecting employment; here we see the reciprocal effect of employment on domestic organisation.

Table 3.1: Division of domestic labour – the impact of the wife's employment experience

	UK		Germany	
Grand mean	0.79		0.86	
Age in years (raw regression	0.001		-0.001	
	No	Effects	No	Effects
Wife's full-time employment, 6 preceding years				
0 full years	1,305	0.02	1,286	0.02
1	116	0.01	89	0.00
2	105	0.01	52	0.00
3	102	-0.02	56	-0.06
4	111	-0.05	59	-0.04
5	71	-0.05	66	-0.08
6 full years	406	-0.05	144	-0.10
Wife's part-time employment, 6 preceding years				
0 full years	1,468	-0.01	1,254	0.01
1	140	0.04	140	-0.02
2	104	0.01	113	-0.03
3	85	-0.01	73	-0.04
4	102	0.02	63	-0.03
5	42	0.02	35	0.00
6 full years	274	0.04	74	-0.04
Couple's joint employment status				
No jobs: unemployed	143	0.01	68	-0.01
No jobs: retaining	419	-0.06	389	-0.06
Husband employed, wife not	461	0.08	548	0.05
Both employed	1,045	0.01	651	0.02
Wife employed, husband not	149	-0.15	96	-0.16
Multiple R squared	0.145		0.141	

Index: 1 = she does it all; 0 = he does it all.

Data source: British Household Panel Study and German Socio-Economic Panel

Towards a multinational research programme

So far we have looked at only a limited part of the long sequence, the events in the spheres of employment and domestic organisation. Just as these interact in complex reciprocal ways, so we find recursive interactions with marital, fertility and family status, and with household income. For example, if households with employed wives fail to adjust their domestic work patterns, there may be marital conflict that culminates in divorce; this type of change in household status has implications for the effective incomes of members of the successor households, which may in turn have consequences for, say, the employment status of those affected. Much of social life may be understood in terms of these types of reciprocal longitudinal interdependencies among different spheres of life.

These lines of argument have major implications for other more general themes in sociology. Take an example from the area of social stratification and differentiation: does the traditional 'class' model of stratification in which life chances are best predicted by the current occupation of the current head of household still hold good in the more changeable world of insecure male employment, growing women's employment, and increasing divorce rates? The arguments set out here provide hints that this may not be so. For instance, the life chances of the 'Allerednic wives' – 40% of whom may well find themselves divorced within a decade or so (Ermisch and Francesconi, 1996), and who have sacrificed career advancement to provide domestic services for their husbands – may well ultimately be more affected by their own domestic work history than by some past episode in their ex-husband's occupational history.

This last example encapsulates the central point of this chapter. The interaction of micro-processes means that sequences of events that once were not significant for subsequent life chances, become so. If, for example, divorce had not become a frequent phenomenon, the domestic division of labour and its implications for women's career attainment would have less significance for women's life chances. It is the growth of divorce that gives the long sequence of domestic work events a social structural significance now that it did not previously have.

This account of a way of thinking about social change has had to be brief, only mentioning influences from the micro to the more macro levels. There are also effects in the opposite direction. There are innovations promoted by actors in social institutions, for example, firms recruiting workers with new characteristics, or governments changing regulations about employment conditions or social security entitlements. There are changed representations of social practices in the media, so that activities that previously appeared to carry negative sanctions lose them. However, the existence of these macro-to-micro influences do not detract from the importance of the micro-to-macro flows. The things we do in our daily lives are aggregated over time into social-structural characteristics. As the balance of activities in the society changes, so new types of structural characteristics become salient in processes of social stratification and differentiation. The new national collections of narrative data – life histories, time budgets, household panel surveys – are the necessary empirical basis for this new type of dynamic thinking about the processes of social change.

There is now a great deal of the type of longitudinal evidence used in the two examples. Many countries collect life history data, but altogether the most promising source of evidence comes from household panel studies (see also Chapter Two). Such a study involves a random sample of households, all of whose members and subsequent co-residents, partners and descendants are repeatedly re-interviewed (typically each year) to build up an event sequence account. These studies accumulate continuous records of employment, income, family status, attitudes and subjective indicators over extended (since such samples are self-reproducing, in principle, limitless) periods. They also often include retrospective studies so that their respondents have continuous records in key fields from the beginnings of their lives. There are currently eight nationally representative studies of this type being carried out in Europe (Sweden, Denmark, The Netherlands, Belgium, Germany, Luxembourg, Hungary, UK) many of these extending back to the early 1980s. There is also the new European Community Household Panel Survey which began in 1994. There are programmes to harmonise these: the PAnel COmparability (PACO) study based in CEPS/INSTED in Luxembourg and the European Panel Analysis (PANEL) programme based in Essex. The data sources that emerge from these programmes will provide the empirical basis for understanding the types of complex processes outlined in this chapter.

Economists have been using panel studies for at least two decades but they have only begun to emerge in the mainstream sociological literature. They provide the opportunity for a major international comparative programme of research in social policy and sociology, a programme of research into the long-term social determinants of advantage and disadvantage. The use of narrative data, in the form of panel studies in a sociological context, has a promising future.[4]

Notes

[1] In saying so, we should bear in mind that causality is a theoretical concept. The terms 'consequential events' and 'inconsequential events' are only defined relative to what we want to know about the subject under consideration.   While carrying out research we are bound to select certain events out of a plethora of events and model them as causal factors according to our theoretical concepts and hypotheses.

[2] In this example, we distinguish between these two types of wives just by whether or not they take substantial breaks in employment for domestic purposes – but the BHPS in fact provides a number of alternative indicators, including attitudes to men's and women's domestic responsibilities, as well as direct measures of couples' domestic work times.

[3] To trace this effect we use dummy variables as apparent from the table.

[4] For a somewhat similar programmatic call, but working from the macro to the micro rather than vice versa, see Mayer and Schoepflin (1989). They expound the concept of 'life course' that aims to link macro and micro (see Chapter One of this volume).

four

Dynamic policy making: an insider's account of reforming US welfare

David Ellwood

Static analysis asks about the who and what of today. Dynamic thinking asks about the past and the future and, at its best, it helps to answer the question of why. As a tool for understanding human behaviour, dynamic analysis brings to bear a great deal more richness and texture. For life is experienced as a series of events, not as a series of static positions. It is those events which often help to define us. As a tool for policy, dynamic analysis is especially potent, for it inevitably points towards helping people to reshape the events in their future. By contrast, static analysis more commonly leads to remediation of the overt manifestations of the current situation. Put differently, dynamic analysis gets us closer to treating causes, where static analysis often leads us towards treating symptoms.

If, for example, we ask who are the poor today, we are led to questions about the socioeconomic identity of the existing poverty population. Looking to policy, we then typically emphasise income supplementation strategies. The obvious static solution to poverty is to give the poor more money. If instead, we ask what leads people into poverty, we are drawn to events and structures, and our focus shifts to looking for ways to ensure people escape poverty.

After working on dynamic poverty and policy issues for most of my professional career,[1] I was given a remarkable opportunity early in 1993. Mary Jo Bane, a colleague and collaborator of many years, Bruce Reed, the issues director for the Clinton campaign, and I, were put in charge of President Bill Clinton's welfare reform initiative. This experience has shaped my view of dynamic research today. I have learned much in the past few years, and I have come to realise some of the limits of dynamic thinking so will suggest here some directions I think this research needs to take to move into the future.

Dynamic thinking and the Clinton welfare reform plan

The USA has a number of different programmes which are sometimes called welfare. The programme that received all the attention, and the one which was the major focus of our reform efforts, was Aid to Families with Dependent Children (AFDC). It was a programme primarily designed for lone parents. In most cases a two parent family did not qualify, although that changed over the years. The costs were shared between states and the federal government. Each state determined its own level of benefits. Benefits for a family of three ranged from $120 per month in Mississippi to more than $600 month in wealthier states. There was no limit on the duration that benefits could be collected. So long as your income was low enough and you were a lone parent with children, benefits continued. There were few, if any, work or training requirements, although the 1988 Family Support Act imposed some requirements for training on both recipients and states. (In addition, we had and still have the Food Stamp Program. It is our only universal programme; it is essentially a low negative income tax where the benefits are paid in food coupons. However, that programme has been less controversial and did not figure prominently in our reform efforts.)

We assembled a team of people from throughout the government to work on the plan. We insisted that team members spend a fair amount of time in welfare offices and that they participate in discussion groups with people on welfare. The process was an eye opener for many members of the team because most had not spent time in welfare offices where eligibility is determined. The stories illustrate the trap that thinking statistically had put us in. One public aid recipient said:

> "I've been on and off welfare for 10 years. I've
> been in and out of the welfare office dozens of

times. Never once in that entire 10-year period
did anyone ask me what I always thought would
be the first question, 'What's the problem, how
can I help you?' Instead they say, 'What's your
income? How many kids do you have? Here's
this form to fill out for your food stamps. Here's
what you do to get your medical card.' I was
happy to have that stuff, but it wasn't what I
really needed."

In the USA, our welfare offices have become the ultimate
caricature of the *who* rather than *why* way of thinking about
poverty. Our income support systems have focused almost
exclusively on determining whether someone is eligible for public
aid, and on deciding what amount they should receive. We have
designed a system of cheque writing rather than a system designed
to help people to help themselves. The system is heavily means
tested, so the question of whether aid recipients are really eligible
is a serious one.

Administrators of this system are preoccupied with accuracy
and fraud. As a result, the system's harshest critics are the poor
themselves: they talk about how the welfare system abuses,
humiliates, isolates and stigmatises them. Europe has escaped
some of the stigma by avoiding such heavy means testing of public
aid. However, means testing is just part of the problem. The
bigger issue is the failure to focus on strategies designed to give
people a brighter future and to link opportunities with responsibility.

When you start asking about the *whys* of poverty, you move
to a very different set of policies. Dynamic thinking played a key
role in the construction of the original Clinton Bill. Two types of
results were particularly potent in developing this plan, both of
which come from focusing on the why and how long of poverty
rather than the who. First, a large fraction of the poor are
working. Unlike the stereotypical image of poverty among
Americans, where unemployment and non-participation are seen
as the key problem, millions work and still have incomes below
the official US poverty definitions. (We use an absolute standard
of roughly $15,000 for a family of four persons.) A full-year, full-
time person earning our minimum wage does not even come close
to earning enough to raise a family of four above the poverty line.
Our health insurance system leaves most working poor families

without coverage, while non-working families on welfare receive such protection. Second, dynamic analysis revealed that a large fraction of public aid was going to people who stayed on welfare for an extended period – even though most people who ever used aid received it during a relatively short period. A focus on longer-term recipients seemed sensible. Given the American emphasis on work, it seemed appropriate to expect that people seeking aid must eventually go to work in order to continue receiving aid.

The reforms we proposed started completely outside the welfare system with support for working families – something we called 'making work pay'. We dramatically expanded the 'Earned Income Tax Credit' (EITC),[2] a refundable tax credit for working families. EITC is based on earnings, so the more you earn the more you receive, up to a maximum, and then it phases out. We introduced and passed legislation increasing EITC to a credit of 40% of earnings so that someone who was in a $4-an-hour job would receive in effect another $1.60 an hour in refundable tax credits from the federal government. We also sought to create universal coverage through health reform. Sadly, this led to a policy and political disaster, but that is not my focus here. Finally, we wanted to expand childcare. If you are asking parents, especially lone parents, to work, childcare is essential.

With respect to welfare (income support), the administration proposed a reformed system where people would be offered the opportunity and responsibility to receive training and/or other support they needed to move towards a job. The goal was to get most recipients off public aid within two years. The refrain 'two years and you're off' was used by some to describe the goal.

Focusing on moving welfare recipients into work within two years is a truly dynamic view of reform. To design an appropriate system you have to know the facts about welfare dynamics. The first thing to understand is that a great many people move off welfare on their own quite quickly. Within the first two years, 60% of aid recipients leave; 90% leave within the first five years. Unfortunately three quarters of them come back. So part of the reason to make work pay when you are thinking dynamically is to help people to earn enough to stay out of poverty when they leave aid.

The second thing dynamic analysis shows is that in spite of the best efforts of administrators and educators, there will always be a great many people who need more than two years aid during the course of their life. There will be people who cannot find work after the two years has ended. The President had made clear that his goal was to get as many people off aid within two years as possible. He also made it clear that he did not want traditional cash aid to continue past two years. So what should happen after two years? There are only two options: cut people off by eliminating support or provide them with a subsidised job as a last resort. The Clinton plan mostly chose the latter, so the plan was 'two years and you work'. After two years if someone still could not find a job, the plan called for using the welfare money that would otherwise have been spent on a welfare cheque to create some form of a subsidised job. After two years, parents could receive aid, but only if they worked for it.

Some may find this sort of two-year limit followed by a work requirement harsh. Implicit in all this discussion is an attitude towards work and public aid that is at the heart of American values, but certainly open to question. Most public aid recipients in the US are single parents with children. Why force people to work? Why not support nurturing children? Is not work inside the home just as important? It is a legitimate question, but literally 95% of the American public believes that at some point people should go to work outside the home if they are to receive government support.

So Clinton called for two years of training followed by a requirement to work. Clinton introduced his Bill in July 1994. The Republicans, seeking to gain the initiative, introduced their own Bill, that was also a 'two years and then you work Bill', but included money for training, work, and childcare. The two Bills were similar in a great many ways, but action could not be taken before the November 1994 elections. When the Republicans swept control of both the House and the Senate in the Republican Revolution, the whole dynamic changed and budget cutting became the paramount goal. The Republicans introduced a new welfare Bill which sought to reduce spending sharply. It focused on limiting the time people could receive aid and, unlike the Clinton Bill and the previous Republican Bill, it simply cut people off after a period and did not offer any sort of work or other support after a time limit was reached. The rest of the story is well known. I gave up my appointment and in August 1996 Clinton signed a Bill that did set time limits.[3] Under the Personal Responsibility and Work Opportunity Reconciliation Act, Aid to

Families with Dependent Children (AFDC) was superseded by Temporary Assistance for Needy Families.

The pitfalls of dynamic policy making

This episode of US policy making illustrates the benefits of dynamic thinking and its risks. The ideas created by dynamics are compelling and potent, but even before the Republican Revolution, I encountered dangers that I had not anticipated inherent in using dynamics for thinking about policy.

The 'and then what?' question

Perhaps the most difficult problem is that dynamic thinking almost inevitably leads policy makers towards implementing time limits of some sort, because the duration of benefits is always considered. When thinking statistically we ask, 'who's poor and how much shall we give them?'; the question of how long benefits continue need not even arise. When you think dynamically, you must confront the 'and then what' question.

Suppose your policy is to give people training and education when they enter the system. The next question is: 'And then what?' You answer that people will be offered a subsidised job if they cannot find an unsubsidised private job. People again ask: 'And then what? How long do we provide that public job? 18 years? A public sector job guaranteed for life! Nobody else in the highly dynamic, highly mobile capitalist US society has a job for life (except tenured professors!).' When Democrats, who would have fought to the death in a Democratic administration for higher benefits to poor families, began thinking dynamically they also said that there has to be a limit on aid, even in work programmes. I tried to argue that limits on subsidised job durations are unnecessary so long as the subsidised job does not pay better than private sector jobs. Yet many policy makers still felt that ultimate time limits had to be imposed. They argued that at some point even a subsidised job would be withdrawn and people should be left to the vagaries of the market. There should be some final cut-off. Ultimately, the Clinton Bill imposed no absolute time limits, but it was a battle I had to fight long and hard within the administration. Eventually it seems, most people believe there is some duration of support after which the answer to the 'and then what' question becomes, 'perhaps we have done enough'.

With the sudden turn to the political right in the US Congress, it is not surprising that there was even more focus on ultimate cut-offs. Under Bills passed by Congress at the time, states would receive a fixed amount of money for public aid from the national government. States could choose to cut people off permanently after as little as six months, regardless of whether or not the person could find a job. That is one danger of dynamic thinking. The answer to the 'and then what' question may be 'we have done enough for this person' much earlier than we might have hoped. Some will wish the 'and then what' question was never asked.

I continue to believe it must be asked. You cannot claim to offer solutions if you do not think in terms of time. To shape and reshape the events of life, each of us must plan and invest. If government is to play an effective role in helping people to obtain a brighter future, it needs to focus on ways of helping people to reshape their lives.

False events

Having to confront the 'and then what' question is the most immediate difficulty with dynamic thinking when applied to policy. There are other, and sometimes larger, intellectual issues which must be confronted. The study of dynamics is ultimately the study of events and processes. Dynamics requires measuring an event which begins and ends. Unfortunately, in our need to find measurable events, we face the real danger of creating *false events*. When researchers focus on particular events, policy will often follow.

The most extreme version of this occurs when you draw an arbitrary poverty line and measure movement into and out of poverty. When you count movements into poverty, you will treat someone whose income had been well above the poverty line and then fell dramatically, on a par with someone whose income was only $1 above and fell by a few dollars. Both are the start of a poverty spell, but these are not comparable events. The person whose income changed so little probably did not experience anything he or she would describe as significant. Thus we have created an arbitrary event. That is less of a problem when you describe dynamics of programme participation. Someone is either on the programme or is not, and an entrance or departure does represent something real.   Still, the movement can represent something more or less significant to different participants.

This mischaracterising of events extends to other dimensions of human behaviour as well.   Increasingly, researchers are looking at the dynamics of family structure changes such as marriage or childbearing.   Marriage or childbearing are surely serious and well-defined events for most people.   Yet these events themselves are significant in part because they represent the culmination of a much longer series of relationships which are likely to extend into the future.   Marriage per se may cause you to change behaviour far less than the relationship that led to it.   If we are using marriage either as a dependent or independent variable, we may focus on the wrong thing.

The reason for this preoccupation with event classification arises in part because of the promise it offers for dynamic analysis. For with longitudinal, dynamic data we begin to pierce the veil of causality, and for social scientists causality is like the Holy Grail. In economics, we have very elaborate models for causality tests using time series data.   We have methods for deciding if event A caused event B or vice versa.   In principle, we can use the same methods to ask whether work leads to marriage, or marriage leads to work.   But if a couple lived together for several years before marriage, is marriage the big event?   Applying such methods to dynamic individual data is very dangerous when false events can create incorrect inferences.   Often you will miss the real causal forces because of misclassification (cf Chapter Three).

Human nature is so complicated that you can easily reject the claim that people changed behaviour in response to some event that just happened.   Behaviour will have changed before the event, in anticipation of it.   The individual knows the event is coming, but the researcher will not see it for months or even years.   So our temptation will be to reject any causal link, even if things are closely connected.   There is no easy resolution of the false event problem, but there is considerable danger that too much of our technical apparatus and thus too much of our policy may focus on establishing the duration of events and not nearly enough time is spent on classifying and understanding the true nature of the events in the first place.   An example of this involves teenage pregnancy – a long-standing preoccupation in the US.   Research is beginning to show that teenage pregnancy by itself is not as dramatically negative an event in people's lives as most policy makers believe. Focusing on just the event may lead us to much larger questions about the lives of young people.

Impact of larger social forces

The biggest danger with dynamic research is its tendency to look to the individual as the critical behavioural unit. When you start doing dynamic modelling, you are essentially forced to look at the events facing an individual. How long did a person receive aid? What events led them on to or out of aid? In theory, you could use any unit of analysis for some form of longitudinal modelling – a family, a firm, or a community. However, it is a lot easier to look at the individual than at any other unit because families, firms and communities change when individuals leave or join the larger unit. The analysis becomes very difficult.

So we follow an individual and measure the events in his or her life. When we do that, we subconsciously move to the person as the relevant economic unit. This focus has significance. Dynamic analysis seems to lend itself more easily to questions such as 'what is wrong with those people' than to questions such as 'what is wrong with that society or economy'. This arises in part because dynamic analysis highlights the heterogeneity of outcomes. Some people made it off of aid, why can't the others? Another part of the problem is that dynamic analysis influences the types of questions we ask. You can ask when a worker lost his job. It is not obvious how you then go and say, 'What feature of the economic system led to this person losing his job rather than someone else?' That is just too difficult. In theory you could do it, but it is just not the type of question researchers tend to ask.

The problem is that individuals are caught in a larger pattern of environmental and socioeconomic forces that we find much more difficult to model. As we focus in on the individual, we do a much better job of modelling individual outcomes. Since we can not do much to understand and measure the larger forces, they receive little attention. In effect, we reproduce the world as it appears to a single economic or social actor. She cannot influence the larger forces. She must cope with them and respond as best as she can. Our models accurately capture *her* individual situation.

However, governments and societies can, in principle, alter the larger forces that influence individuals. Larger structural relationships can be changed with government intervention. If we have a policy tool which myopically hones in on the individual, these larger opportunities will be missed. We may inadvertently aid those who would deny any significance to these forces.

The real challenge for us is to build models that incorporate both individual dynamics and the larger social forces. It is a daunting task, but the simplest versions are already present when we include unemployment rates as an independent variable. Later, we can perhaps create more sophisticated models whereby individual choices feed back into larger economic structures[4] – the way static economic models start with the choices of individual demanders and suppliers and aggregate into a story about how the market clears. Until that time, all who use dynamics for policy should use it carefully.

Conclusion: promise and pitfalls

I continue to believe that dynamic analysis is very exciting and that its promise for policy making is enormous. It is wondrous to see the growing sophistication of both models and analysis.

Still, I feel somewhat glad that I started in a technically simpler era. Mary Jo Bane and I had a mere 300 observations in our first study of welfare dynamics. We were able to print out the data from every one of these people and try to infer just what was happening to them. When we created events or designed classification systems, we could look at each case and see if we thought our designs made sense based on everything we could see in the case record.

Today the technology is so exciting and the possibilities so large that I worry there is too little time or energy for looking at individual cases. If so, those of us who study data can loose track of the realities of the things we seek to study. Then we can make bad inferences and create bad policy. I believe that the pitfalls and the hope for progress in dynamic analysis and dynamic policy making lie mostly outside the technical failures and compromises that inevitably arise in such complicated work. Our technical genius could overwhelm our ability to recognise the human motivations that influence our lives and create a dangerous myopia about the larger political and economic forces at work. The best solution I know is to spend time with the people we study.

Dynamic analysis is the future. Its potential is enormous. I find the work currently being done remarkably exciting. There is so much to learn and so much opportunity for improving policy. Dynamic work is so very ... well, dynamic.

Notes

[1] For summary of Ellwood's analyses of welfare dynamics and of welfare policies and debates, see Bane and Ellwood (1994).

[2] For a comparison of this US scheme with similar options and alternatives for Britain, see Walker and Wiseman (1997). In the summer of 1997 EITC was also discussed as an option for German policy (see Leisering et al, 1997).

[3] See Wiseman (1996) for an account of the provisions of the Personal Responsibility and Work Opportunity Reconciliation Act. For an account of Ellwood's role after the Republican Revolution, see DeParle (1996). For contrasting evidence of welfare reforms in other countries, see Chapter Fifteen.

[4] In Chapters Thirteen and Fourteen such models as called for by Ellwood are developed and implemented. In Chapters Eleven and Twelve the impact of larger social forces on individual benefit trajectories is systematically analysed without using formal macro-micro models.

Part Two

Life course dynamics

Occupational careers under different welfare regimes: West Germany, Great Britain and Sweden

Jutta Allmendinger and Thomas Hinz

Occupational life courses are forcefully shaped by a variety of social institutions: by educational systems, firms, intermediate organisations, labour-management relations, and social policy (Mayer and Müller, 1989). General and vocational training systems define occupational opportunities for entrants to the labour market and influence how people are matched to jobs over a longer term. Firms or intermediate organisations, such as labour unions and trade associations, set wages, benefits, and work conditions. Labour-management relations give structure to the daily life on the shop floor. These factors not only affect the shape of occupational trajectories – duration and stability of jobs held during the life course and hierarchical positions attained – but also pattern norms and expectations with respect to occupational careers.

Our analysis will focus on three of these contextual features: social security programmes, general education, and vocational training, comparing Great Britain, Germany, and Sweden.[1] In doing so we ask whether there are homologies between these three aspects of institutional structure in each country that make for distinct national occupational regimes. Similarly, we ask if different social security, education and training regimes give rise to typical patterns of labour force participation and occupational mobility (job mobility and class mobility[2]). We build on Esping-

Andersen's work (1990) but we emphasise the time dimension of labour force participation and related institutions. Germany serves as a model for a conservative regime; Sweden has a social-democratic welfare state. Among West European countries, Great Britain features a liberal welfare state.

We start with some general remarks about how social policy and occupational life courses interact. We then turn to the educational and vocational training systems of the three countries and discuss their possible effects on occupational trajectories. Next, we show that the social security programmes adopted in each country are homologous with their systems of general and vocational training. Then, after briefly reviewing recent changes that may help to determine occupational opportunities, we analyse patterns of occupational mobility in Germany, Great Britain, and Sweden over the entire life course and between generations. Finally, we ask whether European integration and globalisation may induce change in occupational life courses, and if so, how.

Institutional contexts of occupational careers

Social policy programmes

In asking how social policy interacts with the life course, two *ideal types* of social policy programmes, *situational programmes* and *continuous programmes*, may be distinguished (Allmendinger, 1994). Situational programmes are part of the means-tested 'welfare' state and marked by *life course indifference*, whereas continuous programmes, which are part of the contributory 'social' state, are *based on the life course and centre on it* (Table 5.1).

Table 5.1: Types of welfare state activity

	Situational programmes	Continuous programmes
Life course	Irrelevant	Relevant
Time frame	Present (in real time)	Future (in time to come)
Duration of benefit	One-shot, repeatable (time and again)	Continuous (once and always)
Knowledge	Specific	Atmospheric
Benefits	Concrete	Abstract
	Needs-based	Replacement-based
Prototype	Social assistance	Public pensions

Social policy programmes also have a specific relationship to time ('time frame'). Some policies look only at the present and deliberately ignore the past: social assistance systems are a good example. Other policies work like a perpetual balance sheet, point to the future, and function retrospectively: contributory pension insurance is an example. Moreover, there are differences in *benefit duration*. Some benefits may be received time and again; others once and forever. Time frame and benefit duration are both linked to *knowledge* about the conditions under which benefits may be obtained. Receipt of social security benefit (pension) is for most people a future event. Individual interest and actions are less directly interlinked with such policies, and knowledge is likely to be 'indirect' and 'atmospheric'. Once benefits are received ('once and always'), knowledge gained in obtaining the benefit is of little strategic value for people's future actions. If benefits can be obtained repeatedly the situation is different: here knowledge about the entitlement is likely to be specific and lies within an individual's action space. Because benefits from social assistance systems may be obtained 'time and again', people's learning and experience of benefit receipt can be relevant for, and influence, future actions.

Finally, social security and social assistance programmes also differ in kind. Situational programmes deliver *concrete*, needs-based benefits, whereas continuous programmes are typically about *abstract*, replacement-based benefits (Zacher, 1987). The abstract determination of pension benefits is the outcome of an individual occupational trajectory, it enhances the foreseeability of benefits, and diminishes dependence. A *concrete* determination of benefits focuses on equal treatment for people with similar 'needs' in similar life circumstances, and demands proof of these conditions (one has to be 'deserving'). To determine a benefit concretely, individual circumstances have to be measured against some standard of need, and discretion and judgement loom large. The unclear origin of benefit, discretion, and moral codes of conduct may imply that legal protection is possible only with respect to the process of assessment and not the outcome (that is the level of benefit). Potential recipients have little reliable expectations about the certainty with which they may obtain benefits.

The three countries we studied all share elements of both situational and continuous programmes, but their relative importance varies considerably. The 'social state' is a central European tradition since Bismarck, whereas 'welfare' statism is an Anglo-Saxon heritage.[3] In Sweden (and other Scandinavian countries), programmes based on citizenship combine both situational and continuous programmes. For programmes based on citizenship, the occupational life course is irrelevant, duration is continuous, and knowledge is atmospheric. In non-contributory basic pension schemes knowledge would not even matter, because basic benefits for all build on 'status' parameters that are difficult to change. There is little scope for people to take strategic action. With these differences between programmes in mind, we ask whether general and vocational training can be distinguished along the same lines. However, it will first be necessary to discuss ways in which general and vocational training may pattern occupational life courses.

Education and vocational training

The occupational career that a person will experience depends on his or her educational *environment,* defined in terms of the educational and vocational training systems available. Educational and vocational training each have two dimensions: the degree of *standardisation* of education provisions and the degree of *stratification* of educational opportunities (Allmendinger, 1989; for recent empirical support see Müller et al, 1996). Standardisation is defined by the degree to which the quality of education meets the same standards nationwide; stratification by the proportion of a cohort that attains the maximum number of school years provided by the educational system and by the degree of differentiation within given educational levels (tracking).

Educational systems shape the matching of people to jobs. In standardised systems employers can rely on information given by (standardised) certificates and do not have to screen or train people entering the labour force. Stratification, on the other hand, affects the match between education and social structure. In stratified education systems, there is a tight coupling between the education system and a differentiated occupational structure; in unstratified systems, the coupling is loose.

The dimensions of stratification and standardisation need to be applied separately to educational and vocational training: the former is primarily relevant for general education, the latter for vocational training (see Table 5.2). In highly stratified education systems, people acquire school-leaving certificates that differ according to the time spent in general education. Each level of general education is then matched by specific types of vocational training. People with high certificates may enter vocational training that is of 'lower status', but people in the lower ranks of general education can rarely enter high status vocational tracks without taking a detour back to general schooling to obtain the 'right' certificate, a process that is long and troublesome. Hence a high degree of stratification of general education preserves class lines and makes upward class mobility during the life course unlikely.

Table 5.2: Stratification and standardisation of education and vocational training

	Vocational training (→ stability)	
Education (→ **Boundedness**)	Standardised (dual system) -stable-	Unstandardised (on the job) -unstable-
Stratified -bounded-	G (1)	GB (2)
Unstratified -not bounded-	– (4)	S (3)

Note: G=Germany; GB=Great Britain; S=Sweden.

Standardised vocational training usually takes two to three years, much longer than on-the-job training. During these years, both employers and trainees invest considerable time and money to train and be trained in specific occupational areas. Such a design works only with a high degree of consensus between management and workers and, in turn, enhances labour-management relations, leading to a high degree of reciprocity and generalised trust (Fukuyama, 1996). In standardised systems, considerable auto-nomy and responsibility is given to trainees and future workers, who share a high degree of pride in their work and a sense of professionalism and identification with social class, management, and industry. Standardised vocational training should lead to a smooth transition between the education and occupational sector, and to orderly occupational trajectories with few occupational changes.[4] However, within given occupational areas broad and marketable knowledge eases job changes. These job changes may involve moderate upward (but not downward) mobility, mostly linked to seniority.

In Germany the structures, institutions, curricula and leaving certificates are roughly comparable in all the *Länder*: schooling is relatively standardised.   Germany has a tripartite education system.   Pupils are selected at approximately age 10 for either four, six, or nine years of additional schooling.   This decision is not subject to review, and later transfers to higher levels are difficult.   This stratified educational system – in 1995, only every fourth student of a given birth cohort attained the highest school credentials – is matched at the lower end by the 'dual system' – that is, a standardised vocational training system.   The transition from school to work is sequenced and 'orderly': the education system and the labour market fit within their hierarchical structures, and the standardised vocational training does not confine workers or employees to one single employer.   There are also limitations (Maurice and Sellier, 1979): in the long run, trainees are bound to one occupational field and have restricted access to further training at advanced levels.   The stratified education system requires that higher education – needed for eligibility for higher vocational training – can usually be acquired only by passing advanced levels of general education.   Although stratified general education in itself would allow for downward class mobility, the combination with standardised training – shielding against downward mobility – lead us to expect stability during the working life, with little changes in class positions or occupations.   The German system suggests stable and bounded occupational life courses.

The system of general education in Great Britain differs comparatively little from the German one.[5]   It is stratified and, in 1995, only every fifth student of a given age cohort attained the highest school credentials.   However, vocational training differs sharply.   In Great Britain, vocational training is relatively short and primarily in the hands of firms (Soskice, 1990; 1994; Hutton, 1995).   It qualifies as unstandardised.   Once acquired, vocational training serves for a single job but not for a lifetime; the time horizon is short.   New employers are likely to ask for more and different training, again offered within the (new) firm.   In the British case, we expect many job changes (because of un-standardised training), little upward class mobility (stratified school system), and considerable downward class mobility (unstandardised training). The British system suggests unstable and (upwardly) bounded occupational life courses.

In Sweden, the situation is different again. More than two thirds of each birth cohort attain the highest educational level, so general education is relatively unstratified. Vocational training is unstandardised, pointing towards unbounded and unstable career trajectories. Because vocational training does not have a 'dual system', as in Germany, there is no occupational labour market and frequent job changes are to be expected. Because of the unstratified school system, class position should be less fixed, as even high levels of qualification are within reach without a need to pass and document certification procedures.

In Table 5.2 cell 4 is empty: there is no state with an unstratified education system and standardised vocational training. This is plausible if a state invests in broad and extended education systems; fiscal limitations may steer it away from providing a lengthy phase of vocational training. The age of pupils also matters. If obligatory school age ends at 17, a broad vocational training programme would lead to labour market entry at 20 or even later.

Before moving to empirical evidence of these propositions, we need to ask whether national differences in welfare programmes are related to differences in general education and vocational training.

Integrating conceptual lenses

Continuous social security programmes are more likely to be found in nations where the 'ideal' occupational life course is conceived of as a stable, uninterrupted career with no downward and minimal upward mobility (Mückenberger, 1985). In such systems the policy goal to secure a given position in an occupational hierarchy in times of unemployment or old age can be sensibly pursued. In these nations, education and vocational policies stress continuity, security, expectability, and trust between the social partners. Members tend to share a clear sense of what they may expect and where they stand in the occupational hierarchy, given their educational credentials. People can trust such systems; atmospheric knowledge is sufficient, strategic planning of a life course unnecessary. This culturally deeply ingrained belief in continuity is orchestrated by more than education and social policy: labour unions, trade associations, and other 'communal organisations' (Fukuyama, 1996) play their own part. A different fit between social policy programmes and the education system can be found in nations that mostly employ situational policy programmes. Here, training is often given on the job, with a limited time horizon and limited security, assuming instability and occupational change. In turn, situational programmes are indifferent to the occupational life course. Systems that base their benefits on a snapshot of a given life generate no trust and are not meant to do so.

To summarise, adopting the traditional language of social welfare regimes, the liberal model is market-oriented, vocational training is provided by firms, the role of the state is restrained. Employment relationships are unstable and class positions are less (downwardly) bounded than they are in the conservative regime. In a conservative welfare state stability is the key, and unbounded careers tend not to be welcome. Security against all the risks involved in employment is provided by continuous programmes based on standardised vocational training. The social-democratic model aims at stability, but less by providing for occupational groups and more through social citizenship. Redistribution provides additional degrees of freedom by making social inequality less rigid.

Occupational careers in West Germany, Great Britain and Sweden

Economic structure

Opportunities for social mobility are partly determined by changes in economic structure and in the labour market. Hence it is appropriate to review developments during the period from 1970 to 1990. In 1970, 52% of the British labour force[6] was employed in the *service sector*, but by 1990 the proportion had risen to 69%, higher than in either Sweden or Germany. In 1990, 67% of the Swedish labour force was employed in services, compared with 54% in the 1970s. In Germany, even in 1990, still only 57% of Germans had jobs in the service sector despite an increase of 15% in 20 years. Cross-national differences are even more evident when the type of service jobs are compared. In Sweden, the growth in services was largely caused by an expansion of the public sector providing social and personal services (1970: 27%; 1990: 37%). In contrast, public sector employment in Great Britain rose from 23% (1970) to only 28% (1990); here 'post-industrialisation' took place to a higher degree in the private sector. However, in Germany, expansion of the public sector took place from a low level (1969: 17%) and by 1990 public sector employment (at 25%) was still less than in the other two countries studied.[7] The *industrial sector* decreased markedly in Great Britain: the percentage of workers in industry fell from 45% in 1970 to 29% in 1990 with a comparable decline experienced in Sweden. In Germany, a relatively high proportion of the labour force is still engaged in industry (1970: 49%, 1990: 40%). The *agricultural sector*, in contrast, declined rapidly in both Germany and Sweden during the 1970s and 1980s to levels comparable with those in Britain.

The above evidence suggests that opportunities for structural mobility created by sectoral change were greatest in Great Britain.

Labour force participation

Labour force participation rates are indicators of the transition between education, the labour market, and retirement. An early entry increases the duration of labour force participation and enlarges opportunities for mobility; if labour force participation ends early, the time for which people are exposed to the 'risk' of mobility (the 'risk time') is less.

Labour market activity rates are highest in Great Britain (Figure 5.1). Participation of young British men in the labour market is 15 percentage points higher than in Germany and 20 points higher than in Sweden, although the differences gradually diminish among those of aged 20-25 and 25-30 years. However, remarkable differences in labour force participation persist. In Great Britain the activity rate for the age group of 25-30 years is, at 95%, still 8 percentage points above Germany and 5 percentage points above Sweden. Turning to men aged 55 and above, the activity rates in Germany decline comparatively early and to a greater extent than elsewhere. Among men aged 55-60, participation in the labour force was 73% in Germany, 14 percentage points below that in Sweden, and 6 percentage points below that in Britain. Differences are even greater among men aged between 60 and 65: in Germany only about a third (30%) are still in the labour force, whereas in Britain the activity rate is 53% and, in Sweden, a remarkable 61% are still working.[8]

Figure 5.1: Labour force participation by age cohort, men (1992)

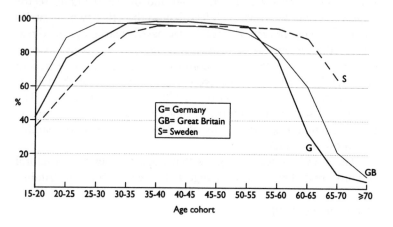

Source: Statistisches Bundesamt (1994); International Statistical Yearbook

The differences in age specific activity rates are closely related to the education, vocational training and social security systems in each country. The British market model is empirically well identified: activity rates of the very young and the very old are both higher than in the two other countries; early entry to the labour force is matched by late exit. There is a longer 'risk time' for upward and downward mobility. The high activity rates of young men (and women) are connected with the emphasis placed on on-the-job training, while the high labour force participation by older people reflects the low level of social security provided by the British welfare system. Germany is the opposite to Great Britain with regard to age-specific activity rates: late entry matches early exit. The German education and vocational training systems result in late labour force entry, but pension entitlements that can be claimed early (notably by the unemployed) cause activity rates to be curtailed at the other end of the life cycle. In Sweden low activity rates among the young are counterbalanced by high rates among older people.

Figure 5.2: Class position of the initial and last job

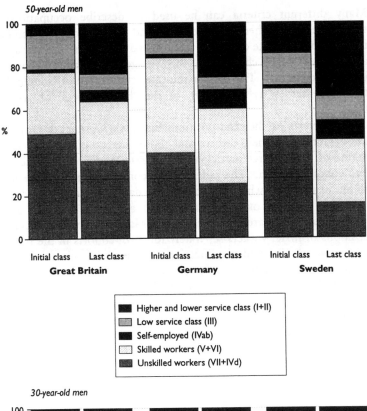

50-year-old men

Legend:
- ■ Higher and lower service class (I+II)
- ▨ Low service class (III)
- ■ Self-employed (IVab)
- □ Skilled workers (V+VI)
- ▦ Unskilled workers (VII+IVd)

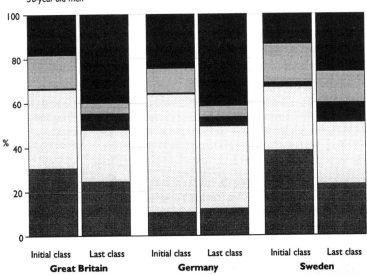

30-year-old men

Job mobility and class mobility

Many different criteria can be used to describe occupational trajectories. For theoretical reasons, and because of constraints imposed by available data,[9] we use just two indicators: the average annual rate[10] of job changes and the average annual rate of change in class position.[11] The former indicates the degree of 'stability', the latter serves as a measure of the 'boundedness' of work trajectories.

To determine the class positions that male workers occupy at the beginning of their careers and those that they reach after a period of labour force participation, we refer to the experience of two cohorts of men. The older cohort comprises men who were about 50 years old when their life course data was recorded, while the other cohort consists of men aged about 30. Figure 5.2 (datasource: Eurocareers project, K.U. Mayer) records the class positions of male workers separately for birth cohorts in the three countries. A five-fold classification of occupation class is used comprising the higher and lower divisions of the service class combined, low service class, self-employed (not in agriculture), skilled workers, and unskilled workers. The first bar for each country indicates the 'initial' class position, based on the job held at the beginning of the occupational career, whereas the second shows the class position at the end of the observation period, when the survey was conducted.

Analysis of the cohort of 50-year-olds reveals that men experience considerable class mobility over the life course in all three countries. The proportion located in the higher and lower service class grew significantly over the occupational life course, most evidently in Sweden where a difference of more than 20 percentage points is apparent. Even more pronounced were the possibilities for upward mobility open to Swedish workers who started as unskilled workers, compared with those in Germany or Britain. These findings testify that life courses are less bounded by class in Sweden than in either of the other two countries with more stratified systems of general education.

Turning to the younger cohort, the 30-year-old men, remarkable differences in initial class position were evident compared with the 50-year-olds who entered the labour market about 20 years earlier. In Great Britain and Germany more men started their occupational life in the higher and lower service class, and fewer began as unskilled workers, than did members of the older cohort two decades beforehand (in Sweden the two cohorts do not differ much). This change is most striking in Germany, indicating the comparatively late expansion of educational opportunities. The later cohort will have had little time in which to change class position: those people who had completed a full academic education will have spent as little as five years in the labour market by the age of 30. Even so, a remarkably high number of men moved into the higher and lower service class, swelling the proportion by 20 percentage points in Great Britain, and by 15 percentage points in Germany. In both countries upward movements in class position seem to occur at the beginning of a career, most likely indicating a degree of (short-term) mismatch between educational credentials and requirement of the first job.

Next we ask whether countries differ with respect to the rate of job and class mobility. Table 5.3, using the same format as Table 5.2 above, provides some preliminary answers: panel 1 presents data for *all* cohorts covered by the three national studies, while panel 2 relates solely to *50-year-old* men.[12] In both cases, we report the rate of job mobility followed by the rate of class mobility.

Table 5.3: Rates of job changes and of class changes

Rates of class changes	Rate of job changes	
	Low	High
All cohorts		
Low	G (0.13/0.07)	GB (0.25/0.11)
High	–	S (0.23/0.14)
50-year-old men		
Low	G (0.09/0.04)	GB (0.17/0.07)
High	–	S (0.16/not provided)

Note: Numbers in parenthesis refer to the rate of job changes (first number) and the rate of class changes (second number); GB=Great Britain; G=Germany; S=Sweden.
Source: Eurocareers project, Karl Ulrich Mayer (see fn 9)

The information covering *all cohorts* reveals that the rate at which *jobs* change over the life course is in line with expectations concerning the labour market consequences of unstandardised and standardised vocational training systems. The rates of change in Great Britain (0.25) and Sweden (0.23), both countries with unstandardised training systems, are similar and considerably higher than in Germany (0.13) which has a standardised system. Class mobility is invariably less than job mobility but also varies internationally: it is highest in Sweden (0.14) and lowest in Germany (0.04), with changes in Great Britain (0.11) falling in between. Again, the results are consistent with expectations based on the consequences of unstratified general education systems (as in Sweden) and stratified ones (such as in Germany and Great Britain). The differences between Germany and Great Britain are explained by the unstandardised vocational training available in Britain which provides little protection against downward class mobility.

Results for the *cohort of men aged 50* are similar: the rate of job mobility is higher in Great Britain (0.17) and Sweden (0.16) than in Germany (0.09). Because data is missing for Sweden, the findings with respect to class mobility are less secure. Nevertheless, the British–German comparison reveals marked differences. On average, 7% of men in the British cohort experienced a change in class position in a given year (a rate of 0.07) compared with only 4% of Germans; the difference is explicable in terms of the higher rates of downward mobility in Britain.

Table 5.4: Men remaining in the initial class position, by occupational class

Class position	Great Britain	Germany	Sweden
All cohorts			
Higher and lower service class	82%	92%	84%
Skilled workers	40%	59%	46%
Unskilled workers	53%	48%	28%
50-year-old men			
Higher and lower service class	74%	90%	–
Skilled workers	32%	56%	–
Unskilled workers	51%	46%	–

Note: Data for Sweden was not available by cohorts.

Source: Eurocareers project, Karl Ulrich Mayer (see fn 9)

The findings can be supplemented by the analysis of mobility tables which again relate to the cohort of 50-year-old men and the two cohorts combined (Table 5.4). The figures presented in the table are limited to the main diagonal of the standard mobility table, and focus on just three of the five class positions: the higher and lower service class; skilled workers; and unskilled workers.[13] The data pertaining to *all cohorts* shows that Germany has the highest proportion of immobile workers. Because Germans are protected against downward mobility, 92% of those starting in the *higher and lower service class* remain in this class. In Britain, class mobility is greater on account of extensive *downward mobility*: close to 6% of those initially employed in the service classes became unskilled workers, six times as many as in either Germany and Sweden.[14] Immobility among *unskilled* workers is also consistent with the predictions: it is considerably higher in Germany (48% immobile) and Great Britain (53% immobile) than in Sweden (28% immobile). More than in any other class, unskilled workers are constrained by the long-term effects of stratified general education – necessitating additional general education before gaining access to higher levels of vocational training. Results for the cohort of men aged 50 are limited to Germany and Great Britain, but reinforce the same conclusions.

Let us summarise the comparative findings on work trajectories (Table 5.5). In Great Britain, situational regulation is characteristic of its liberal welfare state with a stratified educational and unstandardised vocational training system. We find, as expected, unstable work trajectories with many job and relatively few class changes. In this *'deregulated open market system'* (Soskice, 1994), distrust is the basic unit of exchange between the social partners. In Germany, continuous programmes are the major pillars of a conservative welfare state and, together with a stratified education and a standardised vocational system, underpin long-term life course perspectives. Stable and bounded occupational careers predominate with few job changes and limited class mobility. In this *'flexibly coordinated corporatist system'*, trust relations between the social partners predominate. Sweden, in its tradition as a social democratic welfare state with unstratified education and unstandardised vocational training, has occupational careers that are relatively unbounded by class. This structure is caused by an unstratified education system and by a higher level of redistribution within society. The Swedish system, which is characterised by access to the welfare state that is predominately based on citizenship rather than labour force participation, and which achieves high levels of redistribution, might be termed a *'flexible coordinated universal system'*.

Table 5.5: Occupational careers under different welfare regimes

Country	Emphasis of social security	Education: degree of stratification	Vocational training: degree of standard-isation	Job mobility	Class mobility
Great Britain	Situational programmes	+	–	+	–
Germany	Continuous programmes	+	+	–	–
Sweden	Citizenship-based programmes	–	–	+	+

Divergence or convergence?

It has been demonstrated that job and class mobility during the life course are highly dependent upon the national institutional context. An important new question is whether these patterns and relationships are likely to converge or diverge as a result of European integration and economic 'globalisation'.

There are practical restrictions – not legal barriers – to mobility related to the *value* of education certificates. These certificates are granted in a national context: they certify knowledge as well as qualification. However, they also have an 'exchange value' and serve as a necessary passport to occupational positions within the national regime. A smooth transition from an unstratified to a stratified system is impossible, since employers in a stratified system will be unable easily to adjust to the degree of selectivity required. A change from stratified to unstratified systems will expose the employed to yet another selection procedure in addition to that which they have already completed in the stratified system. A move towards an EU-wide recognition of education certificates cannot assure the exportability of the national selection value of these certificates between societies with vastly different structures: certificates will not retain the same value as a passport to a job in a different institutional setting. The link between education system and labour market is overdetermined and structurally immobile.

Divergence or convergence cannot sensibly be studied in isolation by focusing simply on one social institution, or on one societal sector. Fukuyama (1996), for example, points to ingrained cultural differences between nations in the way general training, vocational training, and labour market relations combine to form 'high trust' (Germany) or 'low trust' (Great Britain) societies.[15] Similarly, Soskice (1994) has drawn attention to the fact that transplanting single institutions such as vocational training from Germany to Great Britain is impossible without enormous changes in the functions of the policy in the new country.

European integration is foremost about the markets for goods, services, and capital – and only last and least for labour (Oberender and Streit, 1995). While integration of the first three markets has advanced rapidly since the mid-1980s, labour market and social policy has remained the province of national governments (cf Leibfried and Pierson, 1995). However, intra-European and global competition is likely to intensify resulting, possibly, in the convergence or divergence of occupational career patterns. Four scenarios may be conceived: path dependency, collective dualisation, individual dualisation, and a new synthesis – the 'social investment state'.

Path dependency: intra-European and international competition puts pressure on societies to adjust and reform their existing policies. The result is to increase exclusion from social provision, extending the barriers each country already relies on. In Germany, channels for female employment might be tightened and partly redirected; in Britain, the risks facing all employed people might be intensified and marginalisation might become so extensive that civil society itself is put at risk; in Sweden, dependence upon the state and its fiscal crisis may generalise risks for all participants in the labour market.

Collective dualisation: in all countries an *internal* competition of life course regimes might be introduced, breaking the monopoly of the single model. Two distinct life course regimes, one regulated, one deregulated, would evolve, polarising society. However, the dualisation would be different in each country. In Germany, stability and boundedness would be reserved for the privileged few in the primary labour market, with the burdens on the welfare state being countered by restrictive access and, hence, extensive social exclusion. In Sweden, unbounded mobility would be replaced by a stable stratum and a new unstable one. In Great Britain, two forms of instability and unboundedness would appear: the 'greater' and the 'lesser' would separate in such a way that the less unstable and unbounded patterns would appear as privileged.

Individual dualisation: this scenario entails dualisation or *polarisation* within individual life courses with risks evenly distributed between social strata but differentiated by age. In Germany, the patterns of stability and boundedness could still be cultivated, but at some age, perhaps 55, the pattern of instability and unboundedness would apply, possibly facilitated by means of welfare state programmes. Similar developments could be imagined for Sweden. In Great Britain, systematically increased insecurity and unboundedness could be allocated according to age. Such developments are not without precedent: it is common in Japan to make highly paid workers (and managers), employed by big companies, redundant at age 55 and to re-employ them in the 'secondary sector' at lower wages, mostly in small subsidiary firms (cf Kohli et al, 1992: p 22, note 17). In German history the common decline in productivity of middle-aged manual workers – and its consequence – was one of the triggers for Bismarck's introduction of the welfare state in the late 19th century (Reif, 1982; Weber, 1912).

'Social Investment State': in several essays Myles (1995) has contrasted a conservative polarisation in two life courses with a progressive trajectory towards a new and universal life course pattern. The conservative polarisation would have conservative consequences only in Germany and Sweden, whereas in the UK the benefits of the welfare state – though at a rather low level – would have to be reintroduced.

In our taxonomy we need finally to explore the opposite trajectory: uniform reintegration of life courses via the welfare state. The social investment state would counter the disintegrative consequences of frequent job changes, repeated moves in and out of employment, increasing numbers of 'bad jobs' and would in particular, meet the increased need for basic and continuing education. It would do so by aiming more closely at critical stages and transitions in life and assisting individuals to manage their own life course and by an enabling policy that invests in people via fostering human capital. In such a rebuilding of the welfare state, 'stability' would have to be decoupled from employment and coupled with the status of citizen or resident. Such a scenario is most plausible in Sweden, where egalitarian and universalist traditions seem to provide opportunities for such a qualitative and progressive 'great leap forward', although welfare state reforms in the 1990s do not appear to go this way (Esping-Andersen, 1996).

Authors' acknowledgements

We thank Hannah Brückner, Martin Kohli, Stephan Leibfried, Wolfgang Ludwig-Mayerhofer, Walter Müller, Susanne Steinmann, John Veit-Wilson and the editors of this volume for helpful discussions, valuable comments, and editorial assistance. Karl Ulrich Mayer kindly gave us access to the data of his project on 'Eurocareers'. This paper was completed while the first author was a Fellow at the Centre for Advanced Study in the Behavioral Sciences, Palo Alto. I am grateful for financial support provided by the National Science Foundation Grant #SBR-9022192.

Notes

[1] Because of sparse data on occupational life courses, country selection was severely restricted. Even more consequential, internationally comparative data on occupational trajectories of *women* was not available. Because our data could not systematically cover the issues raised by studying female career trajectories, our conceptual work basically excludes the discussion of female life courses.

[2] For this distinction see, for example, Mayer and Carroll (1987). This classification of Great Britain is justified by the extraordinary market orientation of British social and economic politics since 1979, and macroeconomic indicators (Hoffmann, 1995). We

restrict our analysis to West German life histories because life courses in the former German Democratic Republic (GDR) are a different story altogether (see the analyses by Huinink et al, 1995).

[3] Within central Europe, there is a further tie between the state and the life course. In Germany (and France) it was typically the 'career', the embeddedness of the civil servant's life course, on which social policy was modelled. The life course embedded in social policy is not just a descriptive category but also a normative idea: in central Europe it is about standardising 'normality' according to a civil servant's 'life culture'. This additional layer of 'moral economy' in the life course is completely absent in Anglo-Saxon countries since such a state tradition is foreign to Great Britain (and also to the USA).

[4] It has often been claimed that standardised, occupation-specific training considerably *restricts* workers' flexibility to change occupations. At the same time, such training *increases* flexibility at the level of the shop floor. The former is seen as a severe disadvantage, the latter as a distinct advantage vis-à-vis global competition, because it enhances group work and creative group innovations (Fukuyama, 1996).

[5] Although, since the 1970s the comprehensive system at secondary school level largely avoids irrevocable decisions being taken at the age of eleven.

[6] Unless noted otherwise, data is taken from the International Statistical Yearbook and the Statistisches Bundesamt.

[7] It should be noted that expansion of the public sector creates jobs especially for women. In all three nations, about 20% of male employees are working in the public sector. In Sweden, the proportion of women who were employed in the public sector rose from an already high level (1970: 45.3%) to 56.5% in 1990. In Great Britain, the growth from 34.1% (1970) to 40.8% (1990) turned out to be distinctly smaller than in Sweden, whereas Germany, which had started at a very low level (1969: 22.6%), had the relatively highest growth rate (1990: 35.9%).

[8] Labour force participation by men and women differs remarkably in Germany and Great Britain; in Sweden the gender difference is relatively small. The patterns of women's activity rates look similar for all age groups in Germany and Great Britain but are

very different in Sweden. If we look at the 30-35 age group, labour force participation by Swedish women reaches 88%, whereas the proportion in Germany and Great Britain is about 20 percentage points lower. In the 60-65 age group, the activity rate of German women was 10%, in Great Britain it was 24%, and in Sweden 53%.

[9] Continuous data on work histories, necessary to track the interaction between social structure and individual outcomes, is rarely available internationally. Data considered in this analysis is part of the 'Eurocareers' project, directed by Karl Ulrich Mayer. Members of the study group are Paul de Graaf/Ruud Luikx, David Grusky/Larry Wu, Peter Robert, Michael Tahlin, Colin Mills, Robert Miller, Kirsten Ringdal and Bogdan Mach. Specifically, we used tables from the following data sets: German Life Course Study (West Germany, observation period: 1981-1983; cohorts born 1929-31, 1939-41, 1949-51) Karl Ulrich Mayer; ESRC SCELI (1986; cohorts born 1926-34, 1935-44, 1945-54, 1955-61) Colin Mills; and the Swedish Level of Living Survey (1991, cohorts born 1925-34, 1935-44, 1945-54, 1955-65), Michael Tahlin. All figures reported below are based on information provided by these three researchers, since we did not have access to the data files. Available data led to the following restrictions: comparison of only few nations, different times of observation, and different age groups. We have information on men only, cannot distinguish between class positions I and II, and cannot calculate the ratio number of class positions to number of jobs episodes. Distinction between voluntary and involuntary job shifts is impossible.

[10] We report the *rate* of job and class changes because absolute numbers are misleading as a result of international differences in the 'time of exposure'.

[11] A *job episode* is defined as an employment spell without change in occupation, occupational level, and employer. *Class positions* were classified on the scheme developed by Erikson and Goldthorpe (1992) and available only in a very condensed form: I + II: higher and lower divisions of the service class; III: low service class; IVab: self-employed outside agriculture; IVc: self-employed in agriculture; V + VI: skilled workers; VII + IVd: unskilled workers. Because of its very low absolute numbers, class IVc was not considered in our analyses.

[12] The decision to report numbers based on all cohorts was necessitated by the fact that the Swedish researchers did not provide the rate of class changes by cohort. This problem becomes even more evident in Table 5.4 to follow.

[13] In all three countries, most men working are in these three class positions; for more detail see Allmendinger and Hinz (1997).

[14] In addition, in Great Britain skilled workers suffer the highest risk of moving to the position of unskilled workers (22%), while this percentage amounts to 10% in Germany and 15% in Sweden.

[15] For a related distinction see Soskice (1990). See also Biernacki (1995) for a detailed historical account of the labour-oriented differences between Germany and Great Britain.

six

Intergenerational dynamics in the USA: poverty processes in young adulthood

Martha Hill, Daniel Hill and Robert Walker

Introduction

Students of poverty have long been interested in the question of intergenerational transfer of poverty. Does poverty breed poverty? Is 'rags to riches' just an American myth? Does class trap people or do individual efforts and state support matter? By using dynamic methods of analysis and applying them to the crucial period between youth and adulthood this chapter looks closely at some of the processes involved. Rather than simply comparing a child's socioeconomic status with the status of his or her parents we look more precisely at the paths young adults take and the downward and upward moves at various points of transition.

We trace individuals throughout young adulthood, arguably one of the most complex of the chronological life stages. It is a stage filled with numerous and varied transitions – from adolescence to adulthood, from being a child to being a spouse and parent, from being a student to being a worker, from being someone whose major household responsibility is mowing the lawn or washing the dishes to being the person paying the rent or mortgage. The occurrence or non-occurrence of these types of events, and their timing, may shape the well-being of young adults both immediately and far into the future.

Our focus is on poverty in young adulthood, with poverty defined in the usual US manner as family income falling below a specified minimal needs threshold (see below). As a number of poverty researchers before us have done (see Bane and Ellwood, 1986, for the classic example), we look at poverty as a dynamic process occurring in spells on and off with measurable beginnings and endings. The social sciences, however, are still learning about these processes, and this chapter's unique contribution is three-fold: it accounts for the possibility of repeated spells of poverty by using modulated renewal models; traces poverty transitions throughout an extensive period defining the start of adulthood; and compares the strength of behaviours versus background as predictors of poverty transitions.

Although the repeating of spells has been recognised as a complexity of poverty patterns,[1] it has received relatively little attention from researchers or public agencies trying to alleviate poverty. We attempt to allow for repeated spells by applying modulated renewal models to poverty transitions over a full stage of young adulthood, defined as ages 16-30. Altogether we use a 23-year time span of data from the Michigan Panel Study of Income Dynamics (PSID), which includes observations of young adulthood as well as early adolescence. This allows us to include in our models, and assess the relative importance of, the influences of the past (parental background as reported by the parents) and the present (behaviours of the young adult). This research is part of a broader research programme aimed ultimately at under-standing poverty processes throughout the life course.

Analytical framework

Life-stage approach

The lifetime is a natural time frame for the study of poverty, but existing data does not yet allow us to estimate models of poverty over full lifetimes. Life course analysis teaches us that there are periods of less than a lifetime – life stages – which are meaningful and may differ with regard to poverty processes (Duncan, 1988; Burkhauser and Duncan, 1989; Walker, 1988). A life-stage approach also offers the possibility to avoid a major statistical impediment. Poverty research relies heavily on panel data because measures of income and income needs, the building blocks for poverty status assessment, are not reliably recalled with long retrospection. In the past, panel studies offered only short and arbitrary observation periods, and that resulted in sample censorship, with parts of spells lost to observation. In the USA this is less problematic today because panel data now spans multiple decades, covering full chronological life stages – in contrast to European countries where general household panel surveys have only been established in the 1980s and 1990s (see Chapters Nine and Ten).

We define life stages in terms of chronological age and map the life course into six different 15-year life stages,[2] with young adulthood (ages 16 through to 30) as the stage of interest for this analysis. The 15-year time span circumvents arbitrary sample censorship due to a short observation period but introduces another form of censorship, that of attrition. Our plans for future research aim to address that complication.

Data

The analysis is based on data from the Michigan PSID, a national survey of the US population tracking families and individuals over time (see Hill, 1992, for a comprehensive description). With 23 waves of annual data, the PSID is well-suited to the life-stage approach described above. Because the original focus of the PSID was poverty dynamics, it began, in 1968, with a national sample that included a disproportionately large number of low-income households. Probability-of-selection weights adjusted for differential attrition help to make estimates representative of the US population.

To obtain a sample size capable of producing robust statistics, we selected six cohorts from the PSID (essentially six single-year birth cohorts) and treated them as a single cohort. Our subsample is defined as individuals in an interviewed PSID household in the spring of 1968, aged 8-13 at the time. These individuals all remained in the PSID at least from ages 13 through to 16, with some observed throughout ages 13 to 30. The sample consists of a total of 3,079 individuals, 1,524 males and 1,555 females.

The PSID data enabled us to observe parts of the prior life stage (late childhood) and trace the influence of conditions during adolescence on poverty processes during young adulthood. However, the data is not of sufficient length to show both full childhood and young adulthood as late as age 30. For some measures, such as parental education, the correlation between early childhood level and late childhood level will be high, making the omission of early childhood measurement less critical.

Modelling technique

Since transitions into and out of poverty are repeatable events we base our statistical analysis on a modulated renewal model (Yamaguchi, 1991) which distinguishes between falling in, and climbing out of, poverty (see Appendix A of this chapter for details). The overall likelihood of a transition, be it falling into or climbing out of poverty, could be specified as a single equation yielding fully efficient and consistent parameter estimates. To determine whether to use such a unified equation or separate equations for transitions in each direction, we impose the restriction that parameter estimates for any specific predictor be equal but opposite in sign for transitions into poverty and out of poverty. We then apply a likelihood-ratio test based on the restricted and unrestricted log-likelihoods. If symmetry restrictions are not appropriate, the likelihood function and estimation problem can be greatly simplified by estimating the climbing-out and falling-in portions of the model separately.

Several assumptions are implicit in the modulated renewal model. First, the model assumes independence across time and individuals (conditional on the predictors) in the propensities to climb out of and fall into poverty. Unmeasured individual heterogeneity will violate the assumptions of the model and will impart bias to the estimates. Second, individuals who attrite (leave) from the sample prior to age 30 are treated as right-censored observations. Implicit in this treatment is the assumption that attrition is independent of changes in poverty status. Plans for future research include to explore an alternative treatment of attrition that is free of this assumption.

Defining poverty and poverty transitions

Poverty is defined for an individual as having annual family income below a threshold level needed to satisfy minimal family needs for a family of that size and composition.[3] Entering (exiting) poverty occurs when an individual in a non-poor (poor) family last year is in a poor (non-poor) family this year.

Analyses of poverty transitions during young adulthood face special problems with regard to the treatment of co-residence with parents. When young adults live with their parents, should we count parents' income in our assessment of the young adults' poverty status? If we do, then poverty transitions for some young adults are merely a reflection of their parents' poverty transitions rather than any change in the income of the young adults themselves. In that regard, poverty transitions fail to reflect accurately changes in the young adults' level of economic achievement, and estimates of the influence of predictors such as parental background are upwardly biased. However, poverty transitions counting co-resident parents' income do reflect changes in the young adults' standard of living because young adults living with parents are likely to benefit from the shared consumption that comes from residing with their parents.

The approach taken here is to include all years of young adulthood whether or not they co-resided with parents and to include co-resident family income and needs in the measure of poverty status. Although there are several alternative approaches, none is perfect. Despite the drawbacks of the chosen approach, it does have the advantage of clarity in the direction of its bias – it biases upward the estimated role of parental economic circumstances. To gauge the magnitude of the bias, we do some re-estimation omitting all data relating to periods of co-residence with parents and note how those results differ from our main results based on all years.

Predictors of poverty transitions

Young adulthood is the period during which important additions to human capital are accrued and family formation is begun (Goldscheider and DaVanzo, 1989; DaVanzo and Goldscheider, 1990; O'Higgins et al, 1988). Key events on the social trajectory include leaving the parental home, marriage, marital dissolution, and parenthood. A major determinant of life trajectory seems to be out-of-marriage conception, which often leads the mother, and sometimes both parents, to abandon education in favour of child-rearing or paid employment (McLanahan and Sandefur, 1994a; Hoffman et al, 1993; Brandon, 1993; Pirog-Good, 1993; Marini, 1984). Key events on the human capital trajectory include completion of education and entry into the labour force in a chosen occupation. Statistically there are high costs of low levels of educational attainment in terms of earnings levels (Howe, 1993; Becker and Lewis, 1993; Pencavel, 1993).

Intergenerational transmission may be operative. There is growing evidence that economic disadvantage is passed to a degree from parents to their children, although the precise mechanisms have yet to be determined in detail (Corcoran and Boggess, 1994; Haveman and Wolfe, 1994; Solon, 1992; McLanahan and Sandefur, 1994b). There is also evidence that conditions and stressful events in late, not just early, childhood are important to the child's attainments and achievements (Hill et al, 1996; Gottschalk, 1994; An et al, 1992; Furstenberg et al, 1990; Haveman et al, 1991).

Taking account of findings from the literature and measures available in the data, we constructed the set of predictors listed in Table 6.1 along with their expected association to poverty transitions. The predictors include:

- fixed characteristics (such as sex and race);

- initial conditions (such as the childhood background of the young adult);

- time-varying covariates (such as marrying or giving birth to a child);

- duration of the current spell (which is expected to be negatively associated with chances of a poverty transition in either direction because of 'state dependence').

To capture the influence of the young adult's own decisions and behaviours, the predictors measure major socio-demographic events and accumulations of skills during young adulthood. Each behaviour is measured as of the calendar year just prior to that of the dependent variable. For most of them – but not household establishment and membership – there are clear expectations for the direction of association with poverty transitions. For example, if a person works more hours his or her risk of moving into poverty is lower ('-in' in Table 6.1, first line) and, if poor, his or her chance of moving out is higher ('+out').

The parental situation is also hypothesised to play a role in the poverty processes of young adults, and our model focuses on long-run poverty risks associated with the situation of the parental family during the individual's adolescence (ages 13-15). These conditions are likely to have shaped the individual's development and accumulation of social and human capital during the child-hood life stage and serve as initial conditions at the time of entry into young adulthood.

Table 6.1: Predictors of poverty transitions and expected direction of correlations

Behaviours by the young adult

Hours of work (*work hours*) **[–in/+out] strongest for males**
Accumulated education:
- at least high school level (*HS Grad*) **[–in/+out]**
- completed college (*Col Grad*) **[–in/+out]**

Marital events:
- becoming married (*Marry*) **[?] strongest for females**
- divorce or separation (*Div/Sep*) **[+in] strongest for females**

Child birth events:
- within marriage (*Child in Mar*) **[+in]**
- out of marriage (*Child out Mar*) **[+in] larger than Child in Mar and strongest for females**

Household establishment and membership:
- establish a household separate from the parental household (*Split*) **[?]**
- being a head or wife of a family or subfamily (*Head/Wife*) **[?]**
- sharing a household with another family (*Share HH*) **[?]**

Background factors

Parental family circumstances during the ages 13-15:
- parental family income (*Par Inc 13-15*) **[–in/–out]**
- parental family size (*Par Size 13-15*) **[–in/–out]**
- average amount of AFDC family received (*AFDC 13-15*) **[+in/–out]**
- parental family head's education (*Head Ed 13-15*) **[–in/+out]**
- number of years parental family female-headed (*Yrs Fem Hd 13-15*) **[+in/–out]**
- parental family income* whether established own household (*Head/Wife* Par Inc*) **[+in/–out] opposite in direction to Par Inc**
- parental family size* whether established own household (*Head/Wife Par Siz*) **[–in/+out] opposite in direction to Par Size**

Race:
- whether African-American (*African-Amer*) **[+in/–out]**

State dependence or heterogeneity factor

Duration:
- duration of the current spell **[–in/–out]**

Expected direction of correlation with chances of moving into/out of poverty is indicated in bracket in bold type; AFDC=Aid to Families with Dependent Children.

The measures of parental family circumstances include race, parental family income, and parental family size.[4] To allow for the possibility that the influence of parental circumstances during childhood declines as the young adult gains independence from the parental family, we include additional predictors interacting parental income and size with an indicator of whether the young adult has established a separate household (interaction marked by asterisks in Table 6.1).

Because poverty processes may differ for the sexes, we estimate separate models for males and females and test for overall differences.[5] Expectations are that marital events will be stronger predictors of poverty transitions for females than for males because the economic status of the spouse plays a larger role in women's economic well-being. Labour market work hours, on the other hand, are expected to be stronger predictors for males because of men's generally higher wage levels.

Our models omit several potentially important predictors. They do not include contemporaneous measures of parental family circumstances,[6] some aspects of childhood parental family circumstances (such as step-parent arrangements), or measures of neighbourhood or labour market conditions because construction of such measures is difficult or impossible for a sizeable segment of the sample. Future research will attempt to expand the field of predictors along these lines.

Analysis results

Explaining poverty transitions (parameter estimates)

The analysis (see parameter estimates in Appendix B of this chapter) show that movements into or out of poverty are tied to the actions of the young adult, often in ways that conform to expectations. The major findings about behaviours are the following (for specification of variables see Table 6.1):

- Labour market variables (hours of work) and education (high school, college) have a strong relationship to poverty transitions and in the expected direction.

- Family variables (marriage, separation, divorce, childbirth) show several of the expected patterns. Marriage, marital disruption and out-of-marriage births are all tied to higher risks of entering poverty among young women.[7] Having children in marriage is negatively correlated with chances of climbing out of poverty, but only for men. The lack of a negative association for women is somewhat unexpected. One other pattern is also somewhat at odds with expectations: marriage, for both men and women, is associated with enhanced chances – rather than reduced chances – of climbing out of poverty.

The results regarding the impact of the duration of a current spell in or out of poverty indicate that in young adulthood future poverty experiences are highly correlated with past poverty experiences:

- The longer a young adult has been in a given poverty status, the lower are his or her chances of changing poverty status. This association between duration and poverty dynamics is especially strong for females in poverty, and roughly equally strong for males and females out of poverty.

The interpretation of these associations is unclear without further research because they may reflect either a true causal relationship of state dependence, or they may mirror unmeasured persistent heterogeneity that affects risks of poverty throughout time. 'Heterogeneity' means that some people stay longer in poverty not because they have become 'dependent' in some way – for example, loss of motivation or of self-confidence – but because of some prior characteristic, for example, ill health, which makes it difficult for them to exit but which is not accounted for in our model. The effects of duration are crucial to much of the welfare dependency debate and will require a great deal of further research.[8]

Turning to influences of parental background and race we find that the past is related to young adulthood poverty dynamics in other ways as well:

- Being African-American is associated with a substantially greater risk of becoming or remaining poor during young adulthood.

- Parental family income and family size are also strongly associated with poverty dynamics during young adulthood, and the associations are in the expected direction. As expected, the size of the association declines once the individual establishes a household separate from his or her parents' household (the interaction term is almost always opposite in sign to the main term).

These relationships for parental background hold for males and females, although not necessarily with the same strength. Parental family income and size tend to be of greater importance for males than for females.[9]

Illustrations of risks and chances in young adulthood

Graphical tracking of risks over the life stage can show the impact of the different sets of variables more clearly than the figures of the parameter estimates alone. To illustrate the results graphically, we choose 'pure', exemplary types that make for clear-cut contrasts. Individuals are viewed as having one of two types of background, 'poor' or 'middle class', and one of two types of behaviours, 'poor' or 'middle class'. The two types of background differ mostly in terms of parents' income, parents' education, and amount of childhood spent by the individual in a female-headed family.[10] The two types of behaviours differ mostly with regard to educational attainment, having an out-of-wedlock birth early versus an in-marriage birth latter, not marrying versus marrying, and having different labour market work commitments.[11]

Different combinations of background and behaviour produce four different exemplary types or profiles of individuals. Two have behaviours consistent with their background: PP ('poor' background going along with 'poor' behaviours), and MM ('middle class' background going along with 'middle class' behaviours). Two have behaviours inconsistent with their background: PM ('poor' background but 'middle class' behaviours), and MP ('middle class' background but 'poor' behaviours). We restrict all four profiles to African-American women and apply each of them to our model estimates. Resulting hazard curves that visualise risks and chances of entering or exiting poverty are shown in Figures 6.1 and 6.2.

Figure 6.1 contrasts the predicted risks of entering poverty for the four profiles of women. Let us first look at the two lower curves, showing the two profiles of women from middle class backgrounds but with different types of behaviours. The curve labelled MM represents the pattern of predicted age-specific risks of falling into poverty[12] for an African-American woman from a 'middle class' background who follows 'middle class' behaviours.

The curve shows that such a woman has a 2% predicted probability of becoming poor at age 24 given that she was not poor at age 23. From age 16 on her predicted risk of becoming poor declines with age, but the decline is most distinct at two points – right after she graduates from high school at age 18 and when her work hours increase from very little to full-time at age 25. Her risk of poverty remains at a low level from her mid-20s to age 30.

Figure 6.1: Risks of entering poverty during young adult ages, for individuals with differing backgrounds and differing behaviours

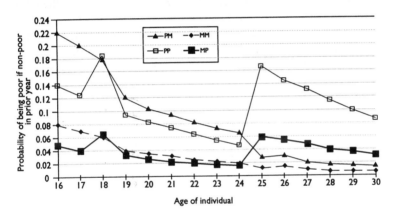

Notes: PM='poor' background but 'middle class' behaviour; PP='poor' background and 'poor' behaviour; MM='middle class' background and 'middle class' behaviour; MP='middle class' background but 'poor' behaviour.
Source: Panel Study of Income Dynamics (PSID); Turbo Pascal programmes used for simulation written by Daniel Hill

Compare that pattern with the MP path, which represents the predicted age-specific risks of becoming poor for an African-American woman with the same middle class background but who engages in poor behaviours. The risks for this middle class background but poor behaviours woman increase (rather than decrease) at two distinct points – when she has an out-of-marriage child at age 18, and when she sets up her own household at age 25. Her young adulthood story is quite different from that of her counterpart engaged in middle class behaviours. It is a story of higher risks of entering poverty in the mid-to-late-20s. Undoubtedly, the sizeable work hours assumed for the early part of young adulthood keep the risk of becoming poor early in adulthood relatively low.

Behaviours matter even more for poor background women (compare curves PM and PP). The curves are of the same general shape as the corresponding ones for women from a middle class background, with sharp changes at the same age markers. However, the two curves for women from a poor background are much further apart at all ages, but especially after age 24, than the curves for women from a middle class background.

Controlling for background, women with poor behaviours are predicted to be at greater risk of entering poverty during the latter part of young adulthood than those with middle class behaviours. This behaviour-generated differential is larger for women from a poor background than for those from a middle class one.

Behavioural differentials also appear in the exiting-poverty paths (see Figure 6.2, which presents those risk paths for all four profiles). The chances of exiting poverty, given that the young woman was in poverty in the prior year, improve substantially for the woman with middle class behaviours after she graduates from high school, again after she graduates from college, again when she enters the full-time work force, and yet again when she marries. The poor behaviours woman who is unable to escape poverty early in young adulthood stands a very slim chance of escaping poverty in the latter part of young adulthood. This behavioural difference in chances of becoming non-poor is stronger for middle class background women (MM versus MP) than for their poor background counterparts (PM versus PP), just the reverse of the findings for hazards of becoming poor.

Controlling for behaviours helps in assessing the role of background. There is evidence of the hazards differing directly with the young woman's background. For a young woman following poor behaviours, chances of becoming poor are substantially higher throughout young adulthood if she comes from a poor background as opposed to a middle class background (compare PP and MP in Figure 6.1). Among women with middle class behaviours, background differences produce sizeable differences in predicted risks of becoming poor during the early adulthood years (compare PM and MM in Figure 6.1). For a

Figure 6.2: Chances of climbing out of poverty during young adult ages, for individuals with differing backgrounds and differing behaviours

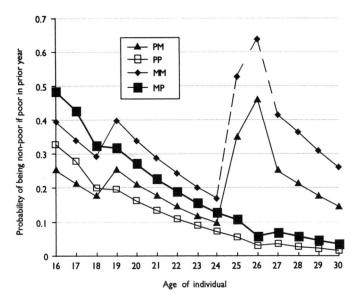

Notes: PM='poor' background but 'middle class' behaviour; PP='poor' background and 'poor' behaviour; MM='middle class' background and 'middle class' behaviour; MP='middle class' background but 'poor' behaviour.

Source: Panel Study of Income Dynamics (PSID); Turbo Pascal programmes used for simulation written by Daniel Hill

middle class behaviours woman, the probability at age 19 of becoming poor is about three times as high if she has a poor background rather than a middle class background (12% probability as opposed to 4%). The difference in risk is still sizeable by age 24 (6% probability as opposed to 2%). With regard to predicted chances of climbing out of poverty (see Figure 6.2), background also tends to make a sizeable difference, with a middle class background producing higher predicted chances of exiting poverty than a poor background.

Only in two types of situations, and then only in the latter years of young adulthood, does background appear to be of little consequence for predicted hazards. One such situation involves the risks of entering poverty for women engaged in middle class behaviours. As Figure 6.1 shows, at age 25, and on through age 30, the predicted hazard for a middle class behaviours woman is very similar whether she is from a poor background or a middle class background compare MM and PM. The other situation in which background makes little difference involves the chances of leaving poverty for women following poor behaviours: their chances of exiting poverty are slim from ages 25 through 30 whether they come from a poor or a middle class background (compare MP and PP in Figure 6.2). In these situations the influence of parental background seems to dissipate by the end of young adulthood.

Relative importance of behaviours and parental background

The results suggest that parental background matters even when controlling for the actions of the young adult and duration of time in the given poverty status. But just how important is parental background? To address this issue more directly, we first examined the extent to which the associations between parental background and poverty transitions were mediated by the behaviours of the young adult. Adding behaviours as predictors of poverty transitions had little effect on the coefficients on the parental background variables, indicating little evidence of parental background influences operating through the behaviours. To more directly assess the relative importance of background versus behaviours, we used a special method of analysis.[13] A clear pattern emerged from the results: for poverty transitions in either direction (entering or exiting poverty) and for men and women, parental background and behaviours were equally important.

Our results based on data for males and females for all ages within the range (person years) probably overstate the predictive power of parental background. As predictors of changes in the level of economic achievement during young adulthood, parental background factors are probably secondary to behaviours. This assertion is supported by the results of additional analysis omitting person years when the young adult was co-residing with parents. When the sample of person years is restricted in that way, childhood parental family income and size tend to be reduced in importance and some behaviours (such as marriage for females) take on more importance.

Summary

Our results indicate that poverty transitions during young adulthood are tied to the behaviours of the young adult. Work and education are strong predictors of poverty transitions, as would be expected for not only the US but many other countries as well. Family behaviours are also strong predictors, but this may be something more unique to the US. Marriage is a somewhat precarious undertaking for US females in that both the initiation of a marriage and the ending of a marriage are associated with higher risks of falling into poverty. At the same time, the initiation of marriage is positively related to chances of climbing out of poverty, both for men and women. Out-of-marriage childbirth, like marital dissolution, is associated with greater risks for women entering poverty. In-marriage childbirth is associated with reduced chances for men of exiting poverty.

However, these behaviours are not the full story with regard to poverty transitions. Parental background factors are also predictors of poverty transitions during young adulthood. The evidence of background being mediated by behaviours is weak, except, as we saw with our hypothetical profiles, when the behaviours are taken to extremes. Even then, the mediation of background by the behaviours did not occur until late in the young adulthood life stage.[14] Young adults from middle class backgrounds are much less likely to stay in poverty in the long run if they do enter it in young adulthood, and it is the young adults from poor backgrounds who are the more likely to find themselves in poverty as adults. The past appears to play an important role not only going into young adulthood but throughout that stage of life.

However, some caution should be taken with regard to our findings about parental background. By counting co-resident parents' income in the poverty status assessment, we find that the predictive power of parental background is equal to that of behaviours. Because our approach tends to bias estimated influences of parental background in an upward direction, this is likely to be an upper limit on the strength of parental background relative to behaviours.

Further research would assist in the interpretation of these findings. As discussed earlier, investigation is needed regarding differing ways of defining economic achievement and the appropriate sample. The specification of some predictors could be improved,[15] and censorship due to attrition over the PSID's panel period could be taken into account more rigorously.[16]

Despite the incomplete nature of the current investigation, the results are promising, and they lend reassurance that the dynamic approach used in this chapter is informative about poverty processes. We would like to apply a similar analytical approach, with refinements along the lines noted above, to other life stages. This would allow us to examine the similarities and differences in poverty dynamics across the life course. In the meantime, while we hesitate to draw strong policy conclusions, we do feel that the findings argue for paying heed to US policies that influence the behaviours of young adults. In the US, behaviours in many life realms appear to shape economic trajectories throughout the young adulthood stage of life. The extent to which the patterns are similar or different in other countries is of substantial interest. In countries, such as Germany, where careers tend to take shape later in the life course, young adulthood may have to be defined in a different way. Having panel data of sufficient length for countries other than the US would facilitate comparative analysis which could substantially further our understanding of poverty processes.

Authors' acknowledgements

The authors are very appreciative of help provided by Pat Berglund in assembling the data. Partial funding for the analysis was provided by the Russell Sage Foundation and the National Institute for Child Health and Human Development grant 1-R01-HD28145-01A2. An earlier draft of the chapter was presented at the Population Association of America annual meeting, April 1995.

Notes

[1] For example, Ashworth et al (1993) found that multiple spells of poverty during childhood were at least as frequent as the pattern of a single poverty spell.

[2] The life stages are: childhood (0-15 years); young adulthood (16-30); early middle age (31-45); late middle age (46-60); early elder (61-75); late elder (76-90).

[3] The threshold varies with family size and composition. It is based on the Orshansky approach of deriving annual needs on the basis of a food needs standard and then incorporating adjustments for diseconomies of scale for small households. The 1985 threshold for a male living alone and aged 21-35 was $5,899 (in 1985 dollars), for a lone female aged 21-35 it was $5,122, for each member of a couple aged 21-35 it was $7,637, and for a lone female aged 21-35 with one child under age 4 it was $5,673.

[4] Parental family resources could have been specified in terms of poverty status. However, the literature suggests that parental resources play a more complex role in shaping children's well-being than that which can be captured by the dichotomy of being poor versus not being poor (see, for example, Corcoran, 1995; Ashworth et al, 1994). For this reason, we include continuous measures of parental family resources and allow for differences in the role of income and needs.

[5] Ideally, the sample would also be disaggregated by race; however, limited sample sizes preclude this differentiation.

[6] After young adults establish a household separate from their parents, access to measures of parental circumstances requires annual matching of parent and offspring records, assuming the parents and the offspring were successfully interviewed. Attrition on the part of the individual of interest or his or her parents means the omission of the case from an analysis of effects of contemporaneous parental family circumstances.

[7] The finding for young men that in-marriage childbirth is more strongly related to poverty dynamics than is out-of-marriage childbirth may reflect a high degree of measurement error in assessments (or true ignorance) of out-of-wedlock fathering of children.

[8] The specification we employ assumes a linear effect of duration *in the current spell* on the hazards of exiting poverty. However, there is no a priori reason to assume the effects are linear and confined to the current spell. In future research we plan to test the sensitivity of the results to these assumptions.

[9] This could be because the level of resources of the parental family during an individual's adolescence are more instrumental in shaping the development of sons than of daughters. Alternatively the measures of parental family resources as of adolescence may be proxying for contemporaneous measures of parental family resources, with contemporaneous levels of parental family resources playing a weaker role in economic dynamics of adult daughters than of adult sons.

[10] Background is defined as the following table indicates:

	'Poor'	'Middle class'
Parental income	$12,076 (80% of poverty level)	$47,095 (median income for family of 4)
Parental family size	4	4
Years in female-headed family	3	0
Average annual AFDC	$7,240	$0
Head's years of education	11	16

Note: $ 7,240 is the average amount of AFDC received by a family of four in 1970, inflated to the 1993 dollar level used for the analysis.

[11] Behaviour is defined as the following table indicates:

	'Poor'	'Middle class'
Graduate high school	not at all	at age 18
Graduate college	not at all	at age 24
Split	at age 25	at age 25
Marry	not at all	at age 26
Have an out-of-marriage birth	at age 18	not at all
Have an in-marriage birth	not at all	at age 28
Annual work hours ages 16-24	1,000	100
Annual work hours ages 25-30	1,000	2,000

[12] We are not dealing with age specific risks of *being* poor but of *becoming* poor after not having been poor in the previous year.

[13] We estimated and compared, for the two sets of variables, the marginal pseudo R-squares adjusted for degrees of freedom. As the name would suggest, the pseudo R-square (also known as the likelihood-ratio index) is interpretable as the proportionate decrease in the log-likelihood value attributable to the predictor variables in question. Our base model for calculating pseudo R-squares adjusted for degrees of freedom included *Duration* as the

sole predictor. To that base we first added the parental background variables and calculated the explanatory power of that addition, adjusted for degrees of freedom. We then repeated that exercise substituting behaviours for background.

[14] Cumulative survival probabilities also show background differences disappearing late in young adulthood.

[15] For example, more work with the data set could reduce the missing data on the educational attainment variables, changes in work hours could be substituted for level of work hours, and at least one interactive term – marriage* age – could be added to allow for differing effects of an event at different ages.

[16] See Hill et al (1993) for a method of estimating event history models with non-independent censoring.

Appendix A: Modulated renewal model

As with other types of event history models, the modulated renewal model is appropriate when analysing discrete events, the occurrence of which can be placed exactly in time. However, poverty depends on whether an income stream falls short of a needs threshold which is also conceived of as a *flow* of required expenditures. The appropriate time frame for measuring these flows is not obvious and, as a result, it is not clear precisely *when* an individual or family falls into or climbs out of poverty. Conventional practice in poverty research is to integrate the income and needs flows over a discrete period of time (either a month or a year) and define people as being poor for the entire period only if the aggregate income exceeds the aggregate needs. Thus we measure and analyse poverty discretely even though the underlying phenomenon is continuous. The event history framework is a convenient and potentially useful approximation to reality.

A modulated renewal model (Yamaguchi, 1991) distinguishes between falling into and climbing out of poverty. The probability of falling into poverty between years t-1 and t, ie, being poor in year t ($Y_{i,t}=1$) given being non-poor in year t-1 ($Y_{i,t-1}=0$), is:

$$Pr(Y_{i,t}=1 \mid Y_{i,t-1}=0) = \exp(\beta'_F X_{i,t})/(1 + \exp(\beta'_F X_{i,t}))$$

where β_F is a vector of parameters relating characteristics of individual i or his/her environment ($X_{i,t}$) to the propensity to enter poverty at time t. The associated likelihood function for falling into poverty can be written as:

$$L_{FI} = \prod_{i=1}^{N}\prod_{t=1}^{T_i} (1-Y_{i,t-1})Pr(Y_{i,t}=1 \mid Y_{i,t-1}=0)^{\delta_{i,t}}(1-Pr(Y_{i,t}=1 \mid Y_{i,t-1}=0))^{1-\delta_{i,t}}$$

where N is the sample size, T_i is the number of years the individual is observed during ages 16-30 and $\delta_{i,t}$ is a dummy variable equalling 1 if a transition occurs between years t-1 and t and 0 otherwise. The probability of climbing out of poverty between years t-1 and t, ie, of being non-poor in year t ($Y_{i,t}=0$) given being poor in year t-1 ($Y_{i,t-1}=1$) is:

$$Pr(Y_{i,t}=0 \mid Y_{i,t-1}=1) = \exp(\beta'_C X_{i,t})/(1 + \exp(\beta'_C X_{i,t}))$$

where β_C is a second parameter vector, this one relating the characteristics $(X_{i,t})$ to the propensity to exit poverty at time t. The associated likelihood function for climbing out of poverty can be written as:

$$L_{CO} = \prod_{i=1}^{N}\prod_{t=1}^{T_i} 1\text{-}Y_{i,t\text{-}1}Pr(Y_{i,t}=0\,|\,Y_{i,t\text{-}1}=1)^{\delta_{i,t}}(1\text{-}Pr(Y_{i,t}=0\,|\,Y_{i,t\text{-}1}=1))^{1\text{-}\delta_{i,t}}$$

Under the assumption of the modulated renewal model, the overall likelihood function of the observed pattern of Ys, Xs and βs is:

$$L = \prod_{i=1}^{N}\prod_{t=1}^{T_i} \frac{Y_{i,t\text{-}1}\exp(\beta'_C X_{i,t})^{\delta_{i,t}} + (1\text{-} Y_{i,t\text{-}1})\exp(\beta'_F X_{i,t})^{\delta_{i,t}}}{1 + Y_{i,t\text{-}1}\exp(\beta'_C X_{i,t})^{\delta_{i,t}} + (1\text{-} Y_{i,t\text{-}1})\exp(\beta'_F X_{i,t})^{\delta_{i,t}}}$$

Fully efficient and consistent estimates of the βs can be obtained by maximising this likelihood function (actually its natural log) with respect to the elements β_F and β_C.

Appendix B: Results of modulated renewal model of poverty transitions in young adulthood (ages 16-30)

	Entering poverty		Climbing out of poverty	
	Males	Females	Males	Females
Work hours	−0.74**	−0.67**	0.30**	0.40**
(1,000s)	(0.11)	(0.05)	(0.08)	(0.10)
HS Grad	−0.47**	−0.32**	0.15	0.68**
	(0.09)	(0.10)	(0.16)	(0.15)
Col Grad	0.12	−0.99**	0.84*	1.14
	(0.13)	(0.24)	(0.34)	(0.93)
MD Ed	0.07	−0.70**	−0.09	0.66**
	(0.09)	(0.08)	(0.13)	(0.12)
Share HH	−2.05**	−1.11**	−0.38**	−0.31*
	(0.09)	(0.07)	(0.14)	(0.12)
Split	−0.95**	−0.04	0.28	−0.42
	(0.32)	(0.16)	(0.28)	(0.29)
Head/Wife	0.27	0.77*	−2.21**	−0.15
	(0.43)	(0.31)	(0.62)	(0.46)
Marry	−0.16	0.27*	1.06**	1.11**
	(0.16)	(0.12)	(0.39)	(0.24)
Div/Sep	−0.18	0.43*	−0.65	−0.38
	(0.32)	(0.17)	(0.56)	(0.40)
Child in Mar	0.12	−0.10	−0.42+	0.01
	(0.15)	(0.13)	(0.24)	(0.24)
Child out Mar	−0.07	0.65**	0.62	−0.21
	(0.42)	(0.25)	(0.61)	(0.36)
Duration	−13.92**	−14.20**	−6.66	−22.87**
(100s)	(1.14)	(1.12)	(4.13)	(3.44)
Intercept	−0.53**	−0.78**	0.22	−0.10
	(0.02)	(0.19)	(0.26)	(0.28)
African-Amer	0.75**	0.56**	−0.55**	−0.64**
	(0.11)	(0.09)	(0.14)	(0.14)
Par Inc 13-15	−0.31**	−0.17**	0.22**	0.05*
(10,000s)	(0.02)	(0.02)	(0.04)	(0.02)
Par Siz 13-15	0.81**	0.86**	−0.78**	−0.40
(10s)	(0.18)	(0.20)	(0.26)	(0.28)
AFDC 13-15	0.54**	0.32*	0.003	0.02
(10,000s)	(0.13)	(0.14)	(0.16)	(0.14)
Head Ed 13-15	0.36**	−0.36**	0.14	0.31*
(10s)	(0.09)	(0.09)	(0.12)	(0.13)
Yrs Fem Hd 13-15	−0.12**	0.06+	0.005	−0.11*
	(0.05)	(0.03)	(0.07)	(0.05)
Head/Wife* Par Inc	0.18**	0.02	−0.002	0.03
(10,000s)	(0.05)	(0.04)	(0.09)	(0.06)
Head/Wife* Par Siz	−1.68**	−0.99*	2.10**	−0.63
(10s)	(0.66)	(0.45)	(0.81)	(0.65)
Log likelihood	−2,152.73	−2,369.31	−833.94	−944.33
N	1,194	1,220	648	711
ρ²	0.268	0.231	0.364	0.352

Notes: Significance levels: *p<0.05, **p<0.01, +p<0.10.
MD Ed: dummy variable (= 1 in case of missing data on both HS Grad and Col Grad).
Intercept: value of hazard rate when all predictors are set to zero.
Figures in brackets: standard errors.
(100s), (1,000s), (10,000s): units of measurement.

The models were estimated using Turbo Pascal programmes written by Daniel Hill, with separate models for exiting versus entering poverty, and estimates performed separately for males and females. Likelihood-ratio tests of the symmetry hypothesis, as well as the hypothesis that a common set of coefficients pertain to males and females, resulted in large χ^2 test statistics, and the hypotheses were soundly rejected.

Source: Panel Study of Income Dynamics (PSID)

seven

Exploring the dynamics of family change: lone parenthood in Great Britain

Stephen McKay

Introduction

It is not surprising that in many chapters of this volume family change is identified as a key factor in welfare dynamics. The likelihood of benefit receipt, for example, may be affected by a family member leaving the household or by the formation of a new household. Changes in family structure may have greater implications for social welfare than changes in employment (as argued by Bane and Ellwood, 1986), although the latter often receive greater attention perhaps because they appear more responsive to changes in government policy. However, to attribute welfare dynamics to family dynamics may just push the analytical questions one stage further back: what caused those changes in family formation in the first place? This chapter takes a different perspective by considering the apparent reasons behind changes in family formation.

It argues that changes in family arrangements respond to systematic factors, rather than being based on simple trends that do not require further explanation. Family change may be analysed as the *effect* of changes in the labour market and in the living standards of men and women – rather than only as the *cause* of such changes. There is a stronger version of this argument, usually associated with right-wing social commentators. This alleges that changes in family formation are actually (or even predominantly) the result of changes in the generosity of welfare programmes (Murray, 1984): a form of 'dependency culture' hypothesis which this chapter does not attempt to evaluate (see Dean and Taylor-Gooby, 1992). However, a recent review of research in this area (Gauthier, 1996) discusses the serious difficulties of reaching definitive conclusions.

In searching for the underlying causes of family change, a number of stances are possible. First, you might argue that such human behaviour is the result of myriad individual circumstances. As a consequence, researchers might analyse the macro-societal trends, but cannot successfully address specific instances of family formation or dissolution, or investigate patterns within different groups. It may be argued that a decline in the importance of shared norms is the underlying cause of increasing family breakdown, anomie (Durkheim's notion of normlessness) being the result of 'progress' in society. However, while changes in patterns of family formation are common enough to many countries to suggest similar social processes, they are not uniform enough to support uni-causal views about the effects of economic development.

Second, people may put forward a range of partial theories. These tend to attribute changes in behaviour to major changes either in social attitudes, or to changes in the legal framework governing family life. It is commonly argued that divorce, lone parenthood, pre-marital childbearing, and so on were socially stigmatised in past decades, but that changing social attitudes have made these phenomena acceptable today. This explanation implies that changes in social attitudes may halt or reverse trends in family structures. It may be partly helpful, but suffers from a number of flaws. It must first be explained why attitudes have moved in similar directions in many countries, although at different rates. It is not only conceivable that changes in attitudes come *after* changes in behaviour, but this is what American research tends to suggest (Cherlin, 1992, p 45). In the USA it seems that attitudes towards divorce only 'softened' some time after divorce rates climbed. An example of changes in the legal framework which have been attributed to change in family formation is that of divorce laws being either introduced, weakened, or the grounds available extended. Changes in the law may enable those separated to become divorced more easily, but of itself this is not a convincing explanation of why people separate in the first place. Instead, a more sophisticated theory would need to use the option of divorce – and particularly of re-marriage – as the driving force behind a higher incidence of separation. Is it not, also, at least as likely that changes in the law followed rather than caused changes in family behaviour? The legal view would also have to deal with some counteractions that might offset legal changes, such as the more widespread availability of contraception.

There are more encompassing theory-based explanations of family change. Some economists and rational-choice sociologists have found inspiration in the work of (Nobel Laureate) Gary Becker (1964; 1976; 1981). This economics of the family approach applies the logic and tools of micro-economic analysis to decisions about family formation and dissolution. It is hypothesised that people are rational, informed individuals who take steps to maximise their level of satisfaction. It is further assumed that marriage becomes more likely the greater the gains from it, which in Becker's particular formulation has much to do with the degree of complementarity between the two partners – men having a comparative advantage in production outside the home, women for production inside the home. The gains to being in a couple are reduced to the extent that men are unable to fulfil such a role, or women can be well-off as individual units. This model has been applied to British data on family formation (Ermisch, 1991).

Whatever the adequacy of the assumptions of this model, a number of testable predictions do result. For example, marital dissolution should be more likely when women are working, or when men are unemployed. Proponents have also suggested that pre-marital childbearing should be more likely when the stock of marriageable husbands is low, and opportunities for women's paid employment relatively poor.

However, the same type of predictions could be consistent with alternative models. For instance, there is considerable overlap with the 'social exchange' theory of marital breakdown which analyses the gains traded between marriage partners. Most commentators on family formation have suggested that the changing life plans and activity patterns of women, and particularly their rising labour force participation, must be a key factor. This applies to decisions about family size, age at marriage, opportunities to live independently, and so on.

In the absence of a universally-accepted theoretical framework, the analyst must draw on a range of resources. The microeconomic approach provides a ready-made set of hypotheses, and is strongly suggestive of which characteristics are likely to be important. It is also crucial to take account of possible trends and major legal changes. Patterns of labour force participation are likely to be an important part of any explanation.

The rest of this chapter focuses on change concerning lone parent families, a family type of particular (and growing) policy interest. In Britain, considerable political attention has been focused on the relationship between rising numbers of lone parent families, and rising expenditure on social assistance (Income Support) for this group (DSS, 1993). The next section provides the British context. We then look at cross-sectional information before considering the dynamics of lone parenthood and looking for key causal antecedents of family change. This element is based on modelling life events, using data on people's lifetime fertility and economic activity.

Lone parents in the UK

The number of lone parents in Britain has increased significantly since the late 1960s and early 1970s. At the time of the Finer inquiry, in the early 1970s there were fewer than 600,000 one-parent families: the most recent figure is around 1.5 million. While the overall number has been on the increase, the composition has also been changing. Up until the mid-1980s, the growth was most associated with increases in separation and divorce among families with children. Divorce had been made easier by the 1971 Divorce Law Reform Act, although this could not be described as a complete move to 'no fault' divorce. In the period since the mid to late 1980s, the number of single (never-married) women having children has grown at the fastest rate.

This increase in numbers of a particular family type was accompanied by relatively low and declining rates of labour force participation among lone parents – when rates for all mothers were increasing – and decreasing rates and amounts of transfers between fathers and lone mothers. The overall result was increasing dependence upon the main British social assistance benefits, especially Income Support.

In charting the increase in the number of lone parents, and more particularly in seeking to explain it, it is important to note the diversity of lone parenthood. The two key dimensions along which lone parents vary are family type, and the time they have spent as a lone parent.

Lone parenthood is a diverse and not a uniform family type. Marital status may be a particularly important source of differences. Put in more dynamic terms, the route of entry to lone parenthood may constitute a key difference within the group, affecting living standards and likely duration. These different routes may have different causal antecedents. The two principal routes into lone parenthood are having a child while single, and separating from a couple in which there are dependent children. There is considerable UK evidence that a much higher proportion of the former group receive social assistance of some kind (see Table 7.1). Nearly nine out of 10 unmarried lone mothers claim social assistance, compared to around three quarters of previously married lone mothers, and fewer than half of lone fathers.

It is worth pointing out that Britain has a 'mass' system of social assistance: for some family groups there is no entitlement to contributory benefits, and they must move directly on to Income Support, which is designed to be the safety net scheme, or last resort. British social assistance has a national system of rules and amounts of payment, and there is little or no discretion. However, there is an important distinction between two different benefits: Income Support (or the income-related elements of Jobseeker's

Table 7.1: Social assistance claimants among lone parents (UK)

Sex	Marital status	Relationship status	Income Support	Family Credit
Mothers	Not previously married	Always single	79%	11%
		Previously cohabited	73%	14%
	Previously married	Divorced	56%	20%
		Separated	49%	20%
Fathers	All groups		35%	7%

Source: Ford et al (1995)

Allowance introduced in 1996) is only available to those working fewer than 16 hours a week; Family Credit requires claimants to be working at least 16 hours a week.[1]

In the USA, never-married mothers are more likely than other mothers to be black, and non-working, while divorcees are more likely to be white, and to hold jobs (Garfinkel and McLanahan, 1986). In Britain, any division by ethnic minority status is less stark, but there remains considerable truth that the never-married mothers are less likely to be qualified, reflecting less advantaged backgrounds, the least likely to receive regular maintenance payments, and the most likely to have a low standard of living (Bradshaw and Millar, 1991).

The second main source of diversity among lone parents is that this family status may be of quite varying durations. An episode may be quite short term, or last 20 or more years. Any change in the number of lone parents may be the result of either more people becoming lone parents, or people staying as lone parents for longer (or both). The policy implications of changes in family status may be quite different depending upon which is the major engine of growth. As others have argued in relation to poverty, optimism that people may rapidly exit a state where their living standard is low should be tempered by pessimism that more people will go through such a condition (see Chapters Two and Fifteen). The evidence largely suggests that time spent as a lone parent has detrimental outcomes for any children involved (McLanahan and Sandefur, 1994b).

Methods: exploring the dynamics of family change

Cross-section information

In Britain, information about lone parents is available from a range of sources, most importantly from three recent surveys of lone parents. These were conducted in 1989, 1991 and 1993 (respectively, Bradshaw and Millar, 1991; McKay and Marsh, 1994; Ford et al, 1995) with funding from the British Department of Social Security. Further research on new cross-sections, and on follow-ups of those cross-sections, continues at the UK Policy Studies Institute.

This substantial body of research has allowed a large number of characteristics of lone parents to be established. It tells us about the proportions in employment, and the main factors which appear to influence decisions about working and the breakdown of relationships. In some cases, samples have been revisited, allowing us to make preliminary remarks about the duration of lone parenthood, and those most likely to make transitions (for example, Ford et al, 1995). However, these surveys were not designed as panel studies.

The 1991 interview sample of lone parents was revisited about one year later. By that stage somewhere between one in 10 and one in 20 had ceased being lone parents. Those least likely to have found a partner were those working full-time. This suggests that workers are able to live an independent life where finding a partner is less important than it may be for other groups. During the same period there was relatively little change in the rates of benefit receipt among this group, and few changes in employment status. Research conducted in 1989 found that half those lone parents who ceased receiving social assistance had moved into work, while half had moved in with a new partner.

While informative, this type of information cannot be used to look at what affects routes into lone parenthood, nor at how long people are likely to stay lone parents because the sample is confined to current lone parents. To analyse routes into lone parenthood requires information on people who do not become lone parents, even though they might face similar circumstances. A cross-section of current lone parents will tend to contain fewer short-term lone parents, and more who have been lone parents for a long time, compared to a group of people who become lone parents at any given point in time.[2] Data on people who are lone parents within a given period, by definition, cannot tell us about those most likely to leave lone parenthood, and the circumstances in which they might do so. Greater information on routes out of lone parenthood may be collected at various follow-up interviews with former lone parents, but this tends to be less informative than panels or life-event data collected from among a more general population.

Life history data

More information on current status is required to look at the inflow into lone parenthood, and the duration of lone parenthood.

A number of British surveys have collected information about life events, covering marriage, divorce, childbearing and so on. By means of such 'life-event' data, it is possible to construct the different routes into lone parenthood, and the duration once people are in that family status. These may be investigated, then linked to changes in employment status, housing tenure, and so on.

The methods used in this chapter are part of 'Event History Analysis', a series of techniques used to look at the length of time it takes for something to happen (cf Chapter Two). This could be the length of time before a machine fails, or the length of time that a person lives. This chapter is concerned with how long people spend in one family type or another, before moving into another family type.

One of the key simplifying assumptions used in such work is that people are in well-defined family types that can be distinguished from other relevant family types. It is beyond the scope of this chapter to question the accuracy of this assumption. However, previous research has found a tendency to date the end of a relationship at an 'official' juncture, such as date of divorce, even though relationships have often effectively ended well in advance of such a date. In other words, survey estimates may misstate dates of effective entry to and exit from lone parenthood. Researchers may analyse family changes such as divorce more as a process than as a discrete, specific event.

The general approach is to consider all the points of time at which people are 'at risk' of an event occurring, and for how many that event then occurs. In Britain, the main application of such methods to family dynamics had been from John Ermisch in a series of articles culminating in a treatise on the area (Ermisch, 1991). Most of this work has been on the Women and Employment Survey conducted on around 5,000 women in 1980.

The results in this chapter are based on the 1986-87 surveys from the Social Change and Economic Life Initiative, a programme comprising detailed fieldwork in six geographical locations.[3] This was the most recent data source with life-history data available when the research began, researchers starting afresh would benefit from subsequent waves of the British Household Panel Study (BHPS), on which research is being conducted, and from the new Survey of Family and Working Lives.

The survey used in this chapter has the benefit of a high response rate (close to 80%) and a considerable academic input into the design of the life-event questionnaires. There were 3,414 women aged 20-60 in the sample. They generated data on both the inflow to lone parenthood, and exits (see Appendix to this chapter).

Transitions into and out of lone parenthood

This section looks at transitions between different family statuses in greater detail relating to pre-marital childbearing, separation among couples with children, and exits from lone parenthood. In each case, a descriptive overview is presented, and briefly followed by a succinct account of modelling work that has been conducted.

Becoming a single lone parent

We refer to women who had a pre-marital birth as 'single lone parents' or 'single parents', in contrast to lone parenthood ensuing from divorce or separation. Women are 'at risk' of becoming a single mother as soon as childbearing is possible, but different datasets tend to begin collecting relevant data from different ages. The Social Change And Economic Life Initiative studies give information on marital and family status from the age of 14 years and onwards. The main alternative life path to having a pre-marital birth is marriage. Some women (probably around 10%) will never marry nor have children, and many more will be observed in this situation at the time of the interview.

It is well known that the number of single lone parents has risen over time. One means of capturing such variation is by look-ing at the hazard rates of different birth cohorts, shown in Figure 7.1. The measure of the hazard rate can be interpreted, more or less, as a probability. It shows the chance that the event will take place – in this instance, a pre-marital birth – given that it has not already occurred. The hazard rate climbs quite rapidly from age 14 onwards, reaching a high plateau during 18-21 years, with a peak in the dataset at around 19 years. Thereafter it drops to a lower level for the late 20s, and down to almost zero in the 30s.

Figure 7.1: Pre-marital first birth by age – hazard rates for different birth cohorts

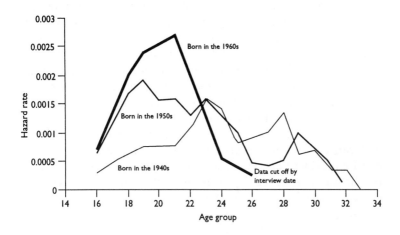

Note: N=3,414 women aged 20-60

Source: Social Change and Economic Life Initiative Study: 1986-87 surveys

Figure 7.2: Pre-marital first birth by age – hazard rates for different forms of tenure at age 14

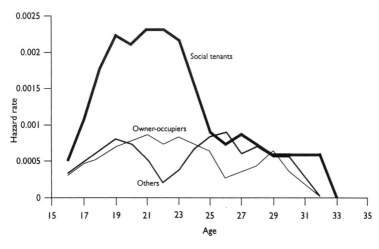

Note: N=3,414 women aged 20-60

Source: Social Change and Economic Life Initiative Study: 1986-87 surveys

If we restrict attention to the ages of 14 to 20, it is clear that later birth cohorts show a much higher hazard rate for entry into 'single parenthood'. For later years, we do not have sufficient years of information on the 1960s birth cohort to make comparisons. However, there seem to be broadly similar hazard rates for births past the age of 22 (or so) for those born in either the 1940s or the 1950s. It is in the teenage years that the chances of having a pre-marital birth have risen during the more recent birth cohorts.

Births to single women are now the fastest growing component of lone parenthood. However, the growth has been most pronounced since the mid-1980s, and is not fully picked up with this data set, nor in Ermisch's earlier work using the Women and Employment Survey. There is some more recent work using the British Household Panel Study, but using a very restricted range of variables (Ermisch, 1995).

Single lone parenthood may also be related to family background, for example, to indicators of disadvantage among the family of origin. As a simple measure of background, we have information on housing tenure when the respondent was aged 14. Figure 7.2 shows the differences by tenure groups. There is a markedly higher risk of single parenthood for those who were social tenants at the age of 14. This may be taken as an early indication that those from relatively poorer backgrounds are more likely to enter single parenthood.

The graphs in Figures 7.1 and 7.2 each look at one factor at a time. Ideally, we would want to look at the simultaneous impact of different characteristics which requires a multivariate setting, and the use of survival modelling techniques. Our research makes use of some information that is fixed over time (such as ethnic group) and others that may vary – such as employment, age, and the year of observation.

Conducting such an analysis allows almost all of the 'trend' towards increased single parenthood to be explained. The trend towards an increase in single parenthood seems to be reflecting changes in employment opportunities and the characteristics of young women. While the 1970s and 1980s appear quite different from the 1960s, there was no evidence for a continuing increase outside of the measured factors in the model. Single lone parenthood is more likely where a young woman is in employment, rather than remaining in full-time education (by a factor of 1.5). There is also a higher incidence where the parents (especially the mother) were of lower socioeconomic status. Women of West Indian background were four times as likely as whites to have births while single, those of Asian background were 10% less likely. The overall picture is one where entry to single parenthood is associated with a number of markers for 'disadvantage'. This supports the view that a lack of alternative opportunities is the key factor at work.

Breakdowns among married couples with children

As is well known, marriages contracted more recently tend to be shorter than those that took place either in the 1960s or earlier, as illustrated by Figure 7.3. The rate at which marriage lengths have fallen is stark.

It has been well established that marriages that take place earlier in life tend to be shorter. Rates of separation are higher where a pre-marital *conception* took place; however, a pre-marital *birth* appears not to have much of an effect. Empirical evidence also permits us to correlate additional characteristics with relationship breakdown. For instance, those who were then living in social rented accommodation were the group most likely to split up. However, the effects of most social and demographic factors appear small compared to dates of conception, age at marriage, date of marriage, and so on.

A modelling approach is needed to analyse the effects of each variable, taking into account the possible effects of other variables of interest. This tended to confirm the importance of marriage and birth timing. Early conceptions, and especially pre-marital conceptions, were associated with shorter durations of marriage. There was a non-linear relationship between marital break-up and age at marriage. However, it seems that marital break-up was more likely for those marrying at younger ages. The more recent the time of marriage, the more likely was a marital break-up, and (in addition) break-up became 20% more likely after 1971, when divorce law reforms became effective. However, the longer the marriage had lasted, the lower the chance it would end.

Those of Asian origin had lower risks of marital break-up than either whites or blacks. Economic activity status, taken as time-varying variables, made no difference to marital splits. Breakdown was least likely for owner-occupiers, but was more likely where the couple shared their accommodation with their own parents. This provides a mixed set of conclusions. Increases in the instability of marriage have often been attributed to the rising economic participation of women, but we found no direct evidence of such an effect. This could be because increases in the number of women working tended to show in individual lives before the actual end of the marriage, rather than just prior, which would make any effect more difficult to identify without some guide as to the time lags involved. Signs of affluence – such as marrying later, a couple being in their own home, and owner occupation – were all associated with marriage stability. Conversely, early marriage, living in rented accommodation or remaining in the parental home were all markers for increased instability.

While some demographic characteristics, as already mentioned, do make a difference, the main effect seems to be one of an inexplicable trend increase which cannot straightforwardly be the effect of more mothers working.

Leaving lone parenthood

People may stop being lone parents for a number of reasons. Usually this is the result of forming a new partnership. The other 'event' that can mean the end of this status is when the youngest child ages beyond dependency (16/18 years) or leaves the household through another route (such as death or going into care). Of 753 instances of lone parenthood in the lives of our respondents, 378 ended in a (re)marriage event (see Appendix). A further 80 spells of lone parenthood ended through children growing older, leaving 295 still lone parents at the time of interview. We were most likely to observe (re)marriages among never-married mothers, and least likely of all for widows.

For those who had pre-marital births, the median time spent as a lone parent was around three years. For those becoming a lone parent on divorce, half had left this state a little over 4.5 years later. There is a rather longer duration for those who separate (8.5 years – see Part C of Table in Appendix). By way of comparison, Ermisch (1991) found a 34 month median duration for single mothers, and 59 months for previously married mothers (here, specified separately for separation and divorce).

Figure 7.4 shows the duration of lone parenthood by the starting decade of that spell. This shows that people becoming lone parents more recently tend to remain lone parents for longer.

Figure 7.3: Duration of marriage since first birth – three marriage cohorts compared

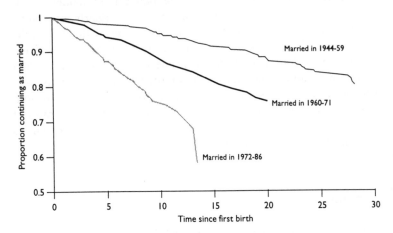

Note: N=3,414 women aged 20-60

Source: Social Change and Economic Life Initiative Study: 1986-87 surveys

Figure 7.4: Duration of lone parenthood – three cohorts compared

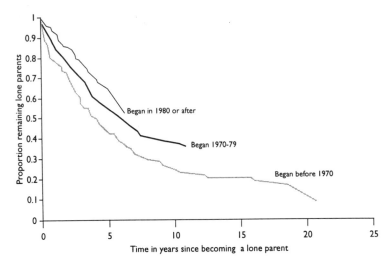

Note: N=3,414 women aged 20-60

Source: Social Change and Economic Life Initiative Study: 1986-87 surveys

There is little literature to draw to aid interpretation of the findings concerning the routes taken out of lone parenthood. Earlier we found that entry to lone parenthood tended to be associated with a disadvantaged background. Similarly, one might expect exits to be more rapid among those with (relatively) advantaged characteristics, and this turned out to be the case. Women were lone parents for less time where they lived in their own homes, and owned rather than rented them. Durations were somewhat shorter for those in full-time work, compared to non-workers, and for those not previously married. However, rates of exit have fallen over time, and the rate of exit tended to fall as lone motherhood continued.

Conclusions

Lone parenthood has been established as a heterogeneous status. There are clear differences according to family type – which, in a dynamic perspective, may instead be labelled differences by the route into lone parenthood. Women are most likely to become single lone parents relatively earlier in their lives; separation of couples with children tends to occur at later ages. There are also differences according to the duration of lone parenthood, with many women remaining lone parents only for relatively short times. Account must be taken of this heterogeneity when researchers seek to analyse or to explain the increase in lone parenthood observed in Britain and elsewhere.

A number of conclusions may be put forward:

- The increasing number of lone parents, at least in Britain, is not only due to more events leading to lone parenthood, but also to an increasing duration of that state.

- Pre-marital lone parenthood appears to be the strongest source of the most recent rise.

- Post-marital lone parenthood is not directly linked to rising labour market participation.

- Early lone parenthood appears not to be the result of rising labour market participation, but of growing inequality of opportunity among young women. Key factors are a disadvantaged background and low participation in education.

How does this leave the various theories we considered at the beginning of this chapter? We found no evidence of particular 'watersheds' in patterns of family change that might be expected to result from legislative or policy changes. These 'theories' seem insufficiently precise to suggest how family change is affected by factors of this type over a longer period of time. We cannot support the centrality that is often given to women's labour force participation in accounting for changes within families. More all-embracing views of human behaviour, based on rational choice, are less susceptible to direct tests but there was no evidence to support the importance of current economic activity. On a more supportive note, the relative future opportunities available to men and women could be part of the best overall explanation of changes in family patterns. The life chances that people anticipate – earnings, quality of employment and so on – affect decisions about family formation. This will be correlated with socio-economic background and education.

Notes

[1] There are a few similar benefits in other countries. Near equivalents are Family Allowance Supplement in Australia, and the American Earned Income Tax Credit (cf Chapter Four). The UK has no minimum wage legislation so employers are largely free to set wages, and Family Credit may 'compensate' for modest earnings or self-employment income.

[2] See the discussion of 'incidence' versus 'prevalence' in Chapter Two.

[3] The areas were chosen to reflect contrasting labour market experience – three areas of improving fortunes, and three of declining fortunes. Most work on the dataset, while acknowledging it is not designed to be nationally representative, assumes that it is a relatively good match to the national situation (see Gallie et al, 1994).

Appendix: Lone parenthood – the key transitions of interest

[a] Separations among married couples with children

Transition	Number of women	Percentage of women
Still married at interview (and not separated)	1,842	79.6
Widowed	67	2.9
Separated	278	12.0
Divorced	126	5.5
Total (married women with a past-marriage child)	2,313	100

[b] Exits from lone parenthood

Category	Still a lone parent at the interview date	No longer a lone parent: children beyond dependent age	No longer a lone parent: (re)marriage (with row percentage)	Total
Never married/pre-marital birth	93	3	190 (66%)	286
Previously married				
Separation	133	40	102 (37%)	275
Divorce	43	10	73 (58%)	126
Widowhood	26	27	13 (20%)	66
Total (spells of lone parenthood in the lives of respondents)	295	80	378 (50%)	753

[c] Duration of lone parenthood

Status on starting lone parenthood	Number of women	Number of exits	Median duration	Mean duration
Pre-marital birth	284	190	38 months	73 months
Separation by married mother	271	102	102 months	139 months
Divorce by married mother	125	73	56 months	71 months
Widowhood of married mother	66	13	–	214 months

Note: N=3,414 women aged 20-60

Source: Social Change and Economic Life Initiative Study, 1986-87 surveys

eight

Income dynamics in old age in Germany

Michael Wagner and Andreas Motel

This chapter investigates how far the German social welfare system succeeds in its aim of ensuring financial security and stability for its senior citizens. Adopting a dynamic perspective allows the discussion to extend beyond the issue of inequality of old age, itself a neglected topic within Germany, to consider the circumstances in which the living standards of older people are likely to deteriorate, and to improve.

Background

> Social Security means freedom from distress and, therefore, constitutes a major element in the freedom of the individual. (Bundesministerium für Arbeit und Sozialordnung, 1994, p 27)

German social policy aims to guarantee this freedom for its senior citizens. Old people who have been in full-time employment for most of their adult lives can expect to maintain an income of between 65% and 70% of their lifelong net income (Hauser and Wagner, 1992, p 583). Their income should reflect the standard of living they enjoyed while in paid employment, enabling them to cope with the negative aspects of ageing.

The state's main method of achieving these aims is through the national pension insurance scheme. Pensions are not regarded as charitable payments; rather they are perceived as an entitlement that elderly people receive in return for contributions made throughout their working lives:

> Pensions are not the bread of charity that is given ad libitum by the state. A pension is an entitlement that is acquired by an individual's own efforts: calculable, protected like property and dynamically adapted to the income level of employees. (Bundesministerium für Arbeit und Sozialordnung, 1994, p 28)

However, the pension system is, in general, an insurance for those in paid employment; raising children does not merit the same consideration.

First drawn up in the 1880s, the current pension structure is based on the 1957 reforms. Pensions were then raised and indexed to the average income of employees, and the system was standardised (Kohli, 1989; Ehmer, 1990). The scheme has three principal components that are at least partly independent. The GRV[1] is the basic German system of compulsory pension insurance, that covered around 30 million workers in West Germany in 1987, both manual and professional. There is also a pension scheme for civil servants and a supplementary scheme for West German public sector employees. Although not part of the core system, especially large private companies provide occupational pensions (Hirvonen, 1993) that often improve financial security in old age. Investments and other individual arrangements can also create extra income.[2]

Insurance for old age is, then, a fundamental principle of the German welfare state.[3] It is complemented by insurance against unemployment, accident, ill-health and, since 1995, by long-term care insurance if required. Of these, accident insurance has little significance for elderly people, although healthcare insurance continues to provide economic and social protection in old age. Apart from accident insurance, all of the state schemes are based on contributions. The contributions to the GRV amount to around 20% of an employee's gross monthly income, half of which is paid by the employer and half by the employee.

In circumstances where the contributory pensions scheme fails to provide financial security, it is supplemented by the state's non-contributory social assistance system. However, payments are means tested and can only be made if there is insufficient income from other sources and little or no wealth. If that proves to be the case, social assistance as a rights-based regime supersedes the principle of state pension insurance. Any individual who cannot maintain themselves by 'his or her own efforts' is eligible, as are those in 'special life situations' (Bundesministerium für Arbeit und Sozialordnung, 1995, p 12).

Pension insurance and, if necessary, social assistance, are the principal means by which the German state secures the economic well-being of its elderly citizens. However, this chapter questions the extent to which the system of social protection achieves its aims. Previous research has addressed this issue in three different ways: the income of different age groups has been compared – typically pensioners' incomes have been contrasted with those of younger employed people (Hauser and Wagner, 1992); researchers have focused on groups of elderly people who are economically disadvantaged (Motel and Wagner, 1993; Mayer and Wagner, 1993); life course research has analysed the cohort-specific association between previous employment history and income in old age (Allmendinger and Brückner, 1991; Maas and Staudinger, 1996).

These studies have produced conflicting results. Hauser and Wagner (1992) concluded from a 1984 comparison of the equivalent incomes of heads of households that the living standards of older people did not differ greatly from those of working age and that the level of social assistance receipt was similar. Likewise, Habich and Krause (1992) investigated the incidence of poverty between 1984 and 1989, and showed that it was lower (between 6% and 9%) among elderly households than among those where the head was less than 65 years old.[4]

However, other studies conclude that the problem of poverty in old age has not disappeared, even if most pensioners do manage to avoid financial hardship (Motel and Wagner, 1993; Bäcker, 1995; Dieck and Naegele, 1993; Backes, 1994; Pfaff, 1992). They have shown that some groups among elderly people, such as very old women and the divorced, have extremely low incomes. Life course studies confirm that income in old age is closely related to income before retirement. There is a marked difference between men and women because of their different employment histories (Allmendinger and Brückner, 1991; Allmendinger, 1994).

How income changes in old age

It is generally assumed that incomes in old age are stable and that the pattern of inequality is constant within a cohort. If this were true, income inequality should be the same among the 'young old' (70- to 84-year-olds), as among the 'old old' (85+). An individual's standard of living, it is claimed, does not change as a person ages after retirement, since any changes in income should be the same for all pensioners. Lastly, it is thought that the association between an individual's previous employment history and their income on retirement does not then alter on ageing. Certainly, the vast majority of elderly people are not employed, therefore they cannot earn additional entitlements to pensions (Kohli and Künemund, 1997; Wagner et al, 1996). Their existing incomes are highly protected; pensions automatically rise in line with increases in general living standards.

An alternative dynamic view of income inequalities emphasises the economic consequences of change, variations in the components of total income, the effects of cohort-specific differential pensions entitlements, and the impact of selective mortality.

Household changes

Change can occur in household composition, for instance, when one partner dies. An elderly person might leave their own home to live with children or move into an old people's home. All of these changes can have an impact on financial well-being.

Little is known about the financial implications of the latter two changes, although both are often the consequence of ill-health. The resources of the first group of elderly people, those who live with their children, remain largely unexplored. As regards the second group, researchers must first tackle the methodological problem of measuring the income of the people in institutions before they can assess the financial implications of moving into residential care (Motel and Wagner, 1993).

Income components

Different developments in the components of an income can be illustrated with respect to the impact of the death of a partner on pension entitlement. Since 1986, both widows and widowers in Germany receive an additional pension equivalent of up to 60% of the pension entitlement of their deceased partner. If the monthly income of the surviving partner is more than 1,094 DM (in 1992, see Bundesministerium für Arbeit und Sozialordnung, 1994, p 251), the widow's or widower's pension is reduced by 40% of the amount by which his or her income exceeds 1,094 DM (Gallon et al, 1994). If this formula results in a negative value, no additional widow's or widower's pension is awarded.

This formula ensures that the loss of a spouse does not increase the risk of poverty for the survivor; it could improve an individual's financial position. Men tend to profit most from this since their own pension tends to be higher than their former partner's due to higher credits amassed during paid employment. In this way, the loss of a spouse further polarises income differences between men and women.

Other components of total income also vary over time, each displaying a different dynamic. The annual increase in occupational pensions, for instance, may differ from the rise in state pensions. This is because occupational pensions are subject to individual contracts, whereas state pensions are linked to increases in the net income of employees. The level of social assistance payments is determined on yet another basis.

Selective mortality and cohort effects

The distribution of income among the elderly population also reflects differential mortality rates, since people surviving into old age will have specific social characteristics. Bearing this in mind, any study which associates differences in income with the movement of old people from private households into residential care might be distorted, as this is a development that mainly affects octogenarians (Lindenberger et al, 1996; Mayer and Wagner, 1996). It is likely, too, that the association between employment history and income in old age varies by cohort. The 'young old' (70- to 84-year-olds) have different employment histories from the 'old old' (85+) (Maas and Staudinger, 1996). The social policies that regulate the income of elderly people are themselves cohort-specific.

Mobility

A major topic in the academic discussion has concerned the apparent increase in inter- and intragenerational mobility and its effects on class, milieu or subculture (Beck, 1983; Bolte, 1983; Hradil, 1990; Mayer, 1987b; Mayer and Blossfeld, 1990; Mayer and Müller, 1989; Strasser, 1987). This research on social mobility has emphasised the importance of introducing a dynamic dimension to the analysis of social inequality and, in particular, has focused attention on the salience of studying social and occupational careers across the life course. Dynamic analysis is also used increasingly in income and poverty research and this provides part of the rationale for publishing this volume (Headey et al, 1990; Rendtel and Wagner, 1991; Hauser and Berntsen, 1992; Leibfried/Leisering et al, 1995; Leisering and Voges, 1996; Zwick, 1994; Buhr, 1995).

However, a dynamic analysis of income in old age in Germany has not previously been attempted (see Burkhauser et al, 1988, for parallel studies in the USA). This chapter seeks to rectify this important omission.

Income dynamics among elderly people

This section divides into four parts: the first describes a new source of information that permits a dynamic analysis of incomes among elderly people; the remaining three sections respectively present evidence on the incomes of elderly people, income inequality in old age and income dynamics.

Source of information

The analysis referred to in this chapter is based on data from the Berlin Aging Study (BASE), an ongoing multidisciplinary investigation of West Berliners with ages ranging between 70 and 105, living both in the community and in institutions (Baltes et al, 1993; 1996; Lindenberger et al, 1996). A description of the specific aims of this sociological study is given by Mayer and Wagner (1993; 1996). The sample was drawn from the city registration office (in Germany, registration is compulsory). It has been stratified by age and sex (Nuthmann and Wahl, 1996), levelling out the extremely uneven age and sex distribution in the population caused by differential mortality rates. The striking effects of the First and Second World Wars are apparent in the sex ratio of the sample; the dramatic fall in the birth rate between

1914 and 1918 means that the cohort of those born in that period is very small.

Half of those surveyed agreed to take part in an intake assessment lasting between one to two hours: these took place between May 1990 and April 1993. Measures of key variables from four disciplines – medicine, psychiatry, psychology and sociology – were included. Out of these respondents 35% agreed to participate in a further 13 sessions for more intensive investigations, held between May 1990 and June 1993. In total, 516 people completed the full programme.

Further data was obtained from a second wave of assessments, carried out between June 1993 and July 1994. Altogether, 362 elderly people (39% of those who had taken part in the intake assessment and 70% of those from the intensive programme) completed the follow-up study. On average, the second study took place 23 months after the first wave, with a minimum time span of 12 months and a maximum of 49 months.

An important question for any researcher is the accuracy of income data obtained through social surveys of elderly people (Wagner and Motel, 1996). Around one in seven of the respondents in this study were diagnosed as suffering from dementia (Helmchen et al, 1996). We know, too, that socio-economic variables, education for example, are associated with dementia (Wagner and Kanowski, 1995). However, a thorough investigation was carried out which indicates that the measurement of income among elderly people is generally reliable. There were, though, many missing or invalid answers from old people in residential care and, for this reason, respondents living in old people's homes were excluded. Both women and the cognitively impaired were less likely to reveal their income, while the presence of a third person during the interview increased the chances that the income questions would be answered.[5]

Elderly people in West Berlin had a monthly equivalent income of around 1,906 DM (Table 8.1). This is slightly higher than the West German average of 1,707 DM (Motel and Wagner, 1993). Women had a lower income than men, and 'very old' people aged 85 or above tended to receive less than those aged 70 to 84, although this age difference was only significant for women.

Table 8.1: Mean equivalent income by age and sex (DM)

	Age 70-84	Age 85+	Total
Men	2,044.-	2,060.-	2,046.-
	1,948.-*		1,963.-*
Women	1,891.-	1,683.-	1,851.-
Total	1,936.-	1,766.-	1,906.-
	1,907.-*		1,883.-*

N=928, valid N=660[†]

Note: * Respondent with an income of 15,000 DM. [†] Because of data editing there are slight deviations from values given by Motel and Wagner (1993). These figures excluded one male.

Source: Berlin Aging Study (BASE) Intake assessment

Age differences in women's income were likely to be a reflection of cohort effects. Despite the fact that the duration of women's employment did not change across the birth cohorts, the proportion of women working as qualified white collar workers increased with each age group, from just over a quarter (26%) of those born in 1887 to 1900, to 38% of those born between 1911 and 1922. Other social changes were apparent from the data. The proportion of 'mithelfende Familienangehörige', that is family members working for a business owned by another family member, decreased in those same birth groups, from 10% to 3%. Similarly, the proportion of women who had never worked more than 20 hours a week also declined, from 14% to 3%. These developments necessarily affected women's pension entitlements with the result that 85% of the youngest age group received a pension based on their own employment, compared to only 67% of the oldest pensioners.

The incomes of men and women were significantly different even when other socioeconomic variables were controlled in multivariate linear regression models (Motel and Wagner, 1993) – see Table 8.2. Women had a lower pension entitlement than men because they were in paid employment for fewer years, and their earnings during those years were lower (Maas and Staudinger, 1996; Allmendinger, 1994). Pensions based on women's paid work were thus less than men's. The income of elderly women fell with increasing age. As would be expected, incomes in old age were related to education and social prestige, variables that

Table 8.2: Determinants of equivalent income in old age[+]

	First wave (intake assessment)			Second wave	
	Total	Men	Women	Total	Total
Age	0.34	9.16	-10.14**	-7.80	-4.01
Sex (1=female, 0=male)	-283.25*	–	–	-402.92***	-405.13***
Living alone (1=yes, 0=no)	–	–	–	–	585.84***
Marital status					
widowed	601.06***	636.26***	388.57***	673.59***	–
divorced	169.85	222.05	-70.79	192.07	–
single	420.87***	-257.65	352.93**	282.97	–
Social prestige of the last job (prestige of the household, estimates included)	10.23***	8.85***	12.04***	6.95***	6.89***
Higher educational level (1=yes, 0=no)	233.08***	297.69**	190.25**	312.55***	272.50**
Occupational training (1=yes, 0=no)	83.67	-27.02	141.12*	138.03	132.59
Constant	885.85*	53.42	1,235.22***	2,348.77***	2,090.17***
N	586	321	265	282	282
R^2	0.22	0.20	0.31	0.20	0.19

Significance levels: *$p<0.10$, **$p<0.05$, ***$p<0.01$

Unstandardised coefficients

Note: [+] Respondent with an income of 15,000 DM is excluded.

Source: Berlin Aging Study (BASE)

indirectly are likely to have an impact on pension entitlement. However, it is also important to note that single women, widows and widowers had more financial resources than married couples.

The potential impact of widowhood, increasing the incomes of widowers rather than widows, has already been alluded to. The following example is similar to the results obtained from empirical analyses of the research data. An elderly couple both receive the average monthly pension for former blue-collar workers: 1,456 DM for the husband and 572 DM for his wife (Statistisches Bundesamt, 1994, p 202). This gives a combined monthly household income of 2,028 DM. Using the weighting factor of 1.8, an equivalent income of 1,127 DM is obtained (2,028 DM ÷ 1.8). If the husband dies, his wife will be entitled to a widow's pension of 874 DM (60% of 1,456 DM). Her total income will thus be 1,446 DM. However, if the wife dies, her husband will receive a widower's pension of 198 DM (60% of 572 DM minus 40% of [1,456 - 1,094 DM]). His total income as a widower will then be 1,654 DM, or 208 DM more than that which would have been received by his widow. Before 1986, this difference would have been even more marked. This feature in German social policy shows that old people's financial resources increase on the death of a spouse, more than compensating for the lost economies of scale achieved by living together. However, it also causes further polarisation of income between men and women, an effect that was even more marked before reforms in 1986.

Income inequality and poverty

Previous research has concentrated on discovering the extent of poverty among elderly people and, hence, has overlooked the possibility that income inequality might be high (Piachaud, 1992). However, there are three reasons why there is likely to be less income inequality among elderly people than there is among the employed. First, the limits set on the assessment of German pension entitlements mean that very high earning employees will not receive a correspondingly high pension. Secondly, very low income before retirement is not reflected in a correspondingly low pension; in fact, such pensions are disproportionately high. Finally, pensions are not simply related to the time spent in employment: they are adjusted to reflect periods of unemployment, or unpaid work, such as childrearing.

The Gini coefficient is used to measure income inequality, ranging from 0 when incomes are equal, to 1 at the other end of the scale (Atkinson, 1983). Table 8.3 shows the Gini coefficients and their confidence intervals by both gender and age. Consistent with the above arguments, income inequality among elderly people in West Berlin (Gini=0.24) is less than that among the total West German population (Gini=0.30, Schlomann, 1992). Gender differences in income inequality are more important than differences due to age. The small apparent increase in income inequality with age is not significant for men or women, but for elderly people aged 85 and above income inequality is greater among men than women.

Table 8.3: Income inequality (Gini coefficients) by age and sex (private households, confidence intervals for p=0.05 in brackets)*

	Total	70-84	85+
Total	0.24	0.22	0.25
	[0.22-0.25]	[0.20-0.24]	[0.22-0.28]
Men	0.26	0.24	0.27
	[0.23-0.28]	[0.21-0.27]	[0.23-0.31]
Women	0.21	0.20	0.22
	[0.19-0.23]	[0.18-0.23]	[0.19-0.24]

Note: * One respondent with an income of 15,000 DM excluded.
Source: Berlin Aging Study (BASE)

Because income inequality does not differ significantly between the two age groups of elderly people, it is unlikely that changes in marital status contribute to changes in income inequality. Inequality could, however, be affected by the transitions into residential care. For example, high-income respondents were more likely to stay in their own homes, while women showed a greater propensity to move into an old people's home. Inequality of earnings might vary according to gender and age cohort and these differences are likely to last into old age.

While income inequality does not increase significantly with age, poverty certainly does. This is not the contradiction that it might seem at first sight. If income inequality is constant across all income groups, poverty would still increase with age if incomes were lower among older cohorts. Motel and Wagner (1993) have discussed this aspect of income inequality extensively. Taking 50% of average income as a threshold, the poverty rate among elderly people in West Berlin was found to be 3.3%. The highest poverty rates occurred among the divorced – more than one in 10 of whom (10.4%) were poor – and among women aged 85 and above (7.8%). In both cases this was likely to be a consequence of broken employment histories, low paid jobs or longer periods of unpaid work. There was less poverty among elderly people who had been widowed, possibly because of the effects of the pension formula discussed earlier in this chapter. Other research has shown that poverty rates in rural areas are higher than those in West Berlin, so it is safe to assume that around one in 10 of elderly people in West Germany are poor.

Income changes

The Berlin Aging Study allows changes in incomes among elderly people to be observed over time, albeit the comparatively short period of 23 months. During this period, pensions increased slightly, but very few respondents experienced large variations in their income (Figure 8.1). Income correlation is high (r=0.82) between the first and second surveys, with around three quarters (72.4%) remaining in the same income bracket (the income brackets were: less than 1,000; 1,000-1,399; 1,400-1,799; 1,800-2,199; 2,200+ DM). Nearly one quarter of those surveyed reported an increase in their income, while only a few respondents dropped to a lower income band. On average, mean equivalent income increased from 1,985 DM by about 100 DM to 2,083 DM per month at the time of the second survey.

Small changes over a short period can have very significant cumulative effects in the longer term. It is important to establish factors associated with both rising and falling incomes in old age. The results of two regression analyses are presented in Table 8.4; these allow the independent effects of several factors to be identified.

As predicted, changes in household composition in old age do precipitate changes in income. For example, beginning to live alone was, on average, accompanied by a rise in equivalent income of around 900 DM per month, compared to those who were living alone at both surveys. Conversely, those who ceased to live alone generally found their income reduced by about 400 DM. Income changes associated with alterations in household composition –

which affected almost 6% of respondents – were less, once the sources of income and its level at the time of the first interview had been added to the models as explanatory variables (regression model 2 in Table 8.4).

The evidence is that income dynamics in old age – in the short term as considered here – are dependent upon the source of income and the overall level. The opposite effect also applies. Households receiving either civil service pensions or pensions from the professions, but no state pension (3.3%), experienced an above average increase in income during the study period. This can be contrasted with households receiving social assistance payments (12%) who were forced to accept a relative loss of income. On the other hand, lower incomes at the first interview appeared to be accompanied by above average increases in income during the subsequent two-year period.

Figure 8.1: Changes in the equivalent income between first wave (intake assessment) and second wave

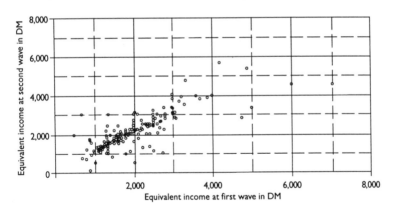

Source: Berlin Aging Study (BASE)

138 Michael Wagner and Andreas Motel

Table 8.4: Determinants of income changes between first wave (intake assessment) and second wave[†]

		Model 1	Model 2[‡]
Age		-1.35	-2.81
Sex (1=female, 0=male)		49.07	18.94
Duration between first and second wave in months		8.43**	6.37**
Change in household composition (ref: always living with others)	Not living alone/living alone	937.64**	848.31**
	Living alone/not living alone	-429.34**	-243.39
	Always living alone	25.42	138.32*
Social prestige of the last job (prestige of the household, estimates included)		-0.23	0.90
Higher educational level (0=no, 1=yes)		-70.45	-10.12
Occupational training (0=no, 1=yes)		-5.56	13.99
Income level at first wave[†]			-0.23**
Pensions from entitlements of own employment (ref group: only state pensions)	Only pensions for civil servants or pensions for professions		230.26*
	State pensions and firm pensions/pensions for civil servants/pensions for professions		97.76
	No pension from own employment		
Social assistance			-164.43*
Constant		-24.29	427.43
R²		0.13	0.24
adj. R²		0.10	0.19

N=264; Significance levels: *p=0.10, **p<0.05, ***p<0.01

Unstandardised coefficients

Note: [†] Two cases were excluded – these had an income difference of more than 4,000 DM. [‡] In model 2 sources and level of income are entered as additional explanatory variables.

Source: Berlin Aging Study (BASE)

Conclusion

This chapter has drawn on a unique survey, the Berlin Aging Study, which attempted to discover the extent of income differences among elderly people, and to determine whether financial resources changed during the course of ageing. The financial well-being of elderly men did not seem to differ between age groups. However, among women, income fell markedly with age for reasons that appear most likely to reflect employment histories related to their birth cohort. Women in West Berlin aged 85 and above were particularly disadvantaged financially.

In contrast to studies on poverty dynamics in younger age groups, the results suggest stability and continuity in the standard of living in elderly people. Older people do not have the opportunity actively to improve their financial position. Only a few continue in paid employment, and hardly any commence new employment. There are other ways to increase income, through the state's social welfare system, for instance, but its use is mainly dictated by need, such as the demand for care. In Germany, such payments are generally made directly to the care provider and appear as benefits in kind to the recipient so do not increase income as measured in most surveys.

It is likely that the assumption about the stable income of the elderly holds true for poverty. Not many respondents reported an income below the poverty line. However, those old people who are poor have little chance of escaping from poverty, especially when they receive social assistance payments on account of having insufficient income of their own to meet the cost of care. Germany's care insurance scheme, newly created in 1994, is not fundamentally changing this position.

However, the longitudinal analysis indicates that living standards are not always stable in old age. Life events, such as changes in household composition, usually the consequence of widowhood, can affect the relative economic position of elderly people. These changes reinforce the lifelong inequality between the sexes since men gain more financially when their spouse dies than women: a widower's equivalent income is around 640 DM higher than that of married men, while this difference is only around 390 DM for widows. This polarisation of income between men and women is an unintended consequence of the pension formula used to determine entitlements.

Elderly people's chances of improving their financial position depend on their sources of incomes.   Senior citizens who receive civil service pensions, or whose pension comes from a number of sources, profit not only from relatively high income levels, but also from comparatively large year-on-year increases in income.   This also applies to those who have additional individual financial arrangements.   In contrast, those who depend on state benefits have been forced to accept a deterioration in their financial circumstances.

The social welfare system and the state pension scheme are currently under economic and political pressure.   Reductions in pensions and social assistance would adversely affect the economic situation of those groups who are already structurally disadvantaged.   The state's social security system creates an economic gap between the more and less affluent in old age.   Action is needed to fill this gap.   At the very least, further discrimination should be prevented.

Authors' acknowledgements

This research was conducted within the context of the Berlin Aging Study (BASE).   The study is directed by a Steering Committee: P.B. Baltes, psychology; H. Helmchen, psychiatry; K.U. Mayer, sociology; and E. Steinhagen-Thiessen, internal medicine and geriatrics.   BASE is a project of the Committee on Ageing and Societal Development working with research centres and institutes attached to the Psychiatric Clinic of the Free University of Berlin and the Virchow Clinic of the Humboldt University of Berlin.   The study is coordinated by the Max Planck Institute for Human Development and Education.   The committee was established in 1987 by the former Academy of Sciences and Technology in Berlin and it has been sponsored by the Berlin-Brandenburg Academy of Sciences since 1994.   From 1989 to 1991, BASE was financially supported by the Federal Ministry of Research and Technology.   Since 1992, financial support has been provided by the Federal Ministry of Family Affairs, Senior Citizens, Women and Youth (314-1722-102/9+314-1733-102/a).

We thank Martin Kohli for his comments to an earlier version of this contribution.   Thanks also to Uli Pötter for his help in computing the confidence interval for Gini coefficients.

Notes

[1] The GRV (Gesetzliche Rentenversicherung) is a compulsory insurance scheme for all employees who are not public servants. It also applies to trainees and apprentices, craftsmen, certain groups of the self-employed, and others in paid employment. It is the basic German pension system.

[2] A comprehensive overview of German pension schemes should also include the smaller system for farmers and the professional pension schemes for doctors and lawyers in private practice.

[3] Old age pension schemes are the most common, but there are early retirement pensions, as well as widow's and surviving dependant's pensions.

[4] Many of the other income studies do not use equivalent scales, making it difficult to compare standards of living among elderly people, or between younger and older age groups (Bundesministerium für Arbeit und Sozialordnung, 1992a; 1992b).

[5] Income was measured by the following questions: 'What is the total amount of your personal monthly income?' (*Wie hoch sind Ihre persönlichen finanziellen Einkünfte im Monat insgesamt?*) and 'What is the total income of the household you are living in?' (*Wie hoch sind die finanziellen Monatseinkünfte des gesamten Haushalts, in dem Sie leben?*). The interviewers were advised to ask only for net incomes. If respondents either refused, or were unable, to specify their exact income, they had the opportunity to provide banded income information. A total of 69% of the respondents living in private households reported their exact income in both waves; 15% reported their exact income at either the first or second interview; 6% provided banded information at each interview. A total of 10% respondents failed to respond on at least one occasion. Response patterns were similar to those on the question on household income. Banded income was assigned the value of the mean for the category.

Information was also collected on the sources of household income. A total of 85% of elderly people were found to be receiving a state pension and a third (32.4%) had income from a company pension. However, respondents rarely had other sources of income. Slightly over 7% had a civil service pension, and just 1.4% were in receipt of a professional's pension, but more than one in 10 old people (11.8%) cited mentioned income from social assistance or housing benefit.   These multiple income sources meant that percentages do not total 100%. Widowhood pensions were not included, as it was not possible to classify them as either state or occupational.

In the transition from the intake assessment to the intensive survey, and subsequently to the follow-up study, respondents were positively selected according to their income. The mean equivalent income in the intake assessment was 1,906 DM in total, but 1,973 DM for those who participated in the intensive programme and 2,017 DM for respondents in the follow-up study.

Part Three

Poverty dynamics

nine

Income and poverty dynamics in Great Britain

Sarah Jarvis and Stephen Jenkins

Measures of poverty table — unreliable (handwritten annotation)

Introduction

How individuals' incomes change from one year to the next in Britain is something little is known about. Are the people poor this year the same people who were poor last year? Are this year's rich the same as last year's? Existing official UK sources such as the Department of Social Security's *Households Below Average Income* (HBAI) reports cannot provide answers to such questions because they are based on detailed 'snapshot' pictures of the income distribution rather than longitudinal income 'movies' (see for example, DSS, 1995). So, too, are virtually all previous UK income distribution studies, for example, Goodman and Webb (1994) or Jenkins (1996). Using data from the first two waves of the British Household Panel Survey (BHPS), this chapter provides new evidence about income dynamics in Britain, focusing on the situations of the poorest.

Our research aims to provide a longitudinal complement to the cross-section income distribution information provided by official UK income statistics. To this end we have taken the HBAI definitions and applied them to BHPS data for wave 1 (1991) and for wave 2 (1992). This provides us with two cross-sectional net income distributions similar to those in HBAI data for 1991 and for 1992, plus the all-important longitudinal income histories with which we can begin to investigate income and poverty dynamics.

Embarking on such a project raises many questions about concepts, definitions and data. We discuss these methodological issues in the second section. In the third section we provide evidence about overall income mobility. To put into perspective information about the extent and pattern of movement or stability in incomes at the bottom of the income distribution, it helps to have a feel for income change throughout the distribution as a whole.

Poverty dynamics per se are the focus of the fourth section. We classify people into one of four groups according to whether their incomes are below or above a wave 1 poverty line and a wave 2 poverty line (low-income stayers, low-income escapers, low-income entrants, and higher-income stayers). Two sets of poverty lines are used to check the sensitivity of results. We discuss both turnover among the low income population, and the income changes which each of the four groups experienced between 1991 and 1992. The fifth section provides a summary and concluding comments. This chapter summarises a lengthy report, Jarvis and Jenkins (1995), to which we refer readers for further details of our methods and results.[1]

Methods: data and definitions

British Household Panel Survey

The BHPS is the only British source which allows analysis of longitudinal changes in a comprehensive measure of income for a large representative sample of the UK population. The BHPS is Britain's first household panel survey, and is similar in structure and content to household panel surveys for other countries (for example, the US Panel Study of Income Dynamics and the German Socio-Economic Panel). In each of these household panel surveys a sample of persons (the 'panel') is followed over time, and data collected from a sequence of interviews ('waves') about one year apart.

The first wave of the BHPS was designed as a nationally representative sample of the population of Great Britain living in private households in 1991. Households were selected by an equal probability sampling mechanism using a design standard for British household social surveys. The achieved wave 1 sample comprises about 5,500 households, which corresponds to a response rate of about 65% of effective sample size (69% if proxy interviews are included). At wave 1 (autumn 1991) more than 90% of eligible adults, approximately 10,000 individuals, provided full interviews. About 88% of eligible wave 1 respondents were successfully reinterviewed at wave 2 approximately one year later.[2] In the research reported here, we use a sub-sample of these base samples, namely the households in each wave in which all eligible members provided complete interviews (more than 4,100 households, about 9,900 persons).[3]

Defining income

Our measure of 'income' mimics one in the official HBAI statistics, and is similar to 'equivalent disposable income' measures commonly used elsewhere. More precisely, we focus on real 'net income' which we define as income from employment and self-employment, investments and savings, private and occupational pensions, and other market income, plus cash social security and social assistance receipts, less income tax payments, employee National Insurance contributions, and local taxes. The components refer to receipts (or payments) during the month prior to the interview (or the most recent relevant period), all expressed on a weekly equivalent basis and in terms of January 1991 price levels.[4] Each household's net income is adjusted using the same equivalence scale as in the HBAI, with scale factors varying with household size and composition, and normalised at unity for a childless married couple household.

To derive the net income distributions we had to manipulate the BHPS data because its data collection focuses on the components of gross income rather than net income. We also had to simulate income tax payments, National Insurance, occupational pension contributions, and local tax payments. We discuss variable construction in detail in Jarvis and Jenkins (1995), and demonstrate the validity of the derived distributions relative to a range of relevant HBAI benchmarks.

The income-receiving unit used throughout is the 'individual': to be consistent with standard practice in the literature, each person is attributed with the equivalent net income of the household to which they belong at the time of the interview.

Defining 'poverty dynamics'

The term 'poverty dynamics' raises important questions about what is meant by 'poverty' and what is meant by its 'dynamics'. In this paper, *being in poverty means having a real income level below a pre-specified low income cut-off.* This income-based definition is in widespread use, though it is not the only possible one. There remains the issue of what low income level should be used as the cut-off to identify who is poor. We use two sets of thresholds to check the sensitivity of our conclusions about dynamics:

- the poorest 1991 decile for the 1991 income distribution (£88 per week), and the poorest 1992 decile for the 1992 income distribution (£92 per week);

- half average 1991 income for both the 1991 and the 1992 income distributions (£109 per week).

There is no official poverty line in the UK (cf the USA), but a specific fraction of average income (for example, one half) is commonly used by academic and other researchers as a benchmark. Our poverty lines are similar to means-tested social assistance benefit levels. For example, the basic Income Support entitlement in 1991 for a married couple with two children aged five and seven was £96.90 per week. Such a family is also likely to be receiving means-tested Housing Benefit to cover housing costs, and a figure of £40 per week would not be atypical. A money income of £136.90 corresponds to an equivalent net income of £96.41 per week, a figure which falls within our various poverty lines.

Given a set of poverty lines for the two BHPS waves, it is straightforward to classify the population into one of four groups according to whether their incomes were above or below those cut-offs in 1991 and 1992:

- (A) low-income stayers: income below the 1991 cut-off and below the 1992 cut-off;

- (B) low-income escapers: income below the 1991 cut-off and above the 1992 cut-off;

- (C) low-income entrants: income above the 1991 cut-off and below the 1992 cut-off;

- (D) higher-income stayers: income above the 1991 cut-off and above the 1992 cut-off.

What we mean by poverty dynamics can be explained with reference to the four groups A to D. There are two dimensions to dynamics which we consider.

First there is *turnover*, that is, the changing composition of the low income population *per se* (cf Chapter Two). This dimension relates to the relative numbers of people in each of the four groups. The proportion in group A measures the incidence of poverty persistence, and it is widely accepted that reduction of such persistence is socially desirable. The larger groups B and C (in a given country), the greater the turnover of people among the poor (it is a maximum when there is no one in groups A and D). The smaller the proportions in B and C, the more concentrated among the same set of people is low income.

The sum of the percentages in groups A, B, and C gives the proportions of the population poor for at least one period during the two year interval – an indicator of the proportion of the population 'touched' by poverty. To put such a statistic into perspective, it is useful to compare it to some reference points. The maximum possible percentage poor in at least one year is the sum of the percentages poor in each of the two years (in which case, the population poor comprises a completely different set of people from one year to the next). The other extreme occurs when the poor are the same set of people from one year to the next, and so the minimum turnover reference point is the maximum of the cross-section percentages of people poor.

The second dimension of poverty dynamics is the *change in real income* experienced by each of the four groups. The questions considered are: by how much does income fall on average for the low income entrants? By how much does income rise for the low income escapers? Are real incomes rising or falling on average among those with persistently low incomes? We summarise group income changes using comparisons of each group's median income in 1991 with that in 1992.

Income dynamics: the overall picture

The relationship between peoples' incomes in 1991 and their incomes in 1992 is summarised by Figure 9.1. Each point in this scatterplot represents the wave 1 income and wave 2 income combination for a person in our longitudinal sample. The more people there are with a given income combination, the greater the concentration, and hence the darker the picture, at that location on the scatterplot. If each person's income in 1992 were the same as his or her income in 1991 – that is, if there were no income mobility at all – then we would not see a cloud of points in Figure 9.1. Instead, all points would lie along the 45° line from the origin (in which case the income correlation coefficient would equal one). At the other extreme, if there were no association at all between wave 1 and wave 2 incomes, then the points in Figure 9.1 would be scattered evenly throughout the picture; there would be no specific areas where persons were concentrated (and the correlation coefficient would equal zero).

Neither of these two extremes apply. What we find is concentration of incomes in the neighbourhood of the 45° line – and so most mobility is relatively short range – and a significant number of points which are distant from the line. There is evidence of upward mobility between 1991 and 1992 (points in the top left) and also of downward income mobility (points in the bottom right). Mobility is experienced by people from all income ranges, rich and poor. The income correlation coefficient is about 0.7.

Figure 9.1 also allows a first look at low income turnover. On it we have drawn a horizontal line (for wave 2) and a vertical line (for wave 1) at the income level corresponding to half average 1991 income (£109 per week). The two lines form a cross with four quadrants. With this threshold, the people with low income in both 1991 and 1992 are those in the bottom left-hand quadrant; those with incomes above the cut-off in both years are those in the top right-hand quadrant. The low income escapers are those in the top left quadrant; the low income entrants are those in the bottom right-hand quadrant. There is a significant number of low income stayers and a considerable number who are higher income stayers. However, at the same time, there is also some considerable turnover in the low income population: the top left and bottom right quadrants are not empty.

Figure 9.1: Income mobility in the UK (1991-92)

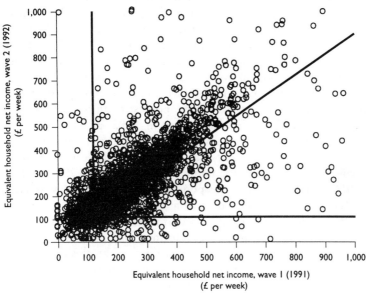

Source: British Household Panel Survey

Mobility between 1991 income origins and 1992 income destinations

To summarise income mobility numerically, we construct mobility matrices defined using decile groups.[5]   That is, everybody is classified into a decile group for 1991 and a decile group for 1992, and then the 1991 and 1992 arrays are cross-tabulated. The resulting mobility matrix summarises relative income mobility because (im)mobility is defined by changes in people's relative positions in the income parade rather than with reference to their income levels per se.   Complete immobility corresponds to the case when everyone's 1991 and 1992 decile groups are the same.

Our cross-tabulations reveal that there was relative stability for most people: almost three quarters (73.5%) of our sample remained in the same decile group in the two waves or moved up or down one decile group.   However, almost 16% experienced downward relative mobility: for about 11% incomes fell by two or three deciles, and for about 5% income fell by more than three deciles. Fewer, 11.6%, experienced upward relative mobility: for

7% income rose by two or three deciles between 1991 and 1992, and for 4% income rose by more than three deciles.[6]

Table 9.1, derived from the decile group mobility matrix, shows the outflow rates to the various wave 2 decile group 'destinations' from each wave 1 decile group 'origin'. Of the people who were in the poorest decile group in 1991, we find that nearly one half (46%) were also in the poorest decile group in 1992, and about one fifth (21%) were in the second poorest tenth in 1992. About two thirds of the poorest tenth in 1991 were in the poorest fifth of the distribution in 1992, and less than one tenth of the poorest 1991 tenth made it into the richer half of the distribution in 1992. Alternatively, the results can be read as saying that, of those in the poorest decile group in 1991, less than half (46%) were still in the poorest decile group one year later, and about one third moved up by more than one decile group.[7]

Whichever perspective is used, it is clear that there is mobility both out of and into the poorest income group. It is also apparent that most mobility is relatively short range. The clustering of the largest probabilities around the leading diagonal shows the prevalence of stability or short-range mobility. This applies to people from other 1991 decile groups, too (as shown by Figure 9.1). Short-range mobility might be all that you might expect in the course of a single year, but until now there has been no concrete UK evidence to confirm this conjecture or to characterise the particular patterns of mobility.

Observe, too, that 58% of those in the richest tenth in 1991 were in the richest tenth in 1992, and more than 80% were in the top fifth. It seems that the mobility process may be asymmetric, with downward relative mobility from the top generally more short-range than the upward relative mobility from the bottom. There are also interesting differences in mobility out of the two poorest 1991 decile groups, suggesting that persons in the poorest tenth have a higher chance of being in the top half of the income distribution one year later than do persons from the second poorest 1991 tenth. The apparently greater mobility at the bottom may be genuine, but it might also reflect the difficulty of reliably measuring very low incomes (see Davies, 1995, and Goodman and Webb, 1995).

Table 9.1: Outflow rates (%) from 1991 income origins to 1992 income destinations

		1	2	3	4	5	6	7	8	9	10
		\multicolumn{10}{Decile income group, wave 2}									

Decile income group, wave 2

Decile income group, wave 1		1	2	3	4	5	6	7	8	9	10
	1	46	21	15	5	4	2	3	1	0	2
	2	23	39	20	11	4	1	1	1	0	1
	3	12	19	28	22	8	3	3	2	2	1
	4	7	9	19	27	20	9	5	2	0	2
	5	2	4	11	15	30	22	7	5	2	1
	6	3	5	5	10	17	25	18	10	5	2
	7	3	1	2	4	11	20	36	14	6	3
	8	2	1	2	2	2	11	19	34	17	6
	9	4	2	2	2	2	6	8	23	41	13
	10	2	1	1	1	1	2	3	7	24	58
	All	10	10	10	10	10	10	10	10	10	10

Notes: Group 1 contains the poorest tenth; group 10 the richest tenth; income = equivalent net household income (£ per week, January 1991 prices).
Database source: British Household Panel Survey

Poverty dynamics

Low income turnover

Our first analyses use the bottom deciles as the poverty line(s): see Table 9.2, column 4. We find that less than one twentieth (4.3%) of our sample had incomes below the poorest decile in 1991 and below the poorest decile in 1992 (group A). For about one twentieth of the cross-wave sample (5.0%), incomes rose from below the poorest 1991 decile cut-off to above the poorest 1992 decile (B). For a slightly greater number of the sample (5.6%), incomes fell from above the bottom decile in 1991 to below the bottom decile in 1992 (C), and more than five sixths (85.3%) of the sample had incomes above the poorest decile in both years (D).[8]

There is a large amount of turnover among the low income population from one year to the next, even though the overall proportion with low incomes remained constant (by construction in this case). A significant proportion of people (almost 15%) had a low income in at least one year during the two-year period. If there were no turnover in the low income population the proportion would have been 10% and if, at the other extreme, there was a complete turnover (no low income stayers), the percentage would have been 20% (10% + 10%). It appears that income variability is such that a significant minority of the population is touched by low income in a two-year period.

Using a poverty line constant in real income terms, that is, half 1991 average income (see column 5 of Table 9.2), about one tenth (10.1%) of our sample had incomes below half 1991 average income during both 1991 and 1992 (group A). Some 7.1% of the sample had incomes below the cut-off in 1991 but above it in 1992 (B), whereas 6.4% had income falls taking them from above the income cut-off in 1991 to below it in 1992 (C). About three quarters of the sample (76.4%) had incomes above the cut-off in both years (D).

Echoing the relative mobility results, using the alternative poverty line reveals a significant degree of turnover among the low income population. If there was no turnover, we would have expected at most about 17% of the sample to have incomes below half the 1991 average for at least one year of the two, but in fact we find almost one fourth (23.6%). This proportion is rather smaller than that if there was a complete turnover (33.7%), but still significant.

Income changes for poverty turnover groups: did the poor become poorer?

So far we have documented the turnover among the low income population but we have not looked directly at the issue of whether 'the poor became poorer'. There has been much debate in Britain about whether real income growth has been experienced by everyone or whether the poorest groups missed out. This debate has typically referred to findings based on cross-sectional comparisons, but now we are able to provide some longitudinal evidence about income changes.

Table 9.2: Poverty turnover in the UK with regard to two poverty lines

Turnover group	Income relative to poverty line		Percentage in turnover group	
	1991	1992	(i) Poverty lines = poorest deciles	(ii) Poverty line = half 1991 average income
A	Below	Below	4.3	10.1
B	Below	Above	5.0	7.1
C	Above	Below	5.6	6.4
D	Above	Above	85.3	76.4
All			100.0	100.0
Percentage poor in at least one year			14.9	23.6
Maximum possible percentage poor in at least one year			20.0	33.7
Percentage poor in 1991			10.0	17.2
Percentage poor in 1992			10.0	16.5

Notes: Income = equivalent net household income (£ per week, January 1991 prices); deviation from 100% is due to rounding.
Database source: British Household Panel Survey

We estimate from our cross-wave sample that the median income among the poorest tenth in 1991 was £73 per week and the median for the poorest tenth in 1992 was about £3 higher at £76 per week (see the top panel of Table 9.3). From this comparison of cross-sections, there appears to be some small improvement over one year in the income of the poorest groups. But we know that there was significant low income turnover, so not everyone would have experienced this increase. So let us now consider the changes over time in income for each of the four turnover groups identified earlier, beginning with the case where the low income cut-offs are the poorest deciles.[9]

For the low income stayers, the people who were in the poorest decile group in both 1991 and 1992 (4.3% of the sample), we find that the increase in group median income was some £5 per week. However, this increase is dwarfed by the increase in median income for the people who escaped from the poorest decile group between 1991 and 1992. For this group (5% of the sample), median income rose by £50 from £74 to £124, an in-

Table 9.3: Changes in median income for poverty turnover groups in the UK with regard to two poverty lines

Wave 1 income group	Wave 2 income group		
	Poor	Not poor	All
	(i) Poverty lines = poorest deciles		
Poor	£71 → £76	£74 → £124	£73 → £95
Not poor	£120 → £75	£210 → £211	£204 → £204
All	£92 → £76	£202 → £207	£191 → £193
	(ii) Poverty line = half 1991 average income		
Poor	£85 → £87	£88 → £136	£86 → £102
Not poor	£145 → £90	£221 → £226	£216 → £215
All	£99 → £88	£211 → £216	£191 → £193

Note: Income = equivalent net household income (£ per week, January 1991 prices)
Database source: British Household Panel Survey

crease of two thirds. However, there were also substantial losers. Among the low income entrant group, those whose incomes fell from above the bottom decile in 1991 to below it in 1992 (5.6% of the sample), median income fell by £45 per week, from £120 to £75. For those with incomes above the poorest decile in both years (85.3% of the sample), median income remained virtually constant.

Using a poverty line of half average 1991 income and taking the cross-section perspective, we see that the median income of those people poor in 1992 was slightly higher than the median income among those poor in 1991: £88 rather than £86. When we unpack this result, we find diverse changes for the different mover and stayer groups (as before). For the two 'stayer' groups, there was also little change in median income: for the higher income stayers (76.4% of the sample) the median increased from £221 to £226, whereas for the low income stayers (10% of the sample) median income increased from £85 to £87. For the low income escapers (7.1%), median income increased substantially, by £48 from £88 to £136. For the low income entrants (6.4% of the sample), median income fell substantially between 1991 and 1992, by £55, from £145 to £90.

Our conclusions are robust to a variation in the definition of the poverty line. Although median income for the population as a whole increased hardly at all between 1991 and 1992, this disguises substantial income rises and falls within the population. *There appears to be no strong evidence that the poor became poorer in Britain between 1991 and 1992.* Instead, it is more accurate to say that those who became poor between 1991 and 1992 experienced big income falls (and those who became non-poor had a large income increase on average).

Conclusions

This chapter has summarised new findings about poverty dynamics and income mobility in 1990s Britain using the first two waves of the new British Household Panel Survey. The evidence provides an important longitudinal complement to the cross-section snapshots of the income distribution provided in the official UK Households Below Average Income statistics.

We have shown that whereas there is a substantial amount of income mobility from one year to the next, much of that mobility is relatively short range. This appears to be the pattern at all levels of income. Although you might have broadly predicted 'not much change' in income during the course of a single year, we have characterised what happened more precisely.

If we focus on the poorest income groups, we find that many of the people who had low incomes when interviewed in 1991 no longer had low incomes when interviewed in 1992. Among the low income stayers, incomes appear to have increased slightly between 1991 and 1992. Among the low income escapers, the increase in income is much larger in absolute terms but counterbalancing this there is also a group of low income entrants, of about the same number, with large income falls. In sum, there is significant turnover amongst the low income population; over this two-year period, a significant minority of people experienced low income at some time during at least one of those years. The essence of all these conclusions about income dynamics stand whether the poverty lines are the poorest deciles, or half 1991 average income.

Our income dynamics analysis can be extended in several directions in future research, taking advantage of subsequent waves of data from the BHPS. For example, we can examine poverty persistence over a longer time period than two years, the incidence of repeated spells of poverty, and in each case the types of people involved and the resulting changes in income levels. We can investigate whether poverty persistence, and spell repetition, is concentrated among specific types of people, or whether the risks of their occurrence are spread more universally across the population. This is useful information for policy design and its targeting. For instance, we found that those with relatively high risks of being low income stayers are those classified in 1991 as belonging to lone parent families, the elderly (mainly single pensioners), and those in families where no one is in work (see Jarvis and Jenkins, 1995, for further details). Further investigation is required to distinguish income (im)mobility due to changes in money income versus that due to changes in a person's household context.

There is also much research which could be undertaken more generally on the causes of income mobility and movements in and out of low income, in particular their relationship to life-course events. What, for example, are the income consequences of taking a job or of losing a job, or a change in employment mix within households? How do these effects compare with the income consequences of household formation, augmentation, and dissolution? These topics are on our research agenda.

Authors' acknowledgements

This chapter is based on Jarvis and Jenkins (1995), a report prepared for the UK Department of Social Security as part of a joint project of the ESRC Research Centre on Micro-Social Change, University of Essex, with the Centre for Research in Social Policy (CRSP), Loughborough University. Financial and other support were also provided by the Economic and Social Research Council and the University of Essex. We thank Karl Ashworth, Richard Burkhauser, Jonathan Gershuny, Dan Murphy and his DSS reviewer colleagues, John Poupore, Gerry Redmond, Steve Webb, Moira Wilson, the editors of this volume and especially Nick Buck, for comments and assistance. Responsibility for the contents of this chapter lies with the authors alone.

Notes

[1] Our research is a significant extension and development of the two previous studies of income mobility based upon the first two waves of the BHPS which used less satisfactory income measures (Taylor et al, 1994, and Webb, 1995).

[2] For a detailed discussion of BHPS methodology, representativeness, and weighting and imputation procedures see M.F. Taylor (1994) and A. Taylor (1994).

[3] This is to ensure we have complete information for income recipients and income sources when we derive our measures of income. As a consequence, we do not use the cross-sectional or longitudinal weights provided in the BHPS data, since they are designed to be applied to samples of all respondent households. Our preliminary investigations suggest that no significant attrition biases are introduced by this. For elaboration of these arguments and sub-sample details, see Jarvis and Jenkins, 1995.

[4] For shorthand convenience we shall refer to 1991 and 1992 incomes and low income status, but the sub-annual accounting period should be kept in mind.

[5] The deciles used to construct the decile groups are estimated using the respective cross-section sub-samples (rather than the longitudinal ones), on the grounds that these provide better estimates of the underlying population figures. As a result, each row (and column) of the mobility matrices shown below does not contain exactly one tenth of the longitudinal sub-sample – although it is very close to one tenth (equal after rounding to two decimal places). It is for this reason (together with sampling error) that Table 9.1 is not a bistochastic matrix.

[6] The opportunities for moving a specific number of deciles are constrained by the decile group you start in. For example, those in the poorest group in 1991 cannot move to a lower decile group, nor those in the richest group move to a richer group in 1992. With our definition of income stability – remaining in the same decile group or changing by one – the proportion experiencing downward relative mobility need not equal the proportion experiencing upward relative mobility.

[7] You could also summarise mobility patterns in terms of inflows and origins as well as outflows and destinations. For example, of those in the poorest decile group at wave 2, almost half came from the poorest decile group at wave 1.

[8] Strictly speaking, the percentages refer to people classified by their income levels at the time of their interviews in 1991 and in 1992, rather than by incomes for each year as a whole. (Remember that we are using the 'year' as a concise shorthand for a sub-annual income receipt period.)

[9] Note that the change in a subgroup's median income does not necessarily equal the median of a subgroup income changes, though in practice the figures are usually similar. The focus in Table 9.3 on a single representative income disguises a substantial spread of income changes within each group. See Jarvis and Jenkins, 1995, for more information about the distribution of income changes.

ten

Low income dynamics in Unified Germany

Peter Krause

One of the most surprising results of the 1969 Michigan Panel Study of Income Dynamics was that poverty was not as persistent as had been previously thought (Duncan, 1984; Bane and Ellwood, 1986; Hill, 1992). Long-running panel data compiled in Germany is now available, giving social scientists the opportunity to compare those US findings with results obtained in another industrialised western country.

Measuring poverty rates in Germany presents special difficulties, since the former East and West have very different social and economic histories. Determining poverty rates was particularly problematic during the transitional period following German unification, as East German incomes rose rapidly. However, the research results detailed in this chapter echo those of the US study. While a surprising number of Germans succeed in escaping from poverty, more people than expected are shown to experience poverty at some point in their lives.

These results imply that poverty can no longer be regarded as a perpetual state of helplessness, requiring long-term social assistance programmes to provide a minimum share of the state's resources. Dynamic poverty research challenges the theoretical ideas on which German social policy has long been based.

Database and methods

German Socio-Economic Panel Study

This chapter is based on a national study, the German Socio-Economic Panel Study (GSOEP), established in 1984. The first wave sample comprised 5,921 households with 16,252 household members, including children; individual interviews were conducted with everyone over 16, yielding 12,245 respondents. Disproportionately large sub-samples were included of the five main groups of foreigners: Turks, Greeks, Spaniards, Italians and Yugoslavs.[1]

The GSOEP was extended to East Germany in June 1990, before the financial, economic and social union of Germany on 1 July, which was followed by formal unification on 3 October. The East German GSOEP sample covered 2,179 households, with a total of 6,253 members, 4,453 of whom were interviewed.

A weakness of many surveys is an under-representation of the poor. However, comparison with the German census showed that low income respondents were not undersampled in the first wave of data (Rendtel, 1990). Further checks have confirmed that the poor are adequately represented even across 10 wave samples (Rendtel et al, 1995).

Defining and measuring poverty

The European Union has defined poverty as follows:

> The poor shall be taken to mean persons, families and groups of persons whose resources (material, cultural and social) are so limited as to exclude them from the minimum acceptable way of life in the Member State in which they live. (Eurostat, 1995, p 4)

This widely accepted definition implies that poverty depends on a broad concept of social and economic well-being, and that poverty is relative in that it is related to a country's general standard of living.

However, most empirical measures use a more restrictive definition based on either expenditure data, which relates to consumption patterns (Eurostat, 1995), or on income data, indicating 'command over resources' (Hagenaars, 1986). In this chapter poverty is defined in these terms, rather than the broader concept proposed by the European Union.

Although disposable household income must be regarded as an inadequate indicator of general individual welfare, it is still the most relevant measure of individual material resources.[2] In many analyses, and this chapter is no exception, it is assumed not only that resources are pooled within households but that they are divided within a household in relation to individual needs, with the result that each member shares the same standard of living.[3] Comparisons between different households are based on equivalent incomes. The equivalence scales used in this chapter are derived from the German social assistance scale rates. The analysis is based on the latest net monthly income.[4, 5]

Germany and most EC countries use 50% of *mean* equivalent income as the main poverty threshold.[6] However, two other thresholds are used in this chapter: 60% of mean income which indicates 'low income', and 40% which is taken to be 'severe poverty'. These provide extra information about the incidence of poverty and are especially valuable when, as here, only the head-count ratio is used. Empirically, the three thresholds correspond roughly to convenient quantiles (Table 10.1). 'Severe poverty' relates to the 5% of the population with the lowest income, the main poverty threshold to the lowest 10% and 'low income' to 20%.

Poverty dynamics in West Germany since 1984

Poverty rates as defined above and based on the GSOEP did not increase in the mid-1980s. If anything, they declined slightly towards the end of the decade, with a sharp decrease at the beginning of the 1990s, followed by an upswing. This is true of the main 50% poverty threshold, and the severe poverty measure based on the 40% line. These trends in relative poverty are similar to the pattern of social assistance receipt for German claimants as revealed by official statistics (see also Chapter Eleven). Poverty rates of recent foreigners are much higher than those of Germans (see Table 10.1).

Table 10.1: Incidence of poverty (%) in West Germany (1984-94)

Year	40%-line Total population	50%-line Total population	50%-line Germans	Foreigners*	60%-line Total population
1984	5.2	12.6	11.8	25.0	21.0
1985	5.0	11.9	11.1	26.0	20.9
1986	5.0	11.9	11.0	27.1	20.1
1987	4.5	10.7	9.7	25.8	19.9
1988	5.3	11.0	10.4	20.8	20.4
1989	4.8	10.3	9.5	23.3	19.5
1990	3.9	10.5	9.5	26.3	18.5
1991	4.3	10.0	8.9	24.5	18.0
1992	4.4	10.0	9.0	24.7	18.6
1993	5.1	11.1	9.8	24.9	19.8
1994	4.8	11.1	10.0	26.6	21.9

Note: * Household members, if head of household was Turkish, Greek, Italian, Spanish, or Yugoslavian in 1984, including the split-offs from these households.
Database: German Socio-Economic Panel Study

Short-term and long-term poverty

The frequency and duration of poverty is revealed by the number-of-times-poor measure (Table 10.2). This shows the number of years in which an individual is recorded as being in poverty during a survey period. Taking the main 50% threshold, just over 30% of West Germans were poor for at least one year between 1984 and 1994, a figure almost three times the maximum number poor in any one year. That is, the incidence of poverty is much lower than the prevalance of poverty (cf Chapter Two). Even so, 70% were not poor at all during the 11 years studied. During the same period, a fifth (20%) had incomes below the poverty threshold for a spell of three years or less, while a further 10% were poor in four or more years. Most people experienced only short spells of poverty: around 35% of those who were poor at all experienced poverty in a single year, whereas only 9% were poor for eight or more years.

The figures for foreigners are substantially different. Only 40% of the foreigners living in West Germany were never poor during this time; around one third (30%) were poor in one to three years, and nearly one in three (30%) suffered four or more years of poverty (compared to just one in 10 of native Germans).

The three different poverty thresholds were also associated with different ratios of short- and long-term poverty (the former defined as being poor in less than four years out of 11, the latter as being poor in four or more years). The ratio of short- to long-term poverty among the nearly 20% of Germans who had experienced severe poverty was 14:4. The same ratio becomes 21:10 at the main 50% poverty threshold and 24:23 at the low income line, which about 45% of the West German population had suffered. Spells of severe poverty were thus less persistent than periods below the 50% threshold which were, in turn, typically shorter than periods of low income.

Table 10.1 showed the marginal decline in poverty rates up until the end of the 1980s, followed by the sharp decrease at the beginning of the 1990s. This decline was largely accounted for by a fall in short-term poverty (Figure 10.1). The percentage of people who were poor only once within a three-year period decreased during the 1980s, reaching its lowest level at the beginning of the 1990s and thereafter increasing (Figure 10.1).

Table 10.2: Duration of poverty (1984-94), full sample ('social policy view')

Number of years in which poor	40%-line Total population	50%-line Total population	50%-line Germans	50%-line Foreigners[*]	60%-line Total population
0	82.4	67.8	69.3	38.9	53.3
1	8.1	10.8	10.7	13.4	12.2
2	4.2	6.1	5.9	10.2	6.3
3	1.7	4.1	3.9	7.7	5.3
4-5	1.6	4.5	4.2	11.4	6.8
6-8	1.5	4.0	3.6	10.2	9.0
9-11	0.6	2.7	2.4	8.1	7.1

Note: [*] Household members, if head of household was Turkish, Greek, Italian, Spanish, or Yugoslavian in 1984, including the split-offs from these households.

Database: German Socio-Economic Panel Study

Figure 10.1: Changing duration of poverty – five three-year periods, West Germany (1984-94)

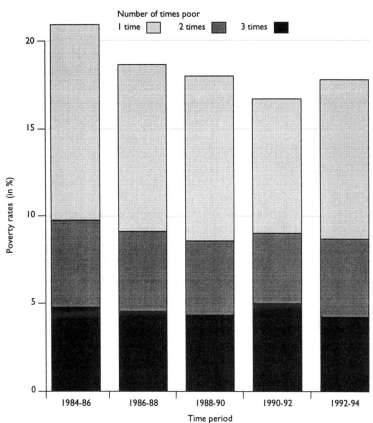

Database: German Socio-Economic Panel Study

Financial status before and after poverty

Social stratification theory and the notion of the 'two thirds' society both assume that most fluctuations in income dynamics are small: while some people may succeed in escaping poverty, their income will remain quite close to the poverty line.

To test this assumption the income of each respondent in each year between 1984 and 1992 was converted to 1992 incomes and averaged over the whole period. The number-of-times-poor measure was then applied. This method was also repeated for periods not spent in poverty (Figure 10.2).

The analysis shows (as expected) that average household income declines as the number of years spent in poverty increases. The two thirds of the population who were not poor during the study period had average incomes well above the national mean. The short-term poor – those with one or two years in poverty – had incomes that fell below the mean, but were still well above the low-income threshold. Those who had experienced longer-term poverty had average incomes that hovered around the 50% threshold, while the incomes of families poor for more than six years fell beneath this threshold when averaged over the entire nine-year period.

The very experience of poverty seems to imply lower incomes even in years when families are not poor; each year of poverty up to four years brought a corresponding reduction in income in periods of comparative prosperity. Human capital, in the form of skills, experience and training, may be reduced during spells of unemployment, and thus account for lower incomes when in work. Alternatively, people experiencing different lengths of

Figure 10.2: Long-term (averaged) income and poverty in West Germany (1984-92)

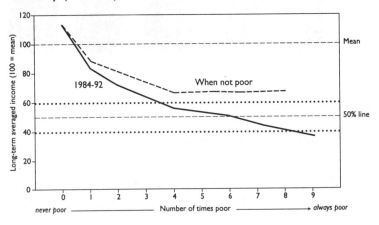

Database: German Socio-Economic Panel Study

poverty may vary in other ways that could account for their differing incomes when they are not poor.

Nevertheless, even people who had been poor in four or more years enjoyed incomes that reached two thirds of the national average when they were not poor; in other words, they were above the low income threshold. This finding undermines a basic premise of social stratification theory, because it shows that the average incomes of even the long-term poor lie well above the poverty line after (or between) spells of poverty. The 'leap' from poverty to non-poverty typically encompasses more than a decile of the income distribution.

Another perspective on income dynamics is provided by using household incomes in 1984 to predict incomes and poverty in future years (Figure 10.3). Although poverty may beget poverty, the affluent are not immune. While 11% of the people in severe poverty in 1984 did not experience poverty again within the next seven years, more than half were poor in four or more subsequent years. Turning to those on or around the margins of poverty, people with incomes of 40 to 60% of the average in 1984, a different picture emerges. A larger number, 35%, were not poor again during the observation period, and one fifth were poor only once more. However, one fifth experienced two or three years of poverty, and one quarter suffered long-term poverty.

Poverty was also to afflict people who had had higher incomes in 1984. One third of those with incomes initially between 61 and 80% of the national average subsequently experienced a spell of poverty. So did 15% of West Germans with lower middle incomes and 5% of those with average incomes.

Roughly the same picture appears when this process is reversed. Income stratification in 1992 was compared with periods of poverty during the preceding seven years. Low income groups were poor for longer and more frequently during this period than those people with higher incomes. However, nearly one fifth of those with incomes between 80 and 120% of the 1992 average had been poor on at least one occasion, as had 8% of those on even higher incomes.

These results are inconsistent with the hypothesis of the two thirds society since individuals can, and do, experience large changes in income from year to year; the leap from poverty to an above-average income is not as extraordinary as stratification

Figure 10.3: Where do they go and where do they come from? Income strata and income dynamics in West Germany (1984-92)

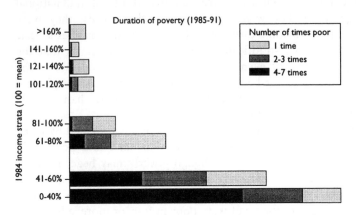

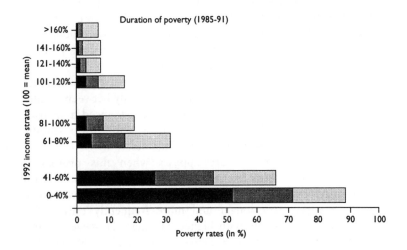

Database: German Socio-Economic Panel Study

theory would suggest. Conversely, those on high incomes can also fall into poverty. However, income dynamics are not a random process. People on lower incomes are much more likely to fall into poverty. Once they have done so, they stay poor for longer periods than those people who have previously enjoyed higher incomes.

Patterns of poverty

The number-of-times-poor measure underestimates the time that people spend in poverty due to the 'censoring' of spells (Bane and Ellwood, 1986; see also Chapter Two); this is because periods of poverty that start before, or end after, the window of observation provided by the study are necessarily truncated. Switching to a more individualistic view on poverty that overcomes this deficiency results in a change in the short to long-term poverty ratio. This was achieved by taking people who were poor in the year 1989 (in the middle of the period 1984 to 1994) and counting the number of years that they were in poverty, thereby producing uncensored profiles of duration for up to five years (and a maximum of 11 years). As anticipated, the proportion of long-term and repeated poverty increases as a consequence (Table 10.3).

Poverty was defined as 'short-term' if a person was poor in less than four years between 1984 and 1994; four or more years in poverty was labelled 'long-term'. Given these criteria the ratio of short- to long-term poverty was approximately 1:2. Just over one quarter (28%) were more or less permanently poor, suffering nine or more years in poverty, another quarter (27%) were below the poverty line for between six and eight years. Even so, 45% of the sample were poor for less than half the observation window. The duration of severe poverty (40% line) was again much shorter than poverty defined with respect to the 50% threshold.

The proportion of the population who had experienced poverty increased as the observation period was extended. As already noted, three times as many people experienced poverty (at the 50% threshold) during the decade than in any one year. The relative importance of different types of poverty varies with the length of the observation period (Figure 10.4). Cross-sectional statistics for a single year reported earlier in this chapter indicate

Table 10.3: Duration of poverty (1984-94) if poor in 1989 ('biographical view')

Number of years in which poor	40% line Total population	50% line Total population	Germans	Foreigners*	60% line Total population
1	16.1	7.5	7.2	9.4	5.8
1-3	43.8	31.1	32.7	18.9	16.4
1-5	66.2	45.3	46.6	35.2	27.8
1-8	91.2	71.8	72.7	64.6	63.7
1-11	100.0	100.0	100.0	100.0	100.0

Note: * Household members, if head of household was Turkish, Greek, Italian, Spanish or Yugoslavian in 1984, including split-offs from these households.
Database: German Socio-Economic Panel Study

that the proportions of people falling below the 40%, 50% and 60% thresholds roughly equated 5%, 10% and 20% respectively ('incidence' of poverty). Over a 10-year period the corresponding figures were roughly 17.5%, 30% and 45% ('prevalence' of poverty). Thus 17.5% of the West German population suffered at least one spell of severe poverty during this period, nearly one third had fallen below the usual poverty threshold, and about a half (45%) of the population had some experience of low income.

The difference between the cross-sectional and 11-year estimates was greatest for severe poverty, a finding consistent with the fact that spells of severe poverty were typically shorter than other types.

The rate of increase in poverty rates that resulted from expanding the observation period was not constant. It was greatest during the first four years. Thereafter the increase remained constant at around 1% for each additional year. This implies that if the study had lasted long enough it would have shown that a high percentage of the West German population would eventually have experienced at least one spell of poverty. This finding also emphasises the short-term nature of most spells of poverty, discussed earlier in this chapter. However, expanding the observation window also increases the proportion of people experiencing repeated spells of poverty. It appears that one experience of poverty increases the probability of suffering poverty on subsequent occasions.

Figure 10.4: Increasing poverty rates with widening observation period – three poverty measures compared, West Germany (1984-94)

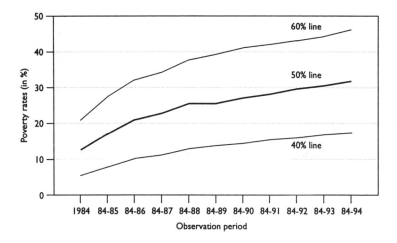

Database: German Socio-Economic Panel Study

This highlights that we need to learn more about the aetiology of different forms of poverty since there may be important associations with life course changes. Further research is needed to determine how the risk of long-term poverty is distributed over a life-time, when an individual is most at risk of falling into long-term poverty, and at what stages it is easiest to escape. The impact of policy cannot be ignored. The role of social policy is of crucial importance in redistributing resources between generations, as well as between social strata. Likewise, attention needs to be paid to the apparent stability of long-term poverty over the study period and the contribution of government policy to the fall and subsequent increase in short spells.

Incidence and duration of poverty in Germany since unification (1990-94)

Increase in disposable income in East Germany

Before unification in 1990, incomes in East Germany were much lower than those in the West, although there was less inequality. Between 1990 and 1994 mean equivalent disposable household income rose steadily from a nominal 727 Mark[7] to 1,381 DM, an increase of 90%. During the same period, the cost of living increased by 46.9%, according to the Statistisches Bundesamt. Even allowing for the controversial 'shopping basket' used to calculate living costs, it is clear that East Germans enjoyed a real and continuous improvement in disposable household incomes during this transition period.

Incomes in West Germany rose by only 17.2% over the same period, while the cost of living increased by 15.3%. The real increase in disposable income achieved in the West between 1990 and 1994 was therefore quite small; positive growth rates in the beginning of the 1990s were followed by a fall in real incomes between 1993 and 1994.

The rate of increase in incomes in East Germany slowed down rapidly, although in 1994 it was still higher than in West Germany. Over the four years, equivalent incomes in East Germany increased from 46.0% to 74.3% of those in the West. Taking account of differentials in purchasing power, 'real' incomes in East Germany rose from 65.9% of those in the West in 1990, to 83.5% in 1994.

At the end of the socialist regime, income inequality in East Germany was much lower than in West Germany. Since unification it has shown a marginal but steady increase, although it is still considerably less than in the former West Germany where income inequality has again been increasing since 1993.

To summarise, real income levels in West Germany remained more or less unchanged between 1990 and 1994, while marked increases in East Germany were accompanied by only a modest rise in income inequality. Average incomes in East Germany increased despite a dramatic growth in unemployment.

Development of poverty in East Germany

Measuring relative poverty for East Germany presents special difficulties since at least three reference points are possible: mean income in East Germany, mean income in West Germany, and the subjective expected mean income in East Germany (Figure 10.5).

When East German mean income was used, poverty rates in the East appeared to be much lower than those in the West. This is because income inequality was lower and relative poverty, by definition, rises as inequality increases. This approach takes no account of unification and was inappropriate after 1990.

Conversely, calculating East German poverty rates using average West German income overstates the extent of poverty rates at the beginning of the transition period. However, this method is becoming more relevant for social policy purposes since it is proposed that social assistance benefits should be the same in the East and West. High poverty rates for East Germany have declined as incomes have converged, and by 1994 poverty rates in East and West Germany were quite similar, at 13.8% and 11.1% respectively.

However, the last method proved the most reliable: measuring average East German income using subjective expected mean income. Explicit account is taken of expectations of rising living standards in the East, and it provides the best means of comparing East/West poverty rates. By 1994, poverty rates in the East were comparable with those in the West.

Duration of poverty in Germany after unification

The aim, in this penultimate section, is to explore poverty dynamics in the immediate aftermath of reunification. As we have seen, poverty rates and trends in East Germany vary widely according to the method used to calculate them. The approach taken here is to use the 'number-of-times-poor' measure based on three thresholds, namely the bottom five, 10 and 20% of the income distributions of the *Länder* that comprised former East and West Germany.

Two, not necessarily incompatible, scenarios are examined. The first assumes that the proportion of long-term poor would be higher in East Germany because only a restricted number of people would benefit during a period of volatile income dynamics.

The second hypothesis rests on the premise that the income volatility in East Germany during the transition period would enable more East Germans than West Germans to escape from poverty. The latter scenario appears to conform better to the facts (Figure 10.6).

The figure shows how many people (in % of the total population in 1990) ranked among the poorest 5% (10%, 20%) at some point during the transformation years 1990-94 (one year, two years, ..., throughout). At first glance the research results bear out the first supposition since it is apparent that more East Germans than West Germans were poor on at least one occasion during the transition period. The difference is perhaps most marked when the numbers of those whose incomes fell into the lowest quintile are compared: 43% of East Germans and 35% of West Germans. Similarly, 25% of the people in the East, compared with 20% in the West, slipped into the lowest decile at some point during the transition. However, differences for experiencing severe poverty (belonging to the poorest 5%) were quite small: 14% and 12% of East and West Germans respectively.

Figure 10.5: Incidence of poverty in Unified Germany (1990-94)

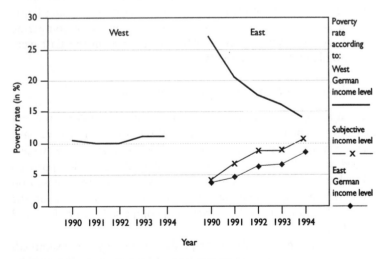

Database: German Socio-Economic Panel Study

Figure 10.6: Duration of poverty during the transformation process (1990-94) – East and West Germany compared with regard to three poverty measures

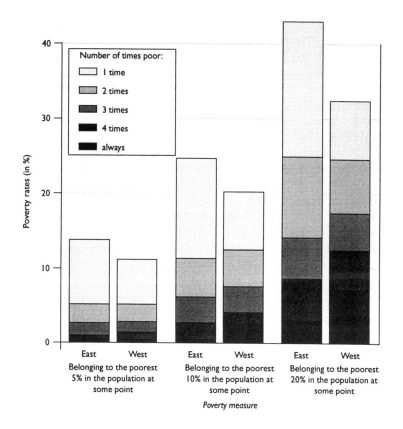

Population: persons who were in the sample throughout 1990-94. Database: German Socio-Economic Panel Study

Turning to the second hypothesis, the percentage of the East Germans suffering long-term poverty was noticeably less than in West Germany during this period. This is apparent in the proportion in the lowest decile of income, which is close to the 50% threshold in West Germany: 13% of East Germans were poor in a single year and 6% in three of the years, that is for more than half the time available; the corresponding figures for the West German *Länder* were 8% and 8%. East and West German experience was fairly similar in respect of the severe poverty defined by the lowest half-decile. In East Germany, 9% suffered severe poverty on one occasion, while only 3% experienced it in three or more years. In West Germany the figures were comparable: 7% and 3%. For the low income range of equivalent income, indexed by the lowest quintile, it is again apparent that incomes were more volatile in the former East Germany. In the East German *Länder* people were more likely to report a low income in one year than in three or more (18% compared with 14%) whereas the opposite was true in the old West Germany (10% and 17% respectively).

To summarise, during the transition process after unification, more people experienced low incomes in the East than in the West. On the other hand, the incidence of severe poverty was no greater or longer lasting. The available evidence suggests that all except the most severe form of poverty was less persistent among the East German population than in West Germany. However, this final conclusion needs to be qualified in that it is sensitive to the effects of spell censorship described above.

Conclusions

Through exploring the dynamics of poverty in Germany before and after unification, this chapter has demonstrated that the experience of poverty is far more prevalent than is generally thought, even in the most affluent of countries. It is not just people on lower incomes who are at risk of poverty, as claimed by proponents of the 'two thirds' society. In Germany, families on middle incomes, and even those further up the income scale, can be thrust into poverty. Within a decade, one third of the West German population has been shown to cross the poverty threshold. During a lifetime, many more Germans will inevitably be confronted by the spectre of poverty.

While most spells of poverty in Germany are comparatively short, more or less permanent poverty still exists. The incomes attained after spells of poverty, even long ones, are on average well above the poverty threshold. However, relatively few of those who escape poverty make it to the upper half of the income range.

Poor people are also much more likely to remain poor than others are to become poor.

The transition period in East Germany, following unification, was potentially a time of enormous personal financial risk. During this time, East Germans were at greater risk of poverty than their West German counterparts. However, the rapid growth that occurred in real incomes, together with other changes, enabled many poor people to escape their situation. That is now more difficult, and perhaps, especially so, for West Germans. Due to the stagnation of real incomes and rising income inequality, the risk of poverty in West Germany is now just as high as in East Germany.

Notes

[1] These five groups represent most of the foreigners to West Germany during the 1960s and 1970s. These are substantially different from the immigration patterns in the late 1980s when the groups came mainly from the former GDR and Eastern Europe and from the Third World countries. Foreigners of the 1980s are covered in two separate sub-samples started in 1984/5 which are not included in this analysis.

[2] Material welfare includes the many types of work done within the house to make living more comfortable. Simply living together improves material welfare due to economies of scale: larger households achieve high levels of individual welfare compared with the same number of people living in single-person households.

[3] For a critical discussion, see Jenkins (1991).

[4] The household questionnaire is answered by the head of household, or the person who can provide answers for all household members. The question about net income is asked after questions relating to state benefits (child allowance, housing benefit, social assistance) and income from assets. These income components should be included in the net income answer.

[5] It might be expected that monthly income figures, used in this research, would fluctuate more rapidly than annual incomes. However, Rendtel et al (1992) showed that estimates of transitions

in and out of poverty are virtually the same regardless of whether annual or monthly income information is used.   Monthly equivalent income is more appropriate given changes in household composition which can occur during a year.

[6] It is usual in the US and in international comparisons with non-European countries, to use *median* rather than mean income to calculate the poverty threshold.   Given that the median is invariably lower than the mean, poverty rates based on 50% of median income are lower than those based on 50% of mean income.

[7] The currency union began after the first wave of the East German sub-sample. Mark and DM are calculated as 1:1.

Part Four

Benefit dynamics

eleven

Social assistance and social change in Germany

Petra Buhr and Andreas Weber

Until recently the dominant public perception of poverty in Germany was that it was predominantly long term. Poverty and the receipt of social assistance were seen as static, unchangeable characteristics of individuals or groups. This is well illustrated by the notion of a 'two thirds' society (Glotz, 1985; Leibfried and Tennstedt, 1985), implying that some groups, the unemployed for instance, are permanently excluded from the mainstream of society. Reliable data on the extent of long-term and short-term poverty, however, was not available.

Since the end of the 1980s, this traditional view of poverty has been challenged. In the process, assumptions about social assistance have also been examined. Dynamic research using new longitudinal data sets has proved that short-term poverty is more prevalent than studies based on cross-sectional data had suggested. One of the first projects to use a dynamic approach was the Bremen Longitudinal Study of Social Assistance (LSA) (Leibfried, 1987; Buhr, 1995; Leibfried/Leisering et al 1995; Ludwig, 1996).[1, 2] The first results of this study were based on an analysis of the city's[3] social assistance claimants from 1983 until 1989 ('the 1983 cohort'). About half of the new recipients left social assistance within a year, and fewer than one in 10 received social assistance continuously for more than five years.

Between 1983 and 1993, Germany experienced huge social, economic and political changes. During those years, the number of people on social assistance[4] doubled from 1.7 million to 3.4

million. The fall of the Berlin Wall and Germany's subsequent unification was the major political event of the era. However, other economic and social changes which may have influenced social assistance must be taken into account.

Immigration from Eastern Europe grew, for instance, and there were changes both in the labour market and in employment conditions. Meanwhile, rents rose, while social benefits were cut and new regulations came into effect. Attitudes towards social assistance changed as well, and lifestyles in general continued to become more individualistic.

We may ask if the results of the Bremen study are still valid. In particular, is it more difficult, as is sometimes supposed by public opinion, to escape from social assistance in the 1990s than it was in the 1980s? To clarify these questions, this chapter compares the 1983 cohort with a more recent cohort of new recipients, people whose first spell of assistance began in 1989 and who were observed until 1994, since the cohorts faced very different political, social and economic conditions.[5] This comparison enables us to explore the effect of social changes on social assistance.

The social and economic situation in Germany during the 1980s

Immigration

In 1960 only around 1% of the population were foreigners. By 1993, that figure had grown to more than 8%: during the 1960s, workers from Southern Europe, particularly Turkey, were recruited to solve the labour shortage in Germany. When German unemployment rose after the oil crisis, recruitment stopped. After 1973, only the families of previous immigrants were allowed entry.

During the 1980s, 'German immigrants' from the German Democratic Republic, and immigrants 'of German origin'[6] from Eastern Europe and the former Soviet Union came to what was then West Germany. Their numbers rose rapidly from 50,000 in 1983 to 700,000 in 1989. The number of refugees and political asylum seekers also grew, from around 20,000 in 1983 to 120,000 in 1989, reaching a peak of more than 400,000 in 1992 (see

Figure 11.1). All of these figures refer only to *new* immigrants who came to Germany in the respective year.

Labour market conditions

Unemployment in the West German *Länder* rose from 3.8% in 1980 to 9.1% in 1983, and 9.3% in 1985. The situation improved slightly during the next few years: in 1989, the unemployment rate dropped to 7.9% and it fell again to 6.3% in 1991. In more recent years it has increased again, reaching 9.2% in 1994.

Long-term unemployment lasting for longer than a year increased dramatically during the 1980s, reaching a peak in 1988 when one third of all unemployment was long-term. That proportion subsequently fell continuously to 26% in 1993, although a marked upswing occurred in 1994 when the proportion of people who had been without work for a year rose again to 32.5%.

Social policy

During the 1980s, entitlement to unemployment benefit was altered, and the level of benefits reduced for some groups of claimants.[7] These changes contributed to creating a new type of poverty among the unemployed (Balsen et al, 1984), and meant that more unemployed people were forced to claim supplementary social assistance.

Three other changes in social policy may have influenced social assistance. First, in 1985, the Employment Promotion Act (*Beschäftigungsförderungsgesetz*) promoted temporary, casual employment, possibly increasing multiple spells of unemployment. Secondly, state employment schemes providing temporary jobs for social assistance claimants (*Hilfe zur Arbeit*) have also increased. Finally, education benefit (*Erziehungsgeld*), introduced in 1985 by the Conservative government, may have lifted some families off social assistance. It is paid to either parent who does not have a full-time paid job for six months after the birth of a baby, irrespective of income. It continues for a further 18 months if the family's income does not exceed the specified threshold.

Figure 11.1: Immigrants in the Federal Republic of Germany (new immigrants in the year of immigration)

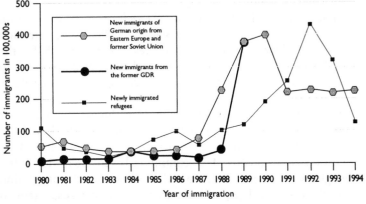

Source: Statistisches Bundesamt (Federal Statistical Office)

Process of individualisation

As in other Western countries, German society is becoming more diverse (Beck, 1986). Individual life courses have become less predictable as the importance of traditional institutions, such as the family, has declined. Attitudes to work have also changed. It is reasonable to assume that this process of individualisation increased during the 1980s, as indicated by the growth in single-person households,[8] the rise in the divorce rate,[9] and the number of babies born to unmarried parents.[10]

However, German social insurance is based on the traditional family model with a male breadwinner in continuous full-time employment, rather than on more diverse forms of the family. Multiple spells of unemployment, divorce and single-parenthood are risks that are inadequately covered by the state's social insurance scheme, and consequently may lead to poverty and the receipt of social assistance.

Changing attitudes towards social assistance

In Germany, social assistance is still associated with charity, and many people try to avoid it for as long as possible. However, the stigma may have lessened during the 1980s, with young people, in particular, being less reluctant to claim social assistance than older generations.

Housing market conditions

The reduction of council house building programmes contributed to the shortage of cheap accommodation evident during the 1980s, especially in large cities. As a consequence, families in particular suffered severe financial problems.[11]

There are three ways in which these social, political and economic changes may have influenced social assistance.

Firstly, the sociodemographic structure of social assistance recipients may have been affected, altering the gender balance and the composition in terms of household type. These structural changes may in turn have affected the average time spent receiving social assistance because duration differs according to social group. Secondly, these changes may also have affected claimants' opportunities to leave social assistance, by finding a job, for instance. Finally, attitudes which are related to the time spent receiving assistance – reluctance to apply, or reapply, for example – may have altered.

Impact on social assistance

Table 11.1 summarises the probable effect of social change which occurred during the 1980s on the average time spent receiving social assistance. The large numbers of German immigrants included among new claimants at the end of the decade may have shortened the average duration. This is because most of them would have been entitled to social insurance, such as unemployment benefits and old age pensions, and would rapidly have left social assistance as soon as their first social insurance payment was made.[12]

Conversely, the increasing numbers of refugees among new claimants during the same period would have lengthened the average time spent on social assistance. Refugees usually have to wait a long time before being granted political asylum (or being deported), during which time they typically receive social assistance continuously. Until 1991, they were not allowed to

Table 11.1: Impact of social change on time spent receiving social assistance during the 1980s

Determinants	Impact on time spent receiving assistance
Immigration	
Increase in number of German immigrants from the former GDR, Eastern Europe and former Soviet Union	–
Increase in number of refugees	+
Labour market	
Decrease in unemployment	–
Decrease in long-term unemployment	–
Social policy	
Employment Promotion Act (promotion of temporary and irregular employment)	+
Employment schemes for recipients of social assistance	–
Childraising benefit	+
Individualisation	+/–
Changing attitudes towards social assistance	+
Housing shortage and increasing rents	+

Source: Authors' data

work. The subsequent relaxation of the rules which then allowed refugees to apply for work permits may also have affected the time spent receiving social assistance benefits.

The decrease in unemployment between 1983 and 1989 would have meant that fewer unemployed people were included in the flow of new social assistance claimants. Low levels of unemployment should have facilitated people finding and holding down jobs, which, in turn, would have reduced the time that they needed to stay on social assistance.

However, by the end of the 1980s there had been a marked increase in temporary, casual employment, and, hence, in the number of people with inadequate unemployment benefit. These changes, largely due to the 1985 Employment Promotion Act, would have increased the proportion of unemployed needing to supplement their incomes through social assistance. It may also have lengthened the total time that people spent on social assistance, although their benefit career may have been characterised by intermittent spells of claiming.

The introduction of education benefit could also have led to longer periods of social assistance, since it does not reduce entitlement to social assistance, but is only payable to persons not in full-time work. Conversely, employment schemes for those on social assistance would have shortened the time spent receiving such benefit; although the programmes themselves only provide temporary employment, participants become entitled to unemployment insurance benefit and so are unlikely to need immediately to reapply for social assistance. Their chances of finding a proper job would also have been improved.

It is difficult to pinpoint the overall effect of individualisation on social assistance (Table 11.2). Certainly you could expect a rise in the proportion of non-traditional families among those joining the social assistance caseload. However, while an expansion in the number of lone parents spending long, unbroken periods on social assistance when their children were small could have increased average duration, the rise in one person households might be expected to have the opposite effect. So, too, might the changed attitudes to work. Greater geographic mobility and an increased preparedness to change jobs voluntarily may have reduced average duration.

Rising rents pushed more people over the poverty threshold, particularly families with several children. This could have led to longer spells on social assistance, since higher rents meant that it was more difficult to escape poverty, even if other sources of income rose. The lessening of the stigma attached to social assistance may also have lengthened duration.

It is far more difficult than it first appears to come to any conclusions about the influence of social change on the length of time spent on social assistance. There is certainly evidence of an increase in duration during the 1980s, but this is balanced by the factors that point to shorter spells of social assistance.

German social assistance dynamics in the 1980s

Having discussed potential influences on the dynamics of German social assistance, it is possible to investigate the changes that actually occurred in the state of Bremen during the 1980s and early 1990s.[13]

Sociodemographic structure of the 1983 and 1989 cohorts

In this chapter we have to distinguish between 'foreigners' and 'immigrants' because many people who immigrated to Germany in the late 1980s and in the 1990s were legally considered to be ethnic Germans. These 'German immigrants' came and still come from Eastern Europe, from the former Soviet Union and, before German unification in 1990, from East Germany. They do not have the status of asylum seekers or of refugees. On the other hand, many 'foreigners' have lived in Germany for many years or were even born in this country. We therefore use the term 'immigrant' to denote people who have newly immigrated in the first year of the observation period (eg, in 1983 or in 1989).

The most marked development was the dramatic increase in immigrants receiving social assistance. In the 1989 cohort, around half of the new recipients were immigrants, both 'refugees' and 'German immigrants',[14] while in the earlier cohort immigrants amounted to less than one in 10 of the total. The proportion of 'native Germans' and 'resident non-German immigrants' (both these groups are called 'residents' for the rest of the chapter) foreign nationals who have lived in Germany for a longer period, showed a sharp fall (see Figure 11.2).

Immigration has come to exert a major influence on the pattern of social assistance receipt. It was entirely responsible for the increase in new recipients recorded during the 1980s. Were it not for the rise in German immigrants and refugees, the total number of new claimants would actually have fallen between the cohorts.

Compared to the dramatic increase in the proportion of immigrants, other differences between the cohorts appear slight. As expected, the proportion of lone parents was greater in the later cohort[15] while, reflecting the improvement in the labour market at the end of the 1980s,[16] unemployment generally declined in importance as a reason for claiming social assistance.

However, it is vital to distinguish between two groups of unemployed: those receiving social assistance while awaiting unemployment benefit,[17] and those claiming social assistance

Figure 11.2: Resident status groups in the 1983 and the 1989
cohorts (refugees and immigrants: newly immigrated in 1983
and 1989)

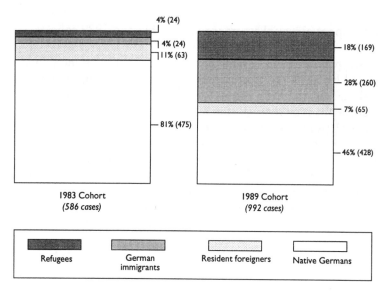

4% (24)

4% (24)
11% (63)

18% (169)

28% (260)

7% (65)

81% (475)

46% (428)

1983 Cohort
(586 cases)

1989 Cohort
(992 cases)

| Refugees | German immigrants | Resident foreigners | Native Germans |

Database: Bremen 10%-longitudinal-sample of Social Assistance Files (LSA);
Department of Women, Health, Youth, Social Affairs and Environment, state
of Bremen; Center for Social Policy Research Center 186, University of
Bremen

because their unemployment benefit is insufficient, or non-
existent. Overall, the proportion awaiting insurance benefit
increased,[18] while those unemployed claiming social assistance for
other reasons decreased. However, in the case of German
residents the opposite trend prevailed, with the proportion of
people lacking, or receiving insufficient unemployment benefit
growing at the expense of those awaiting insurance benefits. This
suggests that native Germans fared comparatively badly as a result
of changes in the labour market which apparently lessened their
access to insurance benefits.

Both the rise in lone parents, and the fall in the number of
social assistance recipients awaiting unemployment benefit, could

have resulted in an increase in the average time spent on social assistance between the two cohorts. However, the reality turns out not to be quite so simple.

Time spent on social assistance in the 1983 and 1989 cohorts

Many people spend several periods on social assistance, interrupted by spells of financial independence. Focusing on a single spell, as did the early research in the USA, can seriously underestimate the total time spent in receipt of assistance.

Therefore two measures of duration are used: 'net duration' refers to the sum of single spells on social assistance, while 'gross duration' is the time period between the first and last social assistance payment, including interruptions. In the absence of a reliable theoretical or empirical definition of short- or long-term poverty, spells of social assistance lasting up to a year are taken to be short-term, while those lasting more than five years are defined as long-term.

Both measures indicate that, contrary to popular belief, in the 1990s people are not staying longer on social assistance than they did in the 1980s (Table 11.2). The proportion of claimants spending a total of less than a year on benefit during the five-year observation period (net duration) increased from 56% in the earlier cohort to 58% in the later one, while long-term receipt fell from 15% to 12%. This decline reflects a fall in the number of claimants experiencing multiple spells on social assistance. Nearly 45% of the 1983 cohort had had two or more spells at the end of the monitoring period (gross duration), whereas the corresponding figure for the later cohort was 35%. However, first spells lasted longer in the 1989 cohort and, largely as a consequence, the median net duration rose slightly from eight to nine months. The pattern of change in gross duration is less equivocal. Short-term receipt rose from 47% to 50%, the numbers on long-term social assistance fell from 19% to 16% and median duration declined markedly from 15 to 12 months.

This decrease in total median duration was mainly caused by dramatic changes in the composition of the two cohorts, rather than by developments in the labour market. This can be seen most clearly when immigrants are excluded (Table 11.3). Among

Table 11.2: Time on social assistance in the 1983 and the 1989 cohorts

Cohort	Median (months)	Years on social assistance					
		0-1	1-2	2-3	3-4	4-5	>5
		First spell (%)					
1983	4	74	9	4	3	2	8
1989	5	72	13	5	2	2	6
		Net duration (%)					
1983	8	56	12	7	5	4	15
1989	9	58	17	7	4	2	12
		Gross duration (%)					
1983	15	47	10	7	6	11	19
1989	12	50	15	6	6	7	16

Based on product-limit-estimation; deviation from 100% is due to rounding.
Data source: Bremen LSA Files; Department of Women, Health, Youth, Social Affairs and Environment, state of Bremen; Center for Social Policy Research and Special Research Center 186, University of Bremen

Table 11.3: Time on social assistance in the 1983 and 1989 cohorts (residents only)

Cohort	Median (months)	Years on social assistance					
		0-1	1-2	2-3	3-4	4-5	>5
		First spell (%)					
1983	4	74	9	3	3	2	8
1989	6	70	14	3	3	2	8
		Net duration (%)					
1983	8	55	13	7	5	4	16
1989	12	51	18	6	4	3	17
		Gross duration (%)					
1983	18	45	10	7	6	11	21
1989	17	41	15	6	7	10	22

Based on product-limit-estimation; deviation from 100% is due to rounding.
Data source: Bremen LSA Files; Department of Women, Health, Youth, Social Affairs and Environment, state of Bremen; Center for Social Policy Research and Special Research Center 186, University of Bremen

German residents, short-term receipt of social assistance actually fell, while long-term dependency rose slightly. Median net duration increased markedly, primarily as a result of the growth in the numbers of German residents spending between one and two years on social assistance.

Continuing to focus on German residents, more detailed analyses have revealed that long-term social assistance is more common among women, young people, elderly people, those with no vocational qualifications, parents with small children, lone parents and the unemployed. Comparing the two cohorts, the total time spent on social assistance increased among nearly all these groups, with young people experiencing the most marked rise.[19]

However, lone parents and elderly people did not show an increase in time spent on social assistance, another result which runs counter to public preconceptions.[20]

Finally, what of the popular notion that the unemployed in the 1990s spend more time on social assistance than they did during the 1980s? At face value the Bremen analysis appears to confirm this supposition since average durations did rise between the two cohorts.[21] However, this result is forged by the experience of one group, those awaiting unemployment benefit, and so reflects the quality of public administration rather than fundamental social change.

Conclusion

The empirical evidence, on which this chapter is based, suggests that spells on social assistance have not lengthened during the last decade. However, the two cohorts do reveal one dramatic difference: nearly half of the new recipients in the 1989 cohort were German immigrants or refugees, compared with less than one in 10 six years earlier. It is immigration which is the major reason for the increasing number of people claiming social assistance in Germany. Had this not happened, the numbers on social assistance in the 1989 cohort would have been much smaller, although the average duration would have been longer.

This evidence shows that unemployment is not the prime mover behind the increase in social assistance, as is often assumed by politicians and social scientists. The rise in the number of social assistance recipients has a political cause, namely the encouragement of German immigrants by the Conservative government over a lengthy period.

Although it is easy to see the impact of immigration, it is more difficult to evaluate the influence of other social and economic forces. Individualisation may have played a part, notably the increase in the number of lone parent families, many of whom have recourse to social assistance. Social policy itself may have had an impact on the number of social assistance recipients. An example is the increased number of resident Germans who, when unemployed, need to supplement inadequate unemployment insurance benefits. Their plight reflects not only the growth of insecure employment but also changes to the eligibility criteria for insurance benefits, some of which have been introduced to curtail rising expenditure.

The research offers little comfort to protagonists at either end of the political spectrum. There is little evidence that it is more difficult to leave social assistance than in the past, as those on the political left might have us believe. Equally, there is little to indicate that social assistance recipients are any less motivated to find work, or more inclined to rely on the welfare state, a repeated claim of right-wing politicians and business organisations. It appears that the German system of social assistance still functions fairly effectively in meeting the statutory obligation to provide transitory help to those who need it. However, social policy makers need to remember that any intervention in social insurance schemes, such as reducing the level of unemployment benefit, has a direct impact on social assistance.

Since the beginning of the 1990s, new factors have come into play. Immigration has declined, while unemployment, including long-term unemployment, has risen to a postwar peak. Not only could this increase the number of people seeking social assistance, it may also lead to an increase in the extent of long-term reliance on means-tested benefit.

Notes

[1] Dynamic poverty research has a longer tradition in the USA (Duncan, 1984; Bane and Ellwood, 1986; 1994).

[2] Since then several other research projects have implemented a dynamic approach, based on other data sources such as the German Socio-Economic Panel (Headey et al, 1990; Rendtel and Wagner, 1991; Krause, 1994) and the Bielefeld data bank of social assistance (Samson, 1992; Andreß, 1994).

[3] Bremen is situated in north-western Germany on the river Weser. It has around 550,000 inhabitants. The city has severe economic problems with a higher than average unemployment rate, due to the decline in its traditional shipyard industries since the end of the 1970s.

[4] Everyone who is in need is eligible for German Social Assistance although since 1993 asylum seekers have a special benefit scheme. Social assistance consists of *Hilfe zum Lebensunterhalt* (basic income support) and *Hilfe in besonderen Lebenslagen* (benefits for those with special needs, such as people with disabilities). In this chapter the term 'social assistance' refers to *Hilfe zum Lebensunterhalt*.

[5] Sophisticated statistical modelling of the causes of long-term social assistance are not provided. (For an analysis of this data compared to Swedish data, see Chapter Fourteen.)

[6] 'Of German origin' refers to those immigrants who are legally recognised as Germans.

[7] The German system of unemployment benefits consists of *Arbeitslosengeld* and *Arbeitslosenhilfe*. In order to be entitled to the former, unemployment insurance must have been paid through contributions from employment for at least a year, while for the latter they must have been paid for at least six months. *Arbeitslosengeld* is usually paid for a period no longer than a year, although special groups such as elderly people may claim it for longer. After that, the unemployed receive the means-tested *Arbeitslosenhilfe* which is paid at a lower level for an unlimited period.

[8] The proportion of single-person households increased from 30.2% in 1980 to 34% in 1989 and 35.3% in 1993.

[9] The rate of divorce per 10,000 existing marriages increased from 61.3 in 1980 to 81.0 in 1990 and 83.0 in 1993.

[10] The ratio of out-of-wedlock births per 100 live births increased from 7.6% in 1980 to 10.2% in 1989 and 11.9% in 1993. The proportion of lone-parent families (with children of all ages) rose from 15.3% in 1982 to 17.6% in 1989 and 17.8% in 1992.

[11] In 1980, a low-income family of four spent on average 23% of their disposable income on rent and energy; in 1989 it was 26%, and in 1994, 29%.

[12] In 1990, entitlement to unemployment benefits was changed for German immigrants.

[13] The data base is the Bremen Longitudinal Sample of Social Assistance Files (LSA), a 10% random sample of all social assistance files in the city of Bremen since 1983. The analysis in this chapter was limited to *Hilfe zum Lebensunterhalt*, with the file – denoted by applicant – being the unit of analysis. In the case of married couples, the applicant is usually the husband. Beside the applicant, several other members of a family may receive social assistance within the same file. The 1983 cohort consists of 586 files, or applicants; the 1989 cohort has 922 cases. The observation period for both cohorts was 69 months, with the 1983 cohort being observed until the end of September 1988, and the 1989 cohort until the end of September 1994.

[14] 'German immigrants', from Eastern Europe and the former Soviet Union (16%), and from the former German Democratic Republic (12%).

[15] The proportion of lone parents increased from 10% to 12% in the total population, and from 10% to 15% in the group of residents.

[16] The proportion of unemployed recipients, or more precisely, recipients who reported unemployment as one cause of social assistance, decreased from 58% to 54% in the total population, and from 60% to 57% in the group of residents.

[17] Those cases awaiting payment indicated poverty that had been inflicted by the welfare state itself (Leisering and Voges, 1992).

[18] This is due to the increase in German immigrants. More than 80% of these are awaiting the payment of unemployment benefit, and another 11% are waiting for other state payments, including old age pensions.

[19] Median gross duration for young people increased from 26 to 41 months.

[20] This holds true for total duration at least. As for lone parents, median gross duration decreased from 36 to 33 months, although the median duration of the first spell increased. For recipients aged 50 and above it decreased from 37 to 12 months.

[21] Median gross duration increased from 10 to 14 months.

twelve

Welfare benefits and recession in Great Britain

Robert Walker and Karl Ashworth

In terms of the numbers unemployed, the recession of the early 1990s in Britain was comparable to that of the 1930s yet it generated considerably less hardship or social unrest. One reason was the panoply of social security and social assistance benefits provided by the welfare state. These benefits will have helped to meet some of the financial needs arising from the loss of employment and the continuing cost of housing and care for dependants. Benefits also serve to even out the fluctuations in aggregate demand that accompany the macro-economic cycle, and may have lessened the depth and length of the recession (Walker and Huby, 1989; Hutton, 1995).

Individual benefits – and, indeed, entire social security systems – are likely to be influenced in different ways by economic recession. The impact on particular schemes, as well as its effectiveness as a response to recession, will probably be affected by the nature of its objectives. Unemployment insurance, for example, is meant as a direct response to recession and the associated rise in unemployment whereas benefits to meet the costs of disability and children ostensibly are not. However, simply because a benefit is designed to meet a particular contingency does not mean that it is effective in doing so. Systems which are funded (that is, with benefits linked directly to moneys collected), or based on contribution records, may buckle in a long recession. In Britain, the unemployment benefit system established by the Liberal government in 1911 was destroyed by the unemployment of the

1920s because many of the unemployed had either exhausted or not acquired entitlement to benefit (Walker et al, 1995). Likewise, the current high levels of unemployment throughout Europe have imposed great pressures on insurance-based schemes and led to the growth of means testing (van Oorschot, 1994).

Benefit schemes that are not intended as a response to the risks inherent in economic recession can nevertheless be affected by high unemployment. The escalating demand for disability and incapacity benefits in Britain is thought to be due, in part, to rising unemployment causing some people to leave the labour force, perhaps attracted by schemes that pay higher benefits than are available to the unemployed. Escalating demand has precipitated reforms designed to reduce expenditures on disability benefits. Even a scheme, such as Child Benefit in Britain, which is essentially unaffected by recession, may become a target as administrations look for ways of curbing total expenditure on benefits that is being driven upwards by unemployment.

This chapter aims to explore how three benefits responded to, and were affected by, the British recession of the early 1990s. These benefits, Unemployment Benefit, Income Support and Housing Benefit, have since been abolished or amended for reasons that are explained below, in part, as a consequence of the recession. Four interrelated questions are addressed:

- How did the system respond to the deepening recession?

- How long did people remain on benefit?

- Where did the new claimants come from?

- Where did those who left benefit go?

Social security benefits

You would expect the three benefits and their dynamics to respond very differently to the onset of recession. Unemployment Benefit (which was superseded by Jobseeker's Allowance in 1996) might be thought of as the first line of defence against unemployment. Eligibility was conditional upon the loss of employment being involuntary and the claimant being available for work and having paid the requisite National Insurance contributions in the preceding two years. The financial circumstances of other members of the benefit unit (broadly speaking the household) were not taken into account when assessing levels of payment. Benefit was payable for a maximum of 12 months,[1] and when exhausted entitlement could only be rebuilt through making further contributions.

On the other hand, Income Support and Housing Benefit were not dependent upon contributions. Instead they were income tested with the financial circumstances of all members of the claimant unit being taken into account when determining levels of payment. In European-speak, Income Support for the unemployed would have been termed social assistance, providing a final safety net to all persons without adequate income from other sources.[2] It could be received alongside Unemployment Benefit. However, Income Support differed from many social assistance schemes in Europe in that it excluded persons employed for more than 16 hours per week. Income Support recipients claiming the benefit on account of unemployment were expected to be actively seeking work. Housing Benefit was (and remains) payable to low-income householders responsible for the payment of rent, including those in full-time employment.

The British system deviates from the European model in the relative importance of social assistance and social insurance benefits (Bolderson and Mabbett, 1995; Eardley et al, 1996). Almost one sixth of the entire British population were receiving Income Support (social assistance) in 1993, one third because of unemployment, whereas less than one quarter of the unemployed received contribution-based Unemployment Benefit (social insurance) (Table 12.1).

Further differences in the characteristics of the people who might have been expected to claim the three benefits could have

Table 12.1: Incidence of benefit receipt, Great Britain (1993)

Benefit	1993
Unemployment Benefit	2.4% of labour force
(Unemployment rate:	10.4% of labour force)
Income Support	17.5% of population
Housing Benefit	20% of households

Source: Various

affected the numbers of new claimants flowing on to benefit as a direct or indirect result of unemployment. Equally, they might also have helped to determine the speed at which people moved off benefit, and hence the rate of growth in the claimant populations.

Evidence will be drawn from the first three waves of the British Household Panel Study and covers the period from September 1990 to August 1993 during which time the official unemployment count rose from 5.7% to 10.4% (Figure 12.1, source: Labour Market Trends). In common with other surveys, the BHPS understates the number of people claiming benefits.

More than two thirds of the claimants who received Unemployment Benefit during the three-year observation period were men (Table 12.2). The majority of these had a partner and, in such cases, more had children than not. Even so almost one quarter of people claiming Unemployment Benefit were lone men. This is in marked contrast to Housing Benefit, and to a lesser extent Income Support, and reflects the labour market orientation of the benefit. Only 45% of people claiming Income Support and 41% of those on Housing Benefit were men. Two fifths of Housing Benefit recipients were retired as were one fifth of Income Support claimants; lone parents accounted for around one sixth of the caseload of both benefits.

Figure 12.1: Unemployment in Great Britain (1988-97)

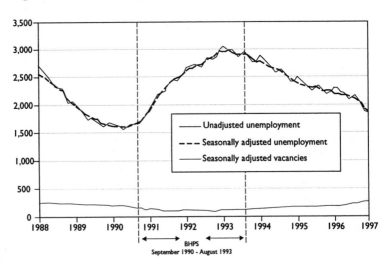

Table 12.2: Characteristics of benefit populations

Family type	Income Support (%)	Housing Benefit (%)	Unemployment Benefit (%)	Total sample (%)
	Respondents receiving benefit some time between September 1990 and August 1993			
Couple no children	12	8	28	27
Couple with children	24	17	36	30
Lone parent	17	18	3	4
Single woman	11	8	8	8
Single man	17	8	23	11
Retired	20	41	2	20
Sample size (=100%)	1,168	801	567	7,809

Note: The total sample refers to all respondents in the BHPS aged 16 and above at the third wave.

Source: Adapted from Ashworth et al (1997b)

About 37% of Unemployment Benefit claimants had no qualifications while 10% possessed a degree or equivalent. While the education and skill levels of this group were less than the general population, they far exceeded those of Income Support and Housing Benefit claimants – 52% of the former, and 72% of the latter, had no qualifications at all. The high proportion of Housing Benefit claimants with no qualifications was a consequence of a larger number of them being elderly and female claimants. Recipients of Housing Benefit were also more likely to report a health problem than either Unemployment Benefit and Income Support claimants. The caseloads of all three benefits, but especially Housing Benefit and Income Support, were characterised by disproportionate numbers of claimants renting local authority housing and hence, falling on the wrong side of the tenure divide that has increasingly come to mark a major disjuncture in the distribution of social disadvantage in Britain (Marsh et al, 1997).

Given the purpose of Unemployment Benefit, the size of the claimant population was likely to be extremely sensitive to the prevailing state of the economy. However, the limited duration of Unemployment Benefit imposed a ceiling on the caseload because people ceased to receive benefit after a maximum of 12 months even if they did not find employment. Such a ceiling applied neither to Income Support nor Housing Benefit since there was no maximum period of receipt.

The Income Support caseload was also going to be markedly affected by recession because it provided a safety net for people not in full-time employment (that is, those working 16 hours or more). On the whole, sections of both the Income Support and Housing Benefit caseloads were likely to be largely immune to the state of the labour market. Pensioners and lone parents, for example, were not expected to be seeking work.[3] Similarly, the financial circumstances of pensioners were likely to be more stable than those of younger people, some of whom would have been engaged in the 'precarious' fringe of the labour market, characterised by low status, poorly paid and insecure jobs. As a consequence, it would be plausible to expect the rate of turnover of the Unemployment Benefit population to have been greater than that of Income Support and Housing Benefit but that the overall rise in the caseload would have been less marked.

How the benefit systems responded

We will now investigate how far these theoretical predictions accord with experience in the early 1990s. Because monthly information on Housing Benefit is not recorded in the BHPS, the discussion concentrates on Unemployment Benefit and Income Support.

Unemployment Benefit and Income Support

The number of respondents claiming Unemployment Benefit in their own right rose from 1.9% in September 1990 to 3.0% in August 1992, but the increase was far from uniform (Figure 12.2). The month-to-month variation was even more erratic (Figure 12.3). Nevertheless, some interesting patterns are evident. New claims were high in the first year, as the recession took hold, but subsequently fell. The number of people moving off benefit increased over time such that the overall caseload, as revealed by the BHPS, was stable for six months in 1992. This outflow was not necessarily a direct reflection of increased labour demand which was still very slack at the time. Some was due to people exhausting entitlement to benefit, the 'self-limiting' component which served to impose a maximum ceiling on the total caseload. This phenomenon was perhaps most marked in 1990/91 when the number of claimants who moved into work after receiving benefit fell from 63% to 30% (Walker, 1994).

The size of the Income Support caseload, as recorded in the BHPS, also increased with the deepening recession, from 7.4% of respondents with families in September 1990 to 10.8% in August 1992 (Figure 12.2). The proportional increase was noticeably less than the rise in unemployment since a significant part of the claimant population was likely to be immune to the downturn in the economy. The growth in the Income Support caseload was comparatively smooth and continued throughout the entire period, although with a gradual reduction in the monthly increase. A small part of the increased caseload was attributable to the secular rise in lone parents claiming benefit.

Figure 12.2: Proportion of BHPS sample receiving Unemployment Benefit and Income Support (September 1990 to August 1992)

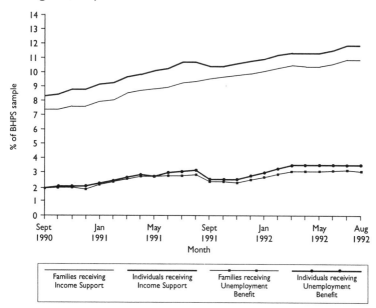

Source: Ashworth et al (1997a)

Figure 12.3: Monthly flows on and off Unemployment Benefit and Income Support (September 1990 to August 1992)

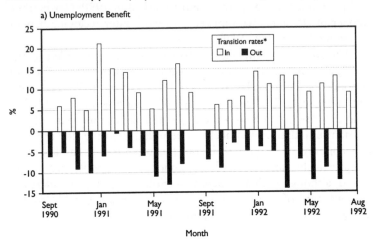

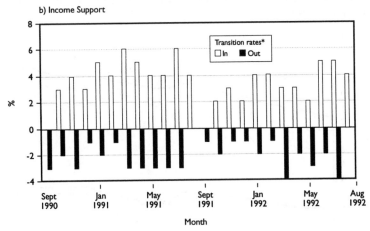

*Flows a as a percentage of recipients in the month indicated. The UB outflow transition rate for August 1991 was 67% (that for IS was 31%) and the inflow rate for September 1991 was 60% (that for IS was 32%). All are subject to seam effects and ommitted from the graph.

Source: Ashworth et al (1997a)

Nevertheless, there was quite marked month-to-month variations in the number of new claims and in the flow of people coming off Income Support (Figure 12.3). The average number of new claims taken each month fell from 4.4% of the caseload in the first year to 3.4% in the second in much the same way as did new claims for Unemployment Benefit. However, while the number of new claims fell, so did the number of people leaving benefit although not to the same extent (from 2.5% to 2.1%). The net result was the slowdown in the rate of increase already noted.

The composition of the flows on and off Unemployment Benefit changed during the first two years of the study period. The proportion of new claims from men with dependants was initially high but fell steadily, while the outflow from benefit remained constant. This led to a slow down in the rate of growth, leading ultimately to a fall in the number of families receiving benefit. On the other hand, claims for Income Support from lone men, many of them young, accelerated, while the outflow fell resulting in a marked increase in the number of claimants.

Comparisons with Housing Benefit

Table 12.3 shows the level (or incidence) of receipt for all three types of benefit at given times and the prevalence, that is the proportion of the population receiving benefit at any time over the three-year observation period. (Figures for Income Support and Unemployment Benefit relate to the benefit unit, family members included in the test of income, whereas those for Housing Benefit necessarily relate to households.)

Whereas the numbers in receipt of Income Support increased by almost two thirds between Autumn 1990 and Autumn 1993, the growth in Unemployment Benefit recipients was limited to only one third. The proportional impact on the Housing Benefit caseload was even smaller (an increase of less than one fifth), reflecting the fact that significant numbers of recipients had already left the labour market altogether.

However, these figures disguise the true importance of Unemployment Benefits as a protection against unemployment. This is indicated by the prevalence, as opposed to the incidence, of claims: the total number of respondents who claimed Unemployment Benefit at some point during the three-year observation period was 2.6 times the number who received it in

Table 12.3: Incidence and prevalence (%)

	Income Support	Housing Benefit	Unemployment Benefit
Prevalence:			
One year (1990/1)	8.3	7.0	2.8
Two year (1990/2)	12.1	8.9	5.5
Three year (1990/3)	14.9	10.1	7.3
Incidence:			
September 1990	5.5	7.0*	1.2
August 1991	7.2		1.8
August 1993	9.0	8.3[†]	1.6

Notes: * Prevalence in the year September 1990 to August 1991. [†] Prevalence in the year September 1992 to August 1993.

Source: Ashworth et al (1997a)

the first year and 4.8 times the number claiming it in an average month. By way of contrast, although the Income Support caseload grew faster than that of Unemployment Benefit, the total number of respondents who received benefit between September 1990 and August 1993 was only 80% greater than the number who claimed benefit in the first year, or 2.1 times the number receiving it in a typical month. The reason for this discrepancy can be found in the comparatively short time for which people received Unemployment Benefit, primarily because most claimants rapidly returned to work but also because some quickly exhausted their entitlement to benefit. Nevertheless, many more people who became unemployed during the recession of the early 1990s were caught by the Income Support safety net than were protected by social insurance. This is unlikely to be the case anywhere else in Europe (with the possible exception of Eire which took the British system as its model).

For Housing Benefit, the three-year measure of prevalence is only 44% greater than the annual one. This is evidence that even in times of deep recession, the Housing Benefit caseload is comparatively stable. Certainly, people made redundant did claim Housing Benefit but they constituted only a small proportion of the total caseload, the majority of which was largely insulated from the recession. Those who did make new claims for Housing Benefit may well themselves have remained on this benefit for longer than those claiming either of the other two benefits (see below).

Staying on benefit

The focus of our enquiry now shifts from the system to the individual and to the time spent in receipt of different benefits. Table 12.4 shows that, as would be expected, spells on Unemployment Benefit are the shortest while those on Housing Benefit last the longest. However, the data presented, which shows the proportions who receive benefit in more than one year, must be treated with caution. For example, not everybody who received benefit in consecutive years was continuously in receipt. Similarly frustrating, a person who received benefit for two weeks straddling the months of August and September is indistinguishable from someone who remained on benefit from one September to the August 24 months later.

Nevertheless, it is apparent that less than one in five (16%) claimants received Unemployment Benefit in more than one year, compared with four out of five (77%) people receiving Housing Benefit, and three out of every five (56%) people on Income Support. One third (30%) of Income Support recipients and more than a half (52%) of households receiving Housing Benefit claimed benefit in each of the three years covered by the survey. The length of individual spells on Housing Benefit meant that comparatively few people had claimed more than once: perhaps 5% of claimants compared with 15% receiving Income Support and 13% on Unemployment Benefit.

Table 12.4 provides further evidence that significant numbers of people claiming Housing Benefit and Income Support received them for substantial periods: 85% of households who were in receipt of Housing Benefit in one year also received it in the next, as did 70% of Income Support claimants. The corresponding figures for Unemployment Benefit were naturally much smaller because of the time-limited nature of the benefit. The proportion also fell significantly over time, probably due to improving labour demand in 1993.

There are at least three ways of conceptualising and measuring the length of time that people spend on benefit. The first is to ascertain how long a person's current spell has lasted to date. The second is to determine how much time the person spends on benefit during a given period, while the third asks how long the person is likely to have spent on benefit by the time they leave.

Table 12.4: Staying on benefit (%)

	Income Support	Housing Benefit	Unemployment Benefit
One wave only[*]	44	23	84
Two waves:[†]			
- continuous	23	20	12
- non-continuous	3	5	2
All three waves	30	52	2
Total = 100%	1,168	801	369
Remaining in receipt between waves 1 and 2[*]	70	85	34
Remaining in receipt between waves 2 and 3[†]	67	85	23

Notes: [*] N=648, 549 and 251 respectively for Income Support, Housing Benefit and Unemployment Benefit. [†] N=750, 609 and 272 respectively for Income Support, Housing Benefit and Unemployment Benefit.

Source: Ashworth et al (1997a)

Summary information covering each of these different perspectives is presented in Table 12.5.

Unfortunately no information is available for Housing Benefit. Also, respondents who were already on benefit when the BHPS began were not asked systematically when they had begun claiming. Consequently, it is impossible to say for how long some people have been receiving benefits. Instead, the first row of Table 12.5 refers to the caseload in August 1993 and reports the time that people had spent continuously on benefit since the survey coverage began in September 1990. The figure for Unemployment Benefit is accurate: the average time that had been spent on benefit was eight months for those who needed to top up their benefit with Income Support and six months for those who did not. The time given for Income Support receipt (at 22 months) is a serious understatement because 35% of the August 1993 caseload had begun their spell on benefit before the survey observation period began.

Table 12.5: Time spent on benefit (months)

	Income Support	Time spent on Benefit Unemployment Benefit	
		With Income Support	Without Income Support
Length of spell for claimants in receipt in August 1993			
Mean*	21.5 (12.7)	8.3 (7.7)	5.9 (5.1)
Median	24	7	4
Total time between September 1990 and August 1993			
Mean*	17.8 (12.3)	6.6 (4.5)	5.9 (4.3)
Median	13	6	5
First spell			
Median†	17	7	4
First spell up until August 1993			
Mean*	10.0 (12.3)	5.7 (4.5)	4.9 (4.3)
Median	8	5	4

Notes: * The standard deviation is the figure in brackets. † Weighted mean of the median lengths for claimants of different ages.

Source: Ashworth et al (1997a)

The second section in Table 12.5 shows the average amount of total time which benefit recipients spent on benefit between September 1990 and August 1993 and so takes account of respondents who experienced more than one spell on benefit. The median length for Income Support recipients was 13 months; that is, a typical recipient spent about 36% of the survey period on benefit. However, because a substantial minority were on benefit virtually continuously, the average value exceeds the median by some five months. As expected, the total length of time that recipients spent on Unemployment Benefit was much less than for Income Support; it also differed relatively little according to whether or not claimants also received Income Support.

For how long respondents receiving a benefit at the time of their last interview will eventually claim is unknown. However, it is possible to derive estimates from information on the proportion of spells of benefit which end each month. These estimates are presented in the third section of Table 12.5. It would seem that more than 50% of claimants who moved on to Income Support at the time of the 1990s recession were likely to claim benefit for more than 17 months, more than twice the time that they had already spent on benefit (shown in the bottom section of Table 12.5). It is predicted that one third would still be on benefit after 36 months but, in contradistinction, 15% left Income Support within three months, 27% within six months and 41% within a year. Most spells on Unemployment Benefit lasted for no more than seven months, but some of these claimants would have exhausted entitlement and transferred to Income Support.

The picture that emerges, then, is one of cohorts of people initially claiming one, or a combination, of the three benefits. Some, although only a minority, stayed on for a very short time and others followed within a matter of months. These were typically people eligible for and receiving Unemployment Benefit. Those who needed to claim Income Support, and, even more so, Housing Benefit, were likely to remain on benefit for longer, sometimes much longer. Other factors discriminated between those who rapidly left benefit and those who did not (Ashworth et al, 1997a). Prior occupation was important; professionals, managers and non-manual workers spent less time than average on benefit and unskilled manual workers considerably more. Educational qualifications, and especially a degree, conferred an additional advantage, although spells on Unemployment Benefit differed little according to schooling. Age was a handicap to leaving benefit and living in local authority accommodation seemed associated with long spells on Housing Benefit although not on Income Support. While the people moving on to benefit shared many characteristics with the population at large, those who remained were characterised by limited skills and experience.

Routes on and off benefit

Nothing has yet been said about the routes that claimants took on and off benefit although the presumption has been one of people losing jobs and subsequently finding new ones. This is now rectified by examining the flows on and off Income Support. For technical reasons it is necessary to focus on individual adults (aged 16 and above) rather than claimant units, who received benefit in their own right as claimants or as members of a larger unit. This means that the fate of a proportion of the sample depends on the labour market status of their partners.

Claiming Income Support

At least 59% of adults newly receiving Income Support between 1990 and 1993 needed to claim benefit as the result of leaving a job (Table 12.6). A total of 30% were made redundant or sacked, 17% ended a fixed period appointment and 4% left for health reasons (Rose et al, 1994). Domestic reasons, to do with the arrival of a child and childcare considerations, were mentioned by another 6% of respondents, retirement by 7% and a mixture of unspecified reasons by the remaining 35%. This means that somewhere between 28% and 48% of new Income Support claims were the direct result of the recession.

Table 12.6 also shows that 13% of people were unemployed for some time before claiming Income Support. Some were receiving Unemployment Benefit. However, no more than a quarter of all unemployed respondents received any Unemployment Benefit and just one fifth of these, 5% of the total, claimed Unemployment Benefit and then Income Support when their entitlement was exhausted. This latter route is the one that is typically followed by the unemployed in the rest of Europe but is rarely trodden in Britain. More people deferred their claim for benefit, sometimes effectively for ever: 10% of the unemployed made no claim at all for benefit during the three years studied. A small proportion of the respondents not initially claiming benefit will have been disallowed on the grounds of 'voluntary unemployment'. Others will not have been eligible for Income Support because they had received large redundancy payments, had other sources of income, or had a partner working 16 hours or more a week. Yet others will have delayed or not claimed through ignorance or due to the fear of stigma.

There was little evidence that Income Support provided a preferred route to early retirement during the recession of the early 1990s. A total of 11% of new Income Support claimants said that they were retired prior to applying for benefit but most were beyond retirement age. The risk of needing to claim Income

Table 12.6: Labour market status of respondents (%)

	Non-recipients of Income Support	Existing Income Support recipients	New recipients of Income Support October 1990-August 1993 Labour market status at:	
	September 1990	September 1990	September 1990	Year moved on to Income Support
a Employed	57	10	47	43
b Self-employed	7	1	6	3
a + b	64	11	53	46
c Unemployed	2	22	8	13
d Retired	19	24	10	11
e Looking after home	9	33	16	18
f Student	4	3	9	6
g Long-term sick	2	8	3	4
h Other	1	1	3	2
f + g + h	7	12	15	12
Total = 100%	6,027	490	804	803

Note: Deviation from 100% is due to rounding.

Source: Ashworth et al (1997b)

Support was only marginally above average for those in the decade before retirement, and only 4% of those who moved on to Income Support before retirement age considered that they had already retired. Presumably early retirement schemes need to be sufficiently generous to provide above-assistance incomes. However, while the BHPS does not provide any suggestion of people choosing to take early retirement funded by Income Support, the evidence was that only a minority of men claiming benefit after the age of 55 would ever return to work (Ashworth et al, 1997b).

The 18% of new claimants who described themselves as looking after a home prior to moving on to benefit were almost all women.[4] At least 39% of these came on to benefit as the result of their partner losing his job and, perhaps, therefore as an indirect result of the recession. It is interesting that the proportion was not higher. However, almost another two fifths experienced a change in their own economic position ahead of claiming benefit and so did their partner. It proved impractical to determine whether this change occurred before or after that of their partner and, therefore, whether it was a reaction to the partner's loss of job. In Britain, economic activity among the wives of unemployed men is very low, partly because their income is offset pound for pound against Income Support with only a small (£5) disregard (Bingley and Walker, 1997).

Table 12.6 also shows that 6% of people claiming Income Support moved straight from education on to benefit. Another 4% said that they had previously been long-term sick.

Leaving Income Support

Table 12.7 focuses on the 53% of people who received Income Support between September 1990 and August 1993 and who had moved off benefit by the latter date. The focus is again on all adults receiving Income Support irrespective of whether or not they claimed benefit in their own right or as a dependant.

By showing their economic status at the time of interview in the year after they left benefit it reveals that while most new claimants applied for Income Support after losing their job (see Table 12.6), only a minority left benefit to take up paid employment. Taken at face value, this comparison suggests that during the early 1990s Income Support served to funnel people more or less permanently out of the labour market. Only later waves of

Table 12.7: Labour market status before and after receiving Income Support (%)

Original labour market status	New labour market status	Retaining status	Changing status to:							Total = 100% ‡
			Self-employment	Employment	Unemployment	Retirement	Looking after home	Student	Long-term sick	
Self-employed •	3	97	–	0	3	0	0	0	0	20
Employed	40	63	8	–	17	2	7	2	2	262
Unemployed	14	27	5	45	–	4	8	6	3	94
Retired	11	82	0	1	0	–	13	0	4	70
Looking after home	19	66	2	18	6	6	–	0	2	126
Student •	6	52	0	40	2	4	0	–	3	40
Long-term sick •	5	81	0	4	15	0	0	0	–	29
Other •	2	20	0	40	7	0	20	13	0	15
Total	100†	60	4	14	8	2	6	2	2	656

Notes: • Note the small base number. † Column percentages based on 656 respondents. ‡ Values in the eight columns to the right sum to 100% except for rounding.

Source: Ashworth et al (1997b)

survey evidence will determine whether this was a temporary phenomenon, perhaps associated with the severity of the recession.

However, the apparent haemorrhaging of the labour market is little more than an illusion. The number employed or in self-employment dropped by only 7% or three percentage points (from 46% to 43%) following a spell of unemployment. People who were apparently unemployed after leaving benefit might well have left benefit for a job only to lose it again before being re-interviewed. The fact that they saw themselves as unemployed suggests that they were likely to be seeking work. Why, precisely, they were not claiming benefit is a mystery although a small proportion may have been eligible for and claiming Unemployment Benefit; those who were not would also have been excluded from the official unemployment count.

A second growth category, those looking after a home, was mainly comprised of women. Some of these will formerly have been lone parents who may have first claimed Income Support long before the survey period began. Because flows off benefit reflect the legacy of successive cohorts of new claimants, you would not expect them to be a perfect reflection of recent claims. Comparatively few people (7%) who had moved on to Income Support after losing their job left benefit to look after a home. Even fewer, 3%, became long-term sick, although small changes such as these can have significant effects if sustained over a long period.

Typically, claimants returned to the economic status that they occupied before claiming benefit (Figure 12.4). Claimants who had worked immediately prior to claiming benefit were almost six times more likely to leave benefit for a job than someone who had been looking after a home. In addition to recent work experience, key factors in determining who would leave benefit and obtain employment were good qualifications and increasing age, at least until age 33, after which negative returns set in. Being single was also significant perhaps because claimants with dependants felt unable to take low-paid jobs.

Figure 12.4: Routes on and off Income Support

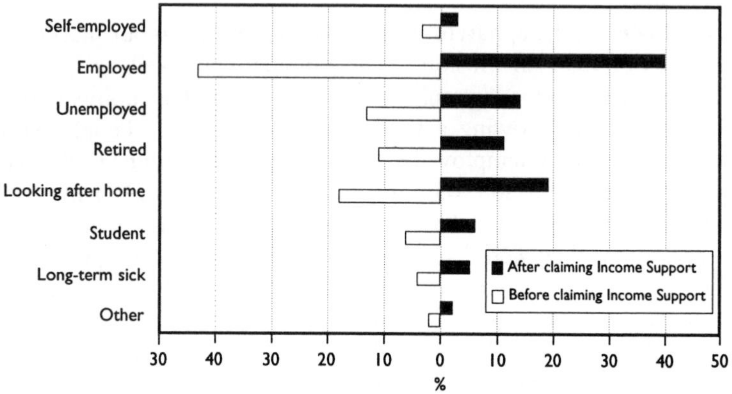

Source: Ashworth et al (1997b)

Conclusions

It is evident that the three benefits had different dynamics and performed differently in the context of the 1990s recession in Britain. Unemployment Benefit, as expected, proved to be very sensitive to the prevailing state of the economy with high flows of people on and off benefit. However, this social insurance scheme served to protect no more than one quarter of those affected by the economic downturn. Housing Benefit contrasted markedly with Unemployment Benefit. The caseload grew slowly and the predominant characteristic was one of stability. Most recipients of Housing Benefit were long-term claimants and the majority were not personally affected by the recession. It was Income Support, social assistance, that made the greatest contribution to protecting people against the worst excesses of rising unemployment. A total of 80% of people who lost their jobs claimed Income Support and more than half continued in receipt for 16 months or more.

Britain's benefits for the unemployed were radically restructured in October 1996. Unemployment Benefit and Income Support for the unemployed were merged into Jobseeker's Allowance (Bottomley et al, 1997) The insurance component was retained but the period of entitlement cut to a maximum of 26 weeks and automatic dependence additions scrapped. The means-tested element remained for those with insufficient means, some of whom also did not qualify for insurance-based provision. In addition to the pre-existing requirement to be actively seeking and available for work, receipt of Jobseeker's Allowance was made subject to the claimant signing an agreement which specifies job-search activity. As before, fulfilment of this labour market conditionality is regularly tested. A key objective of the changes, which formalised the central role played by social assistance in supporting the unemployed, was to reduce the length of time spent on benefit and to get people back to work sooner. Work disincentives inherent in social insurance that require benefits to be paid irrespective of financial need were reduced, while those arising from indefinite benefits were counteracted by tighter monitoring of job search. Changes to Housing Benefit were also introduced between 1995 and 1997, some to smooth the transition into work, others to limit benefits, notably to single persons. The result of these changes is likely to attenuate the different dynamics identified in this chapter.

During the recession of the early 1990s the people who moved on to benefit were almost a cross-section of the British population. However, while the young, the better educated and those unencumbered by children rapidly returned to employment, the most disadvantaged remained behind, spending long periods on benefit. It remains to be seen whether the active labour market initiatives that accompanied the introduction of Jobseeker's Allowance will do anything to rectify this imbalance by focusing remedial resources on those least likely rapidly to return to employment of their own accord.

Notes

[1] Unemployment Benefit is stopped completely after 12 months without any lower rate being paid subsequently as happens, for instance, in Germany.

[2] Income Support provided, and still provides, support for lone parents and people with disabilities who are not expected to be actively seeking work.

[3] A buoyant labour market might attract some lone parents into work and cause some people above pension age not to retire.

[4] 'Looking after a home' describes people not engaged in the labour market such as 'housewives', male non-working partners and carers.

thirteen

Escaping from social assistance in Great Britain

Robert Walker and Andrew Shaw

Increasing expenditure, financial constraints and the apparent reluctance of taxpayers to continue funding welfare have caused policy makers around the world to question spending on social assistance and the time that some families remain on benefit. If the average duration of claims could be trimmed, overall spending would be reduced by a corresponding amount. There is also concern that people who stay on benefit for long periods find it increasingly difficult ever to move off and, instead, become trapped in a state of dependency on welfare. Some have even argued that long-term dependency instils a different perspective on life which contributes to the development of anti-social behaviour and the creation of a perpetual underclass which is detached from the wider society and financed by crime, undeclared earnings and social assistance payments (Murray, 1984; Bane and Ellwood, 1994).

Even without subscribing to the more apocalyptic fears about the social consequences of welfare dependency, it remains important to ask whether too many people spend too long on social assistance. Benefit payments are invariably low compared with average incomes and most claimants would probably aspire to the higher standard of living that moving off social assistance could bring. They would also escape the stigma that is still attached to receiving assistance and which, in some cases, is deliberately re-enforced by society.

A large number of reasons have been suggested why some people seem to remain on benefits for long periods (Deacon, 1996). They can conveniently be divided into two categories: structural or individualistic. Structural arguments are often of two types. The first point to deficiencies in the economy both national and global, that mean that insufficient new jobs have been created to replace those lost in earlier recessions. The second type focuses on the existence of social security and social assistance schemes which, it is argued, create work disincentives by lessening the gap between incomes in and out of paid employment (Shaw and Walker, 1996). Individualistic arguments focus on the human capital resources, attitudes and behaviour of claimants. Some people may simply lose out in the competition for jobs because they lack appropriate skills and experience. Others may choose to remain on benefit for long periods, preferring the life on assistance to actually working. Some may become demoralised in their search for work, and operate according to the principle of least effort. This finding has recently been replicated in a larger national sample of the unemployed (Bottomley et al, 1997). Demoralisation could equally be seen as a personal response to a structural constraint (see the discussion in Chapter Fifteen of Bane and Ellwood, 1994). The obstacles to working, some created by the disjointed interaction between the labour market and the benefits system, may make dependency on social assistance the logical option for some claimants (Field, 1995).

This chapter aims to explore these hypotheses in the context of social assistance receipt in Britain. Political debate about the existence of benefit dependency has been growing steadily since government ministers first used the term in 1987 (Walker, 1994), but, until recently, without any evidence as to its extent. As noted in Chapter Twelve, before 1996, the principal social assistance system in Britain was Income Support which was paid to more than 5 million families with nobody in paid work (for more than 16 hours per week). About 69% of claimants were below retirement age and it is this group which will be the focus of our discussion.

We will begin by briefly noting the characteristics of the claimant population before documenting the time that claimants spend in receipt of benefit. We will then examine the evidence for each of the following factors which constrain people's ability to escape from social assistance:

Structural

- Labour demand

- Disincentives

- Uncertainty

- Benefit administration

Individualistic

- Capabilities

- Attitudes

- Behaviour

Much of the evidence is drawn from a nationally representative survey of Income Support claimants conducted in autumn 1994 (Shaw et al, 1996a). The survey is unique in that it does not relate to a single moment in time but is representative of all people under pension age who received benefit sometime between September 1992 and June 1994. It counteracts the bias towards long-term claimants which would have been present had a cross-sectional sample been drawn and allows estimates to be made of the time that claimants spent on benefit.

Characteristics of claimants

The largest group of claimants, comprising 45% of those on benefit at the time of interview, lived alone without dependants (Table 13.1). Whereas two thirds of British adults had live-in partners, this was clearly not the case among Income Support recipients. Most, but by no means all, of those living alone were young. Lone parents, who did not have to look for work to receive benefit, accounted for just over one quarter of current claimants; 93% of them were women.

Disproportionate numbers of claimants suffered poor health: half of current recipients did so compared with just over one third of the UK population aged between 16 and 64 (OPCS, 1994). Older people, those aged 45 or above, were twice as likely as younger ones to report a long-standing illness or disability. Five

Table 13.1: Demographic characteristics of claimants

| | In % for each characteristic | | |
	Current claimants	Past claimants	All respondents
Gender			
Men	55	62	57
Women	45	38	43
Age			
Under 25	19	31	22
25 to 34	36	30	33
35 to 44	21	23	21
45 to 54	15	12	14
55 and over	11	4	9
Ethnic origin			
White	84	88	86
Black: of African or Caribbean origin	7	3	6
Asian: of Indian origin	1	3	2
of Pakistani origin	2	3	3
of Bangladeshi origin	1	1	1
of Chinese origin	0	0	0
Another group	3	2	3
Long-term health problems or disability			
Yes	50	33	45
No	50	67	55
Family type			
Couple with children	17	26	20
Lone parent	27	8	22
Couple no children	10	11	10
Single no children	24	56	48
Bases	714-722	297-298	1,011-1,020

Note: Subsections may not sum to 100% due to rounding. Source: Shaw et al (1996a)

times as many claimants complained of a health problem as claimed benefit on health grounds.

As a whole, claimants were not disadvantaged educationally. Claimants receiving benefit on grounds of unemployment were overall better educated than the population at large, although claimants with disabilities typically also lacked good qualifications (Table 13.2). However, 60% of older claimants had no qualifications at all compared with 33% of younger ones and just 22% of those aged 25 or below.

Table 13.2: Educational qualifications

	Type of claimant (%)				General population
	Unem-ployed	Lone parent	Disabled	Other	
Higher educational qualifications	18	9	9	15	20
Other qualifications	45	51	27	35	46
No qualifications	37	40	64	50	34
Base (= 100%)	556	230	87	118	14,785*

Note: * General Household Survey (1993)
Source: Adapted from Shaw et al (1996a)

The astute reader will have noted from Table 13.1 that past claimants were on average younger and less likely to suffer a health problem than current recipients of benefit. Likewise, they were also somewhat better educated. These differences hint at the factors that conspire to keep people on benefit for long periods.

Time spent on benefit

As noted elsewhere in this volume (Chapters One, Eleven and Twelve), there are many different ways of measuring the time that people spend on benefit. The most intuitively understandable is to focus on the time between the beginning and end of a spell although, since this is unknown for claimants still in receipt of benefit, modelling is required to provide suitable estimates. The results of such an exercise are presented in Figure 13.1 which shows the cumulative proportion of claimants who had left Income Support within a given time after first claiming benefit.

It is apparent that lone parents, who were not required to look for work until their children ceased to be dependent, left benefit much more slowly than unemployed claimants. About 70% of lone parents were still on benefit after three years. Indeed, for some categories of lone parent the stay on benefit was almost indefinite (Shaw et al, 1996a). An example would be someone aged under 40, with a child under five, who lived in an area of Greater London with an unemployment rate of over 10% and who had no driving licence. Nevertheless, one fifth of the claims made by lone parents lasted for less than six months.

The experience of lone parents can be contrasted with that of claimants on social assistance because of unemployment. One quarter of this group left Income Support within three months and over half within the space of a year. Then, again, over a third of the unemployed were still claiming benefit after two years.

A not infrequent feature in the lives of low-income families is the need repeatedly to rely on social assistance (Walker, 1995b).

Figure 13.1: Cumulative proportion leaving Income Support (by duration and claimant type)

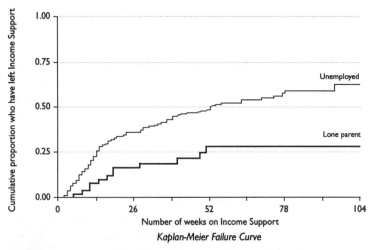

Kaplan-Meier Failure Curve

Note: 308 unemployed claimants, 141 with completed spells; 54 lone parent claimants, 12 with completed spells. Source: Shaw et al (1996a)

One in eight claimants had more than one spell on Income Support during the two-year observation period. The time that lapsed between spells was often not great (Figure 13.2). One in five claimants could expect to be back on benefit within six months but the longer a person stayed off benefit the lower the chance of them returning. A surprisingly high proportion of lone parents, more than half, eventually needed to reclaim Income Support.

So, there was enormous variety in the time that claimants remained on Income Support and it would be wrong to assert that long-term dependency was ubiquitous. Most spells on benefit caused by unemployment lasted for less than a year and one quarter for less than three months. However, a minority of the unemployed, and rather more lone parents, did remain on benefit for longer periods while others repeatedly claimed benefits. We will now consider the reasons for some people leaving benefit quickly whereas others do not.

Figure 13.2: Cumulative proportion restarting Income Support (by number of weeks since previous spell ended and by claimant type)

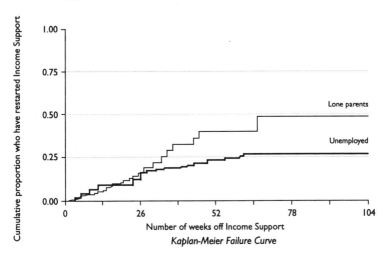

Note: 278 unemployed claimants with an Income Support spell ending, 45 of whom have another Income Support spell; 48 lone parent claimants with an Income Support spell ending, 14 of whom have another Income Support spell.
Source: Shaw et al (1996a)

Structural deterrents to leaving benefit

Labour demand

This is not the place for a treatise on the changing nature of labour demand in advanced western societies. Suffice to say that unemployment in Britain was at historically high levels in the early 1990s, although it had begun to fall before the survey was conducted in 1994 (see Figure 12.1, Chapter Twelve). For over a decade there had also been a tendency for well-paid jobs in manufacturing to be replaced by lower waged jobs in the service sector. Certainly, 79% of claimants believed that their chances of finding permanent full-time work 'were not very good', while 92% thought that it was very difficult to get a 'job with decent pay'. A total of 63% of claimants, predominantly older claimants including lone parents and couples with children, felt 'trapped'; well over half of these pointed to the absence of jobs (26%) and the prevalence of low pay (34%) as reasons.

Disincentives

Claimants' repeated reference to low pay begs a further question: low in relation to what, benefits or other wages? Social assistance acts to provide a financial safety net but may also provide a floor to the wages that people will accept. In Britain, the equation is complicated by the fact that receipt of Income Support acts as a passport to other benefits and that different benefits come into play when a person moves from unemployment to part-time or full-time work.

In investigating this conundrum economists have frequently postulated that people seeking work set for themselves a 'reservation wage': this is the lowest that they would be prepared to accept and is generally assumed to be fixed with reference to benefit rates (Dawes, 1993). A total of 95% of people claiming Income Support because of unemployment were prepared to name a reservation wage; the median was £130 which compares with the average manual earnings of £263 in 1994. The reservation wage cited was typically £30 less than the wage respondents expected to get. However, when asked how they determined their reservation wage only 20% said that they took account of benefit levels – many of these were claimants with families; an equal number mentioned the need to have sufficient to cover the payment of direct taxes. One fifth additionally set their reservation wage in relation to work-related factors: the rate for the job, their experience and skills. The overwhelming majority (87%), though, said that they fixed their minimum in light of the amount that they needed to live on: almost half (47%) took account of nothing else.

What people say, of course, is not necessarily what they do. Invariably reservation wages were more than the benefit that they received. However, multivariate analysis using similar data has shown two primary sets of independent factors: those which were needs driven and those which reflected prior experience with former professionals and managers setting the highest thresholds (Bottomley et al, 1997). More importantly, the same research has shown little difference in the reservation wages stated by claimants who found work and those who did not, and that 44% of claimants leaving benefit took jobs paying less than their reservation wage.

Uncertainty

More recent studies have cast doubt on the use of the reservation wage pointing out that people living on low incomes need to be averse to risk and that taking a job is a risky enterprise (Dobson et al, 1994; Jenkins and Millar, 1989). Not only might the job not last, but it will incur its own costs and take home pay is difficult to calculate. There is also the time which the person has to bridge between the last payment of benefit and receipt of the first wage. Security of income might, Jenkins and Millar argue, be as important as the level.

Respondents who had moved off Income Support (mostly into work) were asked about any worries that they had prior to leaving benefit and the problems that they had actually encountered when doing so. More than one fifth had concerns about whether the job would last and, as demonstrated by Figure 13.2, in a significant minority of cases it did not. Table 13.3 shows that just less than one quarter foresaw the difficulty of managing financially until the first pay day and this turned out to be a real problem for almost as many. However, although uncertainty and the transition from benefit were issues for some claimants, just as many mentioned incentives to stay on benefit, particularly the loss of benefits to cover both housing costs and local taxes (Council Tax Benefit). Even more were concerned about whether they would have sufficient to live on, while travel to work costs emerged as a factor that people had overlooked.

Would these worries be sufficient to prevent a person leaving benefit? Out of the former claimants, 46% said that they might well have moved off Income Support earlier had some such problem been resolved. However, the problems were very diverse; only one, concern about job security, was mentioned by more than one tenth of people (Table 13.3).

Benefit administration

Complexity

With different benefit schemes in Britain applying to different sides of the unemployment-employment divide, there is great scope for uncertainty and error in estimating incomes in work. A total of 43% of claimants did not know that they were allowed to undertake some part-time work while still retaining benefit; a further 28% knew this but not how much they could earn without losing benefit (the earnings disregard). While lone parents were more likely than other people to be aware of the earnings disregard that applied to them, only 13% of claimants receiving benefit because of unemployment could correctly cite their disregard.

As noted previously, Income Support acts as a passport to other benefits, for example free medical prescriptions and eye tests, but only some of these are also available to people in work. Of nine passport benefits presented to unemployed claimants in the survey, five were payable to working people in certain situations but less than 2% of respondents could correctly distinguish one from the other. This would matter less if people were aware of the benefits that applied to them or those which were likely to make a major contribution to their incomes. However, claimants were only marginally more likely to be aware of more pertinent benefits and their knowledge of the details remained low. With Family Credit, a separate in-work benefit for families with children introduced in 1988, awareness was high (92%) but only one third knew any of the precise details. Likewise, knowledge of the details of Housing Benefit, payable on an income-tested basis to people irrespective of employment status, was also limited. Perhaps the degree of complexity of the

Table 13.3: Worries and problems about leaving Income Support[*]

Worries/problems encountered	Before leaving Income Support	Factors slowing move off benefit (%)	After leaving Income Support
	Worries (%)		Problems (%)
Incentives to stay			
Less than on Income Support	12		
Loss of passport benefits	19	7	
Loss of help with rent and mortgages	24	8	22
Loss of Council Tax Benefit	17	7	
Work expenses			
Travel	–		14
Tools and clothes	–	7	5
Cost of living			
Whether enough to live on	30		22
How to meet debts/bills	17	5	13
Transitional			
Sorting out benefits		7	
When would get Housing Benefit	11		7
When would get Family Credit		2	6
Bridging until first wage	24	7	20
Job insecurity			
Length of job	22	12	5
Type of work		9	7
Need to reclaim Income Support	18	5	
Uncertainty			
How much money would get in work	18	8	12
Which benefits would get in work	10		
Caring			
Cost of childcare	3	3	3
Other caring commitments	1		
None	36	62	42

Note: [*] Multiple responses were allowed hence columns do not sum 100%. Source: Adapted from Shaw et al (1996a)

British system is unique.   What is evident is that claimants in Britain were generally unable to make informed choices about the financial utility of remaining on benefit versus taking a job.   Any disincentives created by the British benefit system must be a matter of hunch and impression rather than calculation and precision.

Hassle

Claiming benefit can be stressful.   In Britain, before the introduction of Jobseeker's Allowance, unemployed claimants of Income Support had to deal with two agencies (the Benefits Agency and the Employment Service).   Even now, in-work benefits are administered by different organisations than out-of-work ones. Claiming social assistance may also be stigmatising: a public confession of failure.   A total of 73% of claimants agreed that claiming Income Support could be 'a big hassle' and there was evidence that this could be sufficient to deter people from taking potentially insecure jobs to avoid the risk of having to reapply for benefit (Shaw et al, 1996b).

Benefit administration does not always run smoothly: delays and errors are always more common than would be ideal.   A total of 12% of claimants reported having to wait at least a month for their first payment of Income Support and this caused them problems with the payment of rent and meeting general expenses and even with paying for food.   Then again, 7% of all the people who moved off Income Support experienced problems resulting from delays in the payment of Housing Benefit and 6% waiting for Family Credit (Table 13.3).   Given that only a small minority of former Income Support claimants applied for these benefits, processing delays were clearly prevalent and must have contributed to the uncertainty and insecurity associated with returning to work.

Individual considerations

Attention now turns to the issue of people's attitudes and behaviour and also their capabilities.

Capabilities

People currently claiming Income Support tended to be older, less well educated and more prone to ill health than either former claimants or the population at large. This serves as a priori evidence that these factors inhibit people moving off benefit. Event history modelling (Table 13.4) demonstrates that this is the case. For the unemployed, this shows that the claimants with the following characteristics are likely to have shorter spells on benefit while those without them will experience longer spells:

Education and experience

- A degree
- A-level (pre-university academic qualifications)
- HNC (vocational qualifications)
- Work experience in the two years before claiming benefit

Sociodemographic attributes

- Women
- Aged less than 40
- Has English as first language
- White
- Has good health

Socioeconomic attributes

- Holds a driving licence
- Has a telephone
- The date on which benefit was applied for

The salience of human capital resources is clear in that qualifications would seem to be an important determinant of people's chances of escaping from benefit: each qualification and attribute has a separate independent effect. Prior work experience was also significant while ill health served to slow claimants movement off benefit.

Table 13.4: Explaining weekly movements off Income Support by unemployed claimants (weekly exit rates estimated from a discrete time logistic hazard model)

	'Initial' model		'Final' model	
	Coefficient estimate	Standard estimate	Coefficient estimate	Standard estimate
Educational qualifications (highest):				
Degree	0.599	(0.296)	0.382	(0.228)
A-level	1.305	(0.307)	1.239	(0.262)
GCSE grades A-C	0.123	(0.227)		
GCSE grades D or lower	0.012	(0.284)		
Vocational, technical qualifications:				
Degree equivalent	0.014	(0.641)		
Teaching, nursing, etc	0.603	(0.228)	0.505	(0.199)
City & Guilds pt III, NVQ, OND etc	0.120	(0.250)		
City & Guilds pt I, Scotvec etc	0.206	(0.261)		
Apprenticeship, clerical, commercial	0.292	(0.308)		
YTS, other non-foreign	-0.259	(0.575)		
Has problems with reading	-0.028	(0.552)		
Has problems with writing	0.149	(0.451)		
Has problems with numbers	-0.477	(0.557)		
Has problems speaking English	-0.911	(0.386)	-0.565	(0.331)
No long-term health problems	0.631	(0.186)	0.649	(0.171)
Work experience in 2 years before IS	0.759	(0.218)	0.693	(0.208)
Has driving licence	0.565	(0.199)	0.566	(0.182)
Male	0.483	(0.179)	0.466	(0.163)
No partner present[*]	-0.055	(0.245)		

	'Initial' model		'Final' model	
	Coefficient estimate	Standard estimate	Coefficient estimate	Standard estimate
Age at start of IS spell: 20-29 years				
30-39	0.252	(0.238)		
40+	-0.216	(0.296)		
	-0.408	(0.310)	-0.526	(0.184)
Number of dependant children: [*] 1				
2	0.517	(0.339)		
3+	-0.726	(0.377)	0.798	(0.320)
	0.021	(0.392)		
Ethnic origin is non-European	-0.767	(0.293)	-0.783	(0.271)
Did not seek work in 1st week IS spell	0.148	(0.262)		
Telephone present in household	0.804	(0.259)	0.872	(0.247)
Tenure: Owner	-0.424	(0.658)		
Local authority renter	-0.433	(0.665)		
Housing Association or private rented	-1.324	(0.665)	-1.011	(0.247)
Non-householder	-0.128	(0.636)		
Unemployment rate in local TTWA [*] +	-0.042	(0.045)		
Region: North West	-0.353	(0.564)		
Yorkshire & Humberside	0.260	(0.550)		
East Midlands	0.356	(0.543)		
West Midlands	-0.421	(0.530)		
East Anglia	-0.072	(0.533)		
South East (excl Greater London)	0.061	(0.506)		
Greater London	-0.099	(0.509)		
South West	-0.455	(0.513)		
Wales	0.494	(0.601)		
Scotland	0.161	(0.586)		

	'Initial' model		'Final' model	
	Coefficient estimate	Standard estimate	Coefficient estimate	Standard estimate
Date IS spell began (integer index) +	0.009	(0.002)	0.010	(0.001)
Log (spell duration to date)* +	0.011	(0.086)		
Constant	-5.007	(0.735)	-5.761	(0.290)
-2.logL	2,012		2,038	

Note: Number of respondents = 501. Number of spell weeks at risk of an IS exit = 27, 391. Number of IS exits = 193. All variables are dummy variables except those marked +.

* Time-varying covariate.

TTWA = travel to work area.

For details of the modelling procedures see Shaw et al (1996a).

Women claimants (lone parents excluded) were more likely to move off benefit quickly than men. Why this is so is unclear, but it is consistent with the structural shift to a service economy supplying increasing numbers of comparatively low-paid jobs traditionally held by women. The possibility of racial discrimination in employment is evidenced by the separate inclusion of both language and ethnicity.

Possession of a telephone and a driving licence also seemed to speed up the move off benefit. This might index past affluence and perhaps aspects of work experience and social skills neglected by the other variables. Alternatively, it might reflect the possibility that job search is easier and more effective if you have access to either a car or telephone. A driving licence also seemed to enhance the prospects of a lone mother moving off benefit, although a telephone did not. Older mothers living in areas of low unemployment were the most likely to leave benefit especially when all their children were at school. Even so, spells on benefit were much longer for lone parents than for unemployed claimants. It follows that traditional human capital does appear to differentiate between claimants who manage to escape from benefit and those who are left behind. However, other social factors are also important.

Attitudes and behaviour

There was little evidence that many claimants found life on social assistance to be comfortable. Words such as 'stigma', 'outcast' and 'second-class citizen' were used frequently in claimants' descriptions of how it felt to be on Income Support. Out of the current claimants, 56% had debts and those with children were even more susceptible to getting into financial difficulties (76% had outstanding debts). When asked how well they were managing or had managed when on benefit, 56% said 'not very well' or 'not at all'.

While two thirds of claimants agreed that 'people had to do work on the side' in order 'to make ends meet', very few people appeared to do so. Only 14% undertook paid work of any kind while on benefit and half of the work was irregular. Median earnings for those with regular jobs were just £21 per week, a figure that includes lone parents who were entitled to earn £15 each week before losing any benefit. Less than half of 1% of claimants admitted to working regularly for more than £15 per week during their time on benefit.

It might be that illicit work is ubiquitous and that respondents were simply too coy to admit it. While possible, such coyness fits uneasily with the hypothesis that an underclass exists in which the norm is to defraud the system. It is perhaps more likely that, although people would have liked to have supplemented their benefit, casual work was not readily available without the appropriate skills and access to suitable contacts. There was also the fear of getting caught. These were the two reasons that claimants gave for not working illegally.

Life on benefit was not seen as being easy and claimants generally believed that their chances of finding a job were not very high. In such circumstances did a sense of resignation take over, causing people to retreat from actively looking for work? Is there any evidence of benefit dependency?

Figure 13.1 shows that the chances of moving off Income Support declined with the length of time that a claimant had already spent on benefit. Although, the length of claim did not appear in the list of factors influencing the chances of leaving benefit. The evidence shows that, once account has been taken of the other factors that might cause a person to become trapped on benefit, time itself – benefit dependency – is not important. It would appear that long-term recipients are destined to be on benefit for a long time rather than that people become dependent upon benefit.

Other evidence from the survey supports this contention. Out of the people required to look for work, 91% were in fact doing so. The time that they spent varied quite markedly, but one quarter devoted more than 10 hours each week to the search for work. (Lone parents spent less time on this than unemployed claimants.) However, there was no systematic evidence that people reduced the time that they spent looking for work the longer they had been on benefit; 30% of people had done so, but an equal number had actually increased job-search activity during their spell on benefit.

It would be wrong to presume that claimants either were, or became, inflexible in the type of job they were prepared to take, although most respondents had limits beyond which they would not go. For example, half said that they would not move home to find work, sometimes because of the financial and practical costs of moving but also because of the loss of support networks that helped in the challenge of making ends meet. However, large numbers would accept a temporary job, part-time work or irregular hours and, although very few were seeking to set-up on their own, almost one third said that they would be prepared to try self-employment.

The fact that a large number were not prepared to move because of the loss of informal contacts had a further practical relevance: their social networks served as an important conduit for information about job vacancies. Even more telling is the balance between informal and formal means of finding work. A national

Figure 13.3: Sources of jobs

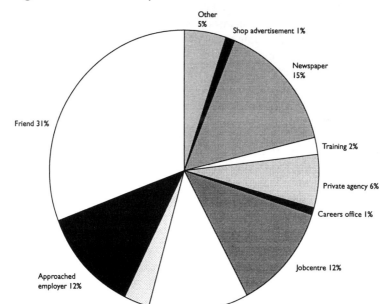

Source: Adapted from Bottomley et al (1997)

survey of the unemployed conducted in autumn 1995 revealed that 31% of those finding work did so through a friend and that at least 58% of placements involved informal contacts with friends, acquaintances or employers (Figure 13.3).

Two final observations return the focus of the discussion to structural factors. Both concern the event history model reported above (Table 13.4). Included in this model was the date of a claimant's application for benefit which suggests that the point in the economic cycle when a person becomes unemployed may be a good predictor of the length of time that they will remain on benefit. Those thrown out of work as a recession deepens and job opportunities are scarce may become part of a 'sinking cohort'. Most well-qualified people rapidly return to work but those in a sinking cohort miss out on this opportunity through little fault of their own. When the demand for labour eventually begins to increase, they may find themselves in a queue behind later cohorts of the unemployed people many of whom will, by definition, have had more recent work experience.

The model excluded any reference to local unemployment rates. The possible reason resonates with the sinking cohort hypothesis. Perhaps employers recruit primarily from among existing employees, from people eligible for insurance-based benefits (see Chapter Twelve) and from people who are ostensibly economically inactive. Social assistance recipients, especially those destined to become long-term claimants, may occupy a substratum within which people's chances of finding employment are much less immediately affected by the prevailing state of the local labour market.

Conclusions

The policy imperative which led to commissioning the survey that has informed this discussion was that British policy makers wished to:

> ... examine the circumstances which permit people of working age to move off Income Support (and to identify those which inhibit movement) so as to provide a basis for developing

> strategies for reducing the length of spells on benefit. (CRSP, 1993)

The aim was to learn in order to act. The predetermined aim was to reduce the time that claimants spent on benefit.

While some commentators and many Income Support claimants would wish an analysis and policy response to focus on means of enhancing aggregate economic demand, the attention of policy makers in Britain, like those in other countries was, and remains, elsewhere. What is evident from the survey is that another traditional focus, on the disincentive effects of benefits, might be misplaced or at least exaggerated. Jobseekers may set a reservation wage but tend to be flexible when presented with the prospect or offer of a job. In the British context with its complex panoply of benefits, few claimants are in a position accurately to compare their potential income in work with that received on benefit.

The research has confirmed the relevance, if not overwhelming importance, of other concerns. The return to work is a time pregnant with uncertainty and risk. Reducing the risks involved, through the design of new benefits, different modes of implementation and better means of communication with people seeking work, is a key challenge for policy.

The discussion has also challenged simplistic views about the generation of welfare dependency. No evidence emerged of large numbers of people adopting social assistance as a permanent way of life. In Britain, at least, the living standards that benefits sustain provide little physical, social or psychological comfort. Instead, the evidence offers two important insights. It appears that the vast majority of claimants are engaged in a determined, continuing struggle to find work so are likely to be receptive to constructive policies that help them in this task, although they would prefer the direct creation of more jobs (Shaw et al, 1996b). Secondly, it seems that people do not become long-term recipients through a process of learning or corruption but because of characteristics that they have, or the circumstances that they face, when first they claim benefit. However, once they have become long-term claimants, the chances of them leaving benefits are very much reduced, even though they typically continue in the endeavour to do so. The policy response must be one of prevention, targeting resources on those likely to become long-term recipients.

As testament to the contribution that dynamic research can make to the policy process, the survey which has formed the empirical heart of this paper was published with an accompanying official press release which listed six policy developments informed by the survey (DSS, 1996). These mostly had to do with smoothing the transition from benefits into employment. Jobseeker's Allowance, which replaced Income Support for the unemployed, aims to enhance the advisory service offered to the unemployed while emphasising the conditionality of benefit receipt upon job search. Only time and experience will tell whether the appropriate balance has been struck between support and deterrence.

fourteen

Contrasting welfare dynamics: Germany and Sweden

Bjørn Gustafsson and Wolfgang Voges

Industrialised countries differ in their welfare systems. Public intervention in the lives of individuals has a wide variety of goals and objectives (Büchel and Hauser, 1998). Not surprisingly, expenditure on social welfare varies as a percentage of GDP between OECD countries, as does the extent of inequality in living standards.

An issue of particular importance to many, if not all, social scientists, is the fate and circumstances of the less privileged in these different societies. An increasingly rich comparative literature exists which examines the extent and experience of poverty. This chapter deals with a related area, the length of time households remain on social assistance, and seeks to understand how this is affected by the welfare institutions and policies of two European countries. Using data from the cities of Bremen in Germany and Göteborg in Sweden, the research focuses on people of working age who have just started to receive social assistance.

Although there are many similarities between Germany and Sweden, their social institutions and policies are not the same. Differences in labour market policies, and in the role of women in the workforce, appear to be the main reason why German households receive social assistance for longer periods than their Swedish counterparts.

Political and social differences

Social assistance is the last safety net provided by the welfare state.[1] Most people earn their livelihood through paid work. When they are old, ill or unemployed, they receive social security if they are eligible. Those without paid work or social security can claim social assistance. The recipients of social assistance are 'generated' by a weak labour demand and gaps in the social security system.

The time that recipients spend on the social assistance safety net depends on how quickly alternatives become available. The welfare state influences in many ways both the number of people on social assistance and the length of time for which they receive it. However, it is the interplay of social policy with the prevailing social and economic climate that exerts a crucial influence on the duration of social assistance.

During much of the 1970s, and throughout the 1980s, the German and Swedish economies differed greatly. Official unemployment, for instance, was considerably higher in Germany than in Sweden, while the reverse was true for inflation. However, there was a marked convergence during the 1990s as Swedish unemployment increased rapidly (Figure 14.1).

The larger Swedish public sector has proved a more durable difference between the two countries. More ambitious Swedish social policies have meant that the sector has more financial resources (Figure 14.2). However, revenue dropped sharply at the beginning of the 1990s when rising unemployment put pressure on public spending, leading to cuts in a number of state benefits, and creating financial difficulties for the Swedish social services.

Unemployment

The availability of paid work is an obvious factor affecting the length of time households spend on social assistance. Swedish research has shown that unemployment influences both the numbers on social assistance (Gustafsson, 1984), and the duration (Gustafsson and Tasiran, 1993). In Germany, too, the risk of becoming a social assistance recipient is greatly increased by un-employment (Voges and Rohwer, 1992). However, in Germany,

Figure 14.1: Standardised unemployment rate in Germany and Sweden (1972-94)

Data source: OECD (1992a, p 234 for the years until 1988); OECD (1995a, p 216 for the later years)

Figure 14.2: Taxes and social security contributions as percentage of GDP (1970-93)

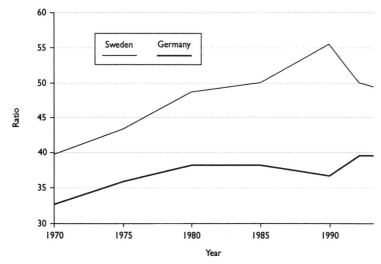

Source: Bundesministerium für Wirtschaft BMWI (1994, p154); OECD (1994)

rising unemployment does not necessarily result in an increase in the median time spent on social assistance, as is the case in Sweden (Buhr, 1995; see also Chapter Eleven)

The lack of a link in Germany between levels of unemployment and lengthening dependency on social assistance has been reported by other writers. Leisering and Voges (1996), for example, used the monthly unemployment rate in an analysis that took account of multiple spells on social assistance. They found that, compared to other factors, the labour market exerted only a slight influence on the time spent on benefit, and that this effect was only apparent during the first spell on social assistance.

This difference in the effect of the labour market in each country is related to the prevalence of different groups among the unemployed.   Each group has a unique chance of finding employment that is influenced by the macro-economic climate, and by government intervention.   At least three groups of unemployed people can be identified in each country: registered short-term unemployed who receive unemployment insurance benefit; longer-term registered unemployed people who receive income-tested insurance benefit; and the long-term unemployed who are eligible for social assistance.   The long-term unemployed on social assistance stand the least chance of finding a job since, in any economic upswing, those on unemployment insurance benefit have the best opportunity of finding employment and 'cream off' the available jobs.   Social assistance recipients can only escape from their situation if an improvement in the labour market is sustained for several months (Voges and Klein, 1994).

The Bremen labour market has been depressed since the beginning of the 1980s, with a stable unemployment rate that only decreased slightly during unification. With a large pool of long-term unemployed, any economic improvement would have had to continue for a sustained period before it benefited social assistance recipients. However, in Göteborg unemployment only increased in 1990/91, thus allowing insufficient time for the accumulation of substantial numbers of long-term unemployed. As a consequence, upswings in the Swedish economy might be expected to have a direct impact on the number and the duration of social assistance claims.

Table 14.1: Public spending on labour market programmes in Sweden and Germany (% of GDP)

Public spending	Sweden			Germany		
	1985/86	1990/91	1994/95	1985	1990	1994
1 Public employment services and administration	0.25	0.21	0.27	0.21	0.22	0.24
2 Labour market training	0.50	0.53	0.80	0.20	0.34	0.42
3 Youth measures	0.21	0.07	0.26	0.05	0.05	0.06
4 Subsidised employment	0.43	0.13	0.81	0.17	0.17	0.34
5a) Measures for the disabled	0.72	0.74	0.82	0.19	0.23	0.26
including:						
5b) Work for the disabled	0.63	0.65	0.73	0.09	0.10	0.12
6 Unemployment compensation	0.75	1.80	2.46	1.41	1.09	2.03
7 Early retirement for labour market reasons	0.12	0.08	0.02	0.01	0.02	0.49
Total	2.98	3.56	5.44	2.24	2.12	3.84
Active measures (1-5)	2.11	1.68	2.96	0.81	1.01	1.32
Passive measures (6-7)	0.87	1.88	2.48	1.41	1.11	2.52

Data source: For 1985/86, OECD (1992b, pp 92, 95, 101); for 1990/91 and 1994/95, OECD (1995a, pp 224, 228)

Sweden also favours greater intervention in the labour market, encouraging shorter spells on social assistance. Table 14.1 shows expenditure on the different labour market programmes as a percentage of GDP. Higher spending is evident in Sweden on training, youth schemes, subsidised employment and work opportunities for the disabled – Sweden spent twice as much as Germany on such measures. It is a fundamental principle of Swedish policy to offer training, both to the unemployed and to people whose livelihoods are considered to be at risk. Swedes are also often paid during training, and as a consequence no longer receive state benefits.

Women and the family

There are also vital differences between Germany and Sweden in official attitudes to working women. Germany comes close to the 'breadwinner' model of social policy, while Sweden follows the 'individual' model (Sainsbury, 1994). Despite changes in the structure of the family that are making the 'breadwinner' model increasingly obsolete in Germany, clear differences remain between the two countries in terms of ideology, family policy, taxation and women's role in the labour force.

The 'breadwinner' model depends on a strict division of labour between husband and wife (Table 14.2). The husband is head of the household and it is his duty to provide for all the members of his family through full-time employment. The wife's role is to make a good home and to care for her husband and children. This family is regarded as a unit for social policy purposes, giving different state benefit entitlements to husband and wife. Indeed, most wives are regarded as 'dependants' for benefit purposes, and they usually lack any entitlements as individuals.

In the 'individual' model, each partner is deemed to be responsible for their own maintenance. Employment policies are directed at both sexes, and the individual, not the family, is entitled to state benefits. Parents share the responsibility for their children, a task that is made easier by the public provision of comprehensive childcare centres.

Table 14.2: Breadwinner model and the individual model of social policy

Dimensions	Breadwinner model	Individual model
Family ideology	Strict division of labour Husband = earner	Shared roles Husband = earner/carer
	Wife = carer	Wife = earner/carer
Entitlement	Differentiated among spouses	Uniform
Basis of entitlement	Breadwinner	Other
Recipient of benefit	Head of household	Individual
Unit for benefit	Household or family	Individual
Unit of contributions	Household	Individual
Taxation	Joint taxation Deduction for dependants	Separate taxation Equal tax deductions
Employment and wage policies	Priority to men	Aimed at both sexes
Sphere of care	Primarily private	Strong state involvement
Caring work	Unpaid	Paid component

Source: Sainsbury (1994)

In Germany, it is most unusual to find full-time childcare provided by the state, although three quarters of German children go to local authority nurseries that cater for the under sixes (Zimmermann, 1993). In Sweden, high quality local authority centres provide care for around half all children aged under six. These centres are also open for schoolchildren after school hours, a provision that is very rare in Germany.

The role of a mother, implicitly and sometimes explicitly prescribed by policy, is also quite different in the two countries. In Germany, the mother is expected to concentrate on caring activities within the home, while in Sweden the emphasis is on paid work.

The tax systems of each country also mirror the prevailing ideology of the family, meaning that the economic incentives for women married to full-time working men are not the same. Sweden introduced separate income tax in 1971. In this 'individualistic' model, the smaller income of one spouse, usually the woman, is taxed at a low rate, while in the German 'breadwinner' model it is added to the income of the full-time worker, subjecting it to a higher rate of tax.   In addition, the German tax system incorporates a substantial 'marriage gain' so that couples are jointly taxed at a lower rate than single people.

Figure 14.3 shows the economic inactivity rate by age for men and women in Germany and Sweden. Inactivity rates are high among all but the youngest German women. But it is motherhood rather than gender per se that explains the differences between Germany and Sweden: inactivity rates are very similar before the birth of the first child. Swedish mothers have greater access to paid work, and their income affects both their own entitlement to benefit and the size of any subsequent social security payment. A Swedish mother is thus much better protected than her German counterpart in the event of any adverse economic circumstances.

Figure 14.3: Inactivity rates by age and gender in Germany and Sweden (1993)

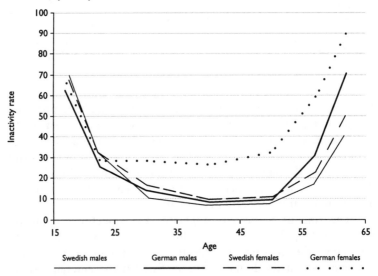

Note: The inactivity rate is defined as the number of people out of employment as a percentage of the population of working age. For Sweden, the age groups are 16-19, 20-24, 25-34, 35-44, 45-54, 55-59, 60-64. For Germany, the first age group differs: it is from 15-19.
Data source: OECD (1995c, pp 481, 499)

Residential segregation

It has been suggested that high concentrations of social assistance recipients in particular neighbourhoods may facilitate the growth of a dependency culture. Different normative standards may evolve which, for example, mean that claiming social assistance may carry less stigma and attachment to paid work may be lessened. This may, in turn, engender different forms of behaviour with more people spending long periods on benefit, and fewer residents working or seeking employment. Such areas may also differ in the opportunities available to residents that further inhibit the chances of people moving speedily off social assistance. For example, welfare facilities – such as public sector childcare – may be less, job openings may be fewer and extra costs may need to be incurred travelling outside the neighbourhood to work.

Systems of social assistance

Differences in the structure and administration of social assistance are important, since they also affect the number and type of recipients. Both the German and Swedish systems are generic rather than categorical, providing support to all residents rather than just to specific groups, such as lone parents. In both countries, benefits are payable subject to a means test and mainly financed by local government. However, in Germany payments vary only slightly between the regions (*Länder*), whereas Swedish social assistance is determined locally, with considerable variation between almost 300 municipal authorities.

When social assistance assessments are carried out, alternative sources of finance are taken into account. In Germany, financial resources are supposed to be transferred between the members of a family according to the subsidiary principle, so that both parents and adult children have a mutual obligation to support each other. If an adult child receives social assistance, for instance, the financing authority can demand a refund from his or her parents. By the same token, an adult child can be forced to refund social assistance paid to elderly parents.

In Sweden, the state assumes the main burden of responsibility for providing social assistance. This is the case in most, but not all, situations. For example, a lone mother is expected to work, rather than depend upon social assistance; this is consistent with social norms relating to family responsibilities and paid work and reflects policies that facilitate the successful integration of paid work with parenting duties.

It might be thought that the level of social assistance payments could influence duration, with higher benefits giving recipients less incentive to work. If this were the case, the time spent on social assistance should be shorter in Germany, since, with the exception of lone parents, payments are more generous in Sweden, (Duncan et al, 1991; Hansen, 1995). However, other comparisons between Germany and the US, for example, show that benefit levels are less important than other factors in influencing the time that claimants stay on social assistance (Duncan and Voges, 1993).

Data sources

While Bremen in Germany and Göteborg in Sweden have many similarities, including size and degree of industrialisation, there are inevitably differences. Perhaps most important, in the present context, are differences in the locations of social assistance recipients. In Bremen they reside throughout the city with some clustering in the central areas. Bremen has implemented a range of policies to prevent the development of residential segregation. In Göteborg, social assistance claimants tend disproportionately to live on the north-eastern outskirts of the town where many recent foreigners are also housed. Other differences between Bremen and Göteborg will, in varying degrees, reflect the unique political and cultural infrastructure of the two countries. Nevertheless, it is probable that comparison of another pair of cities would not yield precisely the same results.

The information is derived from administrative records relating to new social assistance recipients in each city.[2] Claimants older than 64 were excluded as were asylum seekers, but long-standing foreign residents were represented. Claims lasting for less than a month were omitted because of different methods of administering and recording one-off payments.

The Bremen sample relates to people making claims during 1989, the cases being followed up until September 1994. In Göteborg, new claimants were sampled over 12 months from April 1991 after ensuring that they had not received social assistance during the previous two years. Spells on benefit that last longer than a year were treated as censored. The different time periods ensure that claimants were applying for benefit at a similar point in the economic cycle and in each case, a 10% sample was drawn.

For several reasons, this chapter is focused on the experiences of claimants in the 12 months following their first claim. There is some evidence, for example, that, over time, recipients make less effort to re-enter the labour market and resign themselves to being on benefits (Ziegler et al, 1989). In Bremen, claimants are encouraged to take part in work programmes after 12 months in receipt of benefit. Those that participate automatically leave social assistance, while others stop claiming as a result of the pressure to take part in the programme.

Table 14.3: Sociodemographic characteristics of social assistance (%)

Characteristics		Distribution	
		Bremen	Göteborg
All recipients		100.0	100.0
Gender	Men	56.0	50.4
	Women	44.0	49.6
Age	<19	15.9	12.3
	20-29	39.7	51.9
	30-39	23.0	20.5
	40-49	13.7	9.1
	50-64	7.7	6.1
Type of family	Single	74.3	81.5
	Couple	25.7	18.5
Number of	None	62.7	77.0
children	1	22.0	12.1
	2+	15.3	11.0
Nationality	Foreigner	20.1	36.2
	Native	79.9	63.8
Proportion of	Low	8.1	17.9
households in city	Middle	48.7	38.6
district claiming	High	43.0	43.5
social assistance			
Number of cases		1,142	2,315

Note: Any deviations from 100% are due to rounding.

Time spent on social assistance

Social assistance recipients in Bremen and Göteborg were surprisingly similar in terms of their sociodemographic characteristics (Table 14.3). However, there were important differences. More than half (52%) of the Swedish sample had a head of household aged 20 to 29, compared with only 40% in Germany. Reflecting this, a higher proportion of the Swedish sample was comprised of single adult households. Foreigners were disproportionately represented among social assistance caseloads in both countries: they accounted for one in three of the new recipients in Sweden, and one in five in Germany.

It was also apparent that new social assistance claimants in Bremen tend to spend longer on benefit than in Göteborg (Table 14.4). The median length of their first spell on social assistance was six months compared with only around 3.5 months in Sweden. More than one third of German recipients were still on social assistance at the end of the 12-month study (Figure 14.4), which was true for only around one fifth of the Swedish sample.

Many Swedish households escaped social assistance relatively quickly, but significant numbers rapidly reclaimed benefit. Almost 30% of Swedish claimants made a second claim for benefit within the year and 4% a third claim. Even so, the total time spent on benefit during the 12 months of the study was, at 5.7 months, still less than in Germany (6.9 months).

Differences between the two countries become more marked when account is taken of gender, age and nationality. For example, duration varied markedly with the sex of the head of household in Germany, but not in Sweden. German households headed by women faced spells twice as long as those headed by men (Table 14.4), and the majority were still on their first spell of social assistance at the end of the research period. In Sweden, the reverse was true, with male-headed households experiencing slightly longer spells than those headed by females. The net result was that the time spent on benefit by men and their dependants was roughly the same in Bremen and Göteborg. However, no doubt as a consequence of the different models of social policy discussed above, households in Germany headed by a woman stayed on social assistance for twice as long as those in Sweden.

Table 14.4: Duration of social assistance receipt in Germany and Sweden during the initial 12-month period

Characteristics		First episode[a]			Total time[b]		
		GB	SG	p[c]	GB	SG	p[c]
All recipients		6.0	3.5	0.000	6.9	5.7	0.000
Gender	Men	4.4	3.8	0.003	5.0	6.1	0.006
	Women	9.3	3.3	0.000	10.5	5.1	0.000
Age	<19	9.8	3.9	0.000	10.9	6.6	0.003
	20-29	5.5	3.2	0.000	6.2	4.9	0.002
	30-39	4.9	4.3	0.001	5.6	6.2	0.749
	40-49	5.2	3.3	0.000	5.5	5.7	0.821
	50-64	7.9	5.2	0.114	8.6	7.0	0.636
Type of family	Single	6.5	3.5	0.000	7.3	5.5	0.000
	Couple	5.2	4.0	0.024	5.7	6.1	0.605
Number of children	None	5.0	3.4	0.000	5.6	5.5	0.400
	1	9.0	4.0	0.000	10.6	6.1	0.001
	2+	9.5	4.3	0.000	10.8	5.8	0.001
Nationality	Foreigner	6.1	6.0	0.324	7.6	7.7	0.781
	Native	6.0	2.8	0.000	6.7	4.7	0.000
Proportion of households in city district with social assistance	Low	6.7	3.1	0.000	6.7	4.7	0.006
	Middle	5.9	2.8	0.000	6.5	5.0	0.000
	High	6.2	4.7	0.000	7.4	6.5	0.232
Number of cases							

Note: GB = Germany/Bremen; SG = Sweden/Göteborg

In both countries, the duration of claims was associated with the age of the claimant. Spells on benefit were longest for those at the beginning and end of their working lives, but again there were differences between the two countries. Table 14.4 shows that in Germany, the proportion of people beginning their first spell of social assistance before the age of 20 was more than double that in Sweden. This discrepancy can be attributed to more ambitious Swedish labour market policies that promote work programmes for young people, enabling them to earn an income.

In Bremen, the length of a first spell on social assistance was the same for foreigners and resident Germans. However, in Göteborg, foreigners remained on benefit for more than twice as long as Swedish residents. They spent the same amount of time on social assistance as foreigners in Bremen (Table 14.4). The lengthy spells suffered by foreigners in Sweden were not unexpected, since Göteborg, in common with other large Swedish cities, has had an influx of foreigners during the 1990s, and their chances of finding a job have deteriorated (Aguilar and Gustafsson, 1994). Even so, the relative deprivation suffered by foreigners to Sweden, who

Figure 14.4: Duration of first episode and total time on social assistance for Germany/Bremen and Sweden/Göteborg during the initial 12-month period

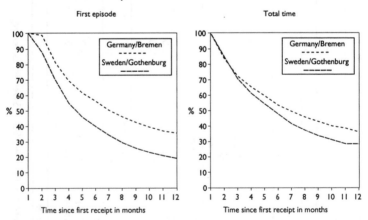

Note: A social assistance episode is assumed to have ended only if we observe two consecutive months of non-receipt.

comprised more than one third of social assistance recipients in Göteborg, was marked compared with that in Germany.

The impact of different housing policies with respect to residential segregation was also apparent. In Bremen, it was difficult to determine any differences in the time spent on assistance according to residential areas. In Sweden, on the other hand, households in neighbourhoods with a high concentration of social assistance recipients did on average suffer noticeably longer spells. The total time that these households spent on social assistance during the study period was as great as the average Bremen claim.

Modelling

Consideration has so far been limited to the association between the pattern of benefit claims and specific individual characteristics. While these have revealed important pointers to differences between Germany and Sweden, it is essential also to explore the combined effect of individual associations. To achieve this, a series of statistical models was developed which linked the likelihood of leaving benefit to a large number of 'predictor' variables, including the sociodemographic characteristics of claimants, job availability and binary 'dummy' variables, indicating calendar months, to assess the impact of any seasonal factors (see Table 14.5). Models were created for Göteborg, Bremen and, uniquely, for all claimants in both cities.

Many of the earlier results were repeated in the statistical models. For example, the combined model confirmed that the chances of leaving benefit were lower in Bremen than in Göteborg and that spells on benefit were consequently, on average, longer. The model also threw further light on the impact of different policy models of the experiences of women claimants. In Germany, households headed by women were less likely than men to move off benefit quickly. If they had children, their stay on benefit was extended and increased with the addition of every child. In Sweden, women were marginally more likely than men to move off benefit and it was parenthood, rather than motherhood, that

Table 14.5: Termination of first social assistance episode in Germany/ Bremen and Sweden/Göteborg by characteristics of the recipients and of the local labour market

Variables	Termination of first social assistance episode					
	All recipients		German recipients		Swedish recipients	
Women	0.036	(0.046)	-0.329**	(0.094)	0.160**	(0.054)
Women x children	-0.439**	(0.076)	-0.732**	(0.141)	-0.181*	(0.096)
Foreigner	-0.904**	(0.090)	-0.571**	(0.151)	0.051**	(0.114)
Foreigner x single	0.191*	(0.103)	0.356*	(0.194)	0.243**	(0.128)
Age 16-20	-0.350**	(0.063)	-0.656**	(0.112)	-0.211**	(0.076)
40-49	0.189**	(0.064)	0.120**	(0.105)	0.054*	(0.081)
50-64	-0.476**	(0.086)	-0.613**	(0.147)	-0.456**	(0.107)
Number of children	-0.001	(0.033)	-0.139**	(0.057)	-0.062	(0.043)
Singles	-0.678**	(0.082)	-0.673**	(0.127)	-0.611**	(0.108)
Couples x children	-0.436**	(0.102)	-0.307*	(0.167)	-0.543**	(0.130)
High recipiency district	-0.210**	(0.041)	-0.081	(0.074)	-0.268**	(0.050)
Vacancies/ unemployment	0.003**	(0.001)	-0.013	(0.046)	0.018	(0.010)
Germany/Bremen	0.900**	(0.060)				
Period effects						
January	-0.762**	(0.097)	-0.224	(0.179)	-1.051**	(0.121)
February	-0.837**	(0.052)	-0.374**	(0.186)	-0.071**	(0.117)
March	-0.519**	(0.087)	-0.129	(0.172)	0.720**	(0.102)
April	-0.663**	(0.091)	-0.132	(0.168)	-0.931**	(0.107)
May	-0.673**	(0.089)			-1.023	(0.109)
June			-0.339*	(0.179)		
July	-0.519**		-0.362**	(0.181)	-0.616**	(0.095)
August	-0.170**	(0.085)	-0.250	(0.175)	-0.201**	(0.089)
September	-0.444**	(0.080)	-0.213	(0.173)	-0.569**	(0.100)
October	-0.595**	(0.087)	-0.067	(0.166)	-0.871**	(0.111)
November	-0.430**	(0.086)	0.210	(0.242)	-0.546**	(0.099)
December	-0.502**	(0.088)	-0.094	(0.242)	-0.695**	(0.105)
First quarter	-2.330**		-3.571**		-2.252**	
Second quarter	-2.003**		-3.103**		-1.952**	
Third quarter	-2.457**		-3.522**		-2.408**	
Fourth quarter	-2.792**		-3.732**		-2.824**	
Number of splits	20,395		8,291		12,074	
Number of events	2,554		755		1,799	
Log likelihood	-12,791.94		-4,131.21		-8,537.04	
χ^2 (df)	1,236.91(29)		273.43(26)		836.13(26)	

Notes: Reference group: men aged 21-39, no children, natives, couples, low and middle recipiency districts, labour market situation in June (for Bremen: May). The estimated model is a Piecewise-Constant-Model. Significance $p < 0.05$: **, $p<0.10$: *. Standard error in parenthesis. Likelihood-ratio test statistic (χ^2) against the constant-rate model without covariates. Characteristics of the recipients measured for the monthly sub-episodes.

seemed to curtail the chances of leaving social assistance, while the number of children appeared to be immaterial.

The models showed that, in both countries, living alone and being young independently and additionally increased the time spent on benefit, although young people below the age of 21 were especially disadvantaged in Germany. Older people, towards the end of their working lives, were also likely to spend longer time on benefit than most other claimants and this was true of both Sweden and Germany.

The disadvantaged position of foreigners was evident in all the models but was particularly marked in Sweden where the effect is twice that in Germany. It is also apparent that foreigners without dependants moved off benefit rather more quickly than other groups. Whether this reflects greater flexibility, such as being more prepared to be residentially mobile, or a propensity to return to their country of origin at times of economic adversity, cannot be deduced from the evidence at hand.

It is not only personal factors that conspired to keep people on assistance. There was evidence of some structural effects. For example, in Göteborg, although not in Bremen, living in a neighbourhood with a high concentration of social assistance claimants appeared to reduce the likelihood of leaving benefit quickly. The processes involved are not transparent. It might be that residential segregation generated a common culture of benefit dependency or, alternatively, that residents faced a common set of barriers preventing them from finding work or otherwise moving off benefit. For example, it is possible that jobs locally were scarce. There was evidence in Göteborg that the buoyancy of the local labour market did affect the speed at which claimants moved off benefit. However, in Bremen this was not true, presumably because of the effect of creaming, with employers recruiting from among the ranks of the unemployed who received social insurance and who had probably been out of the labour market for shorter periods. In Bremen, lower levels of residential segregation may mean that concentrations of social assistance recipients did not reach some critical threshold above which any deleterious effects of concentration might become apparent.

Seasonal effects were very important in Sweden, if not for immediately interpretable reasons, but were much less so in Germany. Labour demand is typically most buoyant in spring and summer and certainly movements off benefit were at a particularly low ebb in January and February in Göteborg and in February in Bremen. However, surprisingly, flows off benefit were also low in Sweden in May and July which suggests that any links which exist between movements off social assistance and the seasonal state of the labour market is either complex or indirect.

Conclusions

The aim of analysing data from Bremen and Göteborg on the length of time that households received social assistance was to provide insight into the workings of the welfare state in Germany and Sweden, as well as to shed light on the lives of the less fortunate. It emerges that in both cities the majority of claimants leave social assistance within a year, although households in Bremen tend to spend longer on benefit, particularly during their first spell. Although this finding is consistent with earlier research (Duncan and Voges, 1993), it is still notable since benefits are set at a higher level in Sweden than in Germany so might have been thought likely to provide a greater incentive to remain on benefit. A considerable proportion of households in both cities claimed social assistance on more than one occasion during the study period.

In Göteborg, the time spent on benefit appeared to be affected by the prevailing state of the local labour market but this was not the case in Bremen, presumably because claimants were typically more distant from the labour market or lacked the equivalent help to re-enter employment. Labour market policies are far more active in Sweden than in Germany and this probably explains why younger people, in particular, typically spent a far shorter time on social assistance than do their German counterparts.

The differences in the pattern of social assistance receipt between the two cities can also be traced to the role allotted to women in the workforce. Most Swedish mothers are in paid employment which is not the case in Germany, a discrepancy that probably relates to policy differences, including a comprehensive system of childcare and family-centred employment policies, and in tax regimes. These differences in philosophy and welfare provision probably partly explain the finding that households headed by a woman in Bremen typically experienced long periods on social assistance, especially if they have children, which was not the case in Sweden.

Overall, Swedish social policy appears to have been more successful in reducing periods on social assistance. Nevertheless, the system has some unattractive features. For instance, foreigners spent much longer periods on welfare in Sweden than did those in Germany. The damaging effect of residential segregation on the duration of social assistance was also much more marked in Göteborg than in Bremen.

Notes

[1] The German information was taken from the Bremen Longitudinal Study of Social Assistance (LSA), which is part of the Special Research Programme 186, (*Sonderforschungsbereich*) funded by the German Research Council (*Deutsche Forschungs-gemein schaft*) (Voges and Zwick, 1991; Buhr and Voges, 1998). This data is also used in Chapter Eleven. It was supplemented with geographical information on the receipt of social assistance derived from the Federal Bureau of the Census annual micro-census based on a 1% sample. The Swedish data was drawn entirely from the administrative register of all social assistance claimants in Göteborg, the *Socialbidrag* (Gustafsson and Tasiran, 1993). No account is taken of claimants who leave Göteborg and Bremen with the result that estimates of the time that people spend on benefit might be slightly understated.

[2] For a description of these state 'safety nets' in Germany and Sweden, '*Sozialhilfe*' and *Socialbidrag*, see Voges and Rohwer (1992) and Gustafsson and Tasiran (1993) respectively.

Part Five

Policy

fifteen

Making the future: from dynamics to policy agendas

Lutz Leisering and Robert Walker

The aim in publishing this volume is to contribute to the new, increasingly dynamic science of society. To understand modern society we need movies, not stills. We also need a new agenda of 'dynamic' policy making that takes account of the new realities which dynamic studies reveal and, in a political sense, create.

New concepts

The dynamic approach to society and poverty is both a theory and a method. It is a theory that explores the dynamic character of modern society and modern lives and, at the same time, provides a method needed to capture these dynamics. In Chapter One we noted that members of modern communities, unlike their ancestors in traditional societies, are subject to continual change throughout their life times – changes that ensue from the dynamics of markets, technologies, science and the large scale organisations that tinge all aspects of life. The modern individual is perpetually faced with the task of constructing a life amid external pressures for change. The 'life course' is not simply a description but has become a project in which individuals are actively and consciously engaged. Social institutions expect and ensure that people plan their lives and, in part, establish the states, events and transitions that define the life course. A crucial agency in this process is the welfare state: public policies are to a large degree 'life-course policies' aiming to sustain 'normal' life courses in a society in which risks have become a way of life.

When social life is intrinsically dynamic then dynamic methods of inquiry are naturally superior to the static approaches which have dominated earlier research. A case can be made that such approaches are indispensable since the concept of causality implies a temporal order that is fully unfolded only through longitudinal analysis. The structure of causality inherent in social processes can be reconstructed as a specific *sequence* of events leading to a certain state rather than the simplistic assumption that 'a is a cause of b' which is made in conventional analysis. For example, Jonathan Gershuny in Chapter Three depicts the use of 'narratives', life histories created from panel or event history data, as a means of reconstructing what he terms the 'recursive determination of action'. At the same time narratives provide a means to tackle the 'macro-micro problem' in social science, that is to disentangle the processes by which structural changes of society impinge on individual lives and, vice versa, how individuals' actions change large structures. While grand theories, such as historical materialism or the liberal theory of capitalism, may continue to help explain society in aggregate terms, life course studies focus on critical events and transitions in individual lives where the interaction between action and structures can be closely observed.

With the advent of appropriate data and methods the dynamic approach is transforming long established areas of social research. In Chapter Seven, Stephen McKay casts new light on the increase in lone parenthood in Britain, revealing that it is not only due simply to the rise in premarital births, separations or divorce, but also to the fact that spells as lone parents last longer. Lone parenthood may be better thought of as a life phase or state (lasting an average of six years in Britain) rather than as a means of defining a social category. Likewise, Michael Wagner and Andreas Motel in their chapter on old age from the German perspective (Chapter Eight) find not only the high degree of income stability that one might expect but also that widowhood exacerbates gender inequalities. This, it appears, is an unanticipated consequence of social security provisions which cause widowers to gain more financially through widowhood than widows.

In Chapter Five, Jutta Allmendinger and Thomas Hinz employ the new approach of dynamics to mobility studies and embrace the concept of the life course. They discover that, while class mobility is fairly similar in Britain, USA and Germany, 'job mobility' differs markedly. The reason appears to relate to the different forms of vocational training and to recruitment and promotion criteria in these countries. By looking at birth cohorts, rather than cross-sections of the population at a given point in time, Allmendinger and Hinz are in a position to trace employment trajectories while controlling for the effects of age. Cohort analysis is an indispensable part of the tool kit of dynamic analysis[1] and is also used by Petra Buhr and Andreas Weber in their study of German social assistance (Chapter Eleven). They follow cohorts of new claimants before and during the reunification of Germany and employ event-history analysis to determine both the probability of leaving social assistance and the time taken to leave. Doing so adds clarity to our understanding of the processes involved whereas focusing on the caseload at any single point would have wrought confusion by replicating the haphazard accumulation of very disparate trajectories among the claimant population.

Poverty dynamics

Since, as Simmel (1908) once remarked, poverty is a mirror or seismograph of changes in society at large, it ought to be a key focus of the dynamic study of society. As the chapters on poverty and benefit dynamics show, applying the dynamic approach to the analysis of poverty and social assistance has yielded substantive results that challenge ingrained views of the subject. The dynamic approach has not simply added the telling insight, it has established a new paradigm in the study of poverty, unemployment and other social risks.

Redefining poverty

The *measurement* of poverty, a traditional matter of concern for poverty researchers, is changed by the use of new units of reference: flows rather than stocks, spells as well as poor persons. The dynamic perspective changes the parameters of the debate adding its own new realities. For example, Peter Krause shows in

Chapter Ten that while cross-sectional measures suggest that about one tenth of Germans live below the 50% mean income line, almost one third of the German population suffered at least one spell of poverty between 1984 and 1992.

The causal *explanation* of poverty is also recast and broadened to take account of the routes through and out of poverty. The focus is on the triggers that precipitate spells of poverty as well as on the factors that mediate the impact of the triggers. So, for example, it would appear that in Britain most spells of unemployment eventually result in a period on social assistance whereas in Germany most people rely first on social insurance (see Chapters Eleven and Twelve). Dynamic analysts would also recognise that the pattern of causality can change throughout a spell of poverty, shifting from triggers to both exogenous and endogenous constraints. While the characteristics that poor people have when they enter poverty appear to be good predictors of the time they are likely to spend in poverty, the actual duration is determined by the opportunities for boosting their incomes and by their ability and willingness to take these opportunities (Chapters Thirteen and Fourteen). The ways leading out of poverty do not necessarily reflect the initial cause. It follows that a complete explanation of poverty demands an understanding of the changing pattern of causation before, during and at the end of a period of poverty.

The *classification* of the poor is equally transformed. Conventional classifications are usually based on the standard and essentially static sociodemographic variables such as employment status, household type, age or gender. This gives rise to classifications of 'problem groups' including, for example, 'the unemployed', 'single mothers', 'the elderly', that may sometimes be refined by reference to a combination of variables as in the case of 'the young unmarried single mother'. However, an unemployed person bridging a few months to their next job is in a very different life situation than someone who has been on the dole for years. Each of the conventional 'problem groups' is highly heterogeneous and time is a key dimension of this heterogeneity. Classifications of poverty based on temporal criteria such as duration and continuity of living in poverty lead to a different conception of the life situation of the poor and to different policies. Ashworth et al (1993; 1994), for example, have identified six different forms of childhood poverty based on the number, spacing and length of spells: transient, occasional, recurrent, persistent, chronic and permanent. Poverty has many faces.

Understanding poverty and dependency

The application of the new paradigm in Chapters Nine to Fourteen generates four central findings that reframe our understanding of the nature of poverty:

- *poverty is more differentiated and dynamic than allowed for in traditional accounts or generally recognised in the public debate:* there are considerable flows in and out of poverty and on and off social assistance;

- *poverty and the receipt of social assistance is not restricted to traditional marginal groups:* as a more or less transitory experience both reach well into the middle class;

- *a section of the poor population is less mobile and suffers long-term or recurrent spells of poverty:* although the proportion is much smaller than is normally assumed;

- *although poor families risk being socially excluded, many of them retain some leverage over their circumstances:* the evidence is that the majority of poor people continue as active agents rather than lapsing into a state of inert dependency upon the state.

The initial response to these findings may be that the high degree of mobility at the lower end of society is good news, whereas the advance of poverty and its associated risks into the middle class is not. Yet, these are two sides of one coin that shows that the experience of poverty is widespread and that the role of social assistance is more wide-ranging and varied than is usually thought. Whereas social assistance provides long-term income maintenance for a few, it serves variously as a safety net, springboard or trampoline for many more. As such, it emerges more often as a success story than as a failure of state intervention, although the enhanced role of social assistance points to the failings of other social institutions.

The recognition that a group of those who experience poverty suffer it for a long-term period is not in itself new. What is original is the meaning that attaches to this finding. It is evident from Chapters Nine and Ten that a large minority of the population, even in advanced industrial countries, is at risk of poverty over the medium term. Those who are afflicted, say by the trigger of unemployment, differ little from the population at large. However, the attributes that fate and life history have dealt them act powerfully to discriminate between those who rapidly leave poverty and those who stay for a longer period of time. While analyses show that the probability of escaping from poverty or benefits decreases with time, the simple assertion that this is evidence of dependency, of morally enervating effects of being on benefit, receives little support.

Three models of dependency have been distinguished in the public debate in the USA which have more general applicability (Bane and Ellwood, 1994): the rational model – generosity of benefits as compared to wages makes it irrational for claimants to leave assistance; the psycho-social (or 'expectancy') model – people want to get off benefit but they cannot because they have lost faith in their own abilities; the cultural model – people do not want to leave assistance because they have developed values different from the rest of society that endorse a life on benefits.

While the cultural model may yet apply to specific deprived areas (Chapter Fourteen provides evidence of the potential for this in Sweden) and perhaps to groups that suffer simply from social exclusion – topics not considered thoroughly in this volume – the validity of the two other models looks questionable in light of the evidence presented in Chapters Eleven to Fourteen.

Long-term claimants who provide the evidence for dependency constitute only a minority of those newly in receipt of social assistance benefit or of those who ever receive it: in Bremen (Germany), for example, only 6% of all applications for assistance made in 1989 led to an uninterrupted claiming period of six years or more (Chapter Eleven). In Germany, as in Britain, the likelihood of leaving benefit decreases the longer claimants draw benefit but this is largely due to external factors rather than pressures produced by the benefit system itself (Chapters Eleven and Fourteen). People remain on benefit for a long time because their situation of need – such as unemployment, sickness or lone parenthood – lasts for a long time (Leibfried/Leisering et al, 1995). Similarly, in Britain, there is no evidence that the time already spent on benefit has any influence on a person's propensity to remain on benefit even longer, once account is taken of the socioeconomic and demographic characteristics they had when first claiming (Chapter Fourteen). This conclusion also appears to hold for recipients of AFDC (Aid to Families with Dependant Children) in the USA (Bane and Ellwood, 1994).

Likewise, the British data reported in Chapters Twelve and Thirteen offers little evidence that benefit receipt corrupts. While life on benefit is bare and demeaning and people can become demoralised, those expected to look for work do so in large measure and some people may have cut back on the time spent seeking work just as many have increased it. Job-search continued even when the chances of finding work appeared bleak. In Britain, as in Bremen, Germany, flows off benefit into work are not greatly affected by variations in labour demand which suggests that social assistance recipients may be excluded from the mainstream labour market.

All this is not to deny that there can be 'rational' reasons for staying on benefit. These undoubtedly include uncertainty as to whether a new job will last long, whether extra costs of employment, tools, transport and so on can adequately be met from wages and whether the time until the first pay day can be bridged. However, these concerns point to problems associated with the labour market, such as insecurity and low pay, rather than to the overgenerosity of social assistance (Chapter Thirteen). The comparison between Germany and Sweden – spells are longer in Germany despite lower benefits – indicates that benefit level is less important than other factors in determining the time spent on benefit (see also a similar comparison between Germany and the USA, Duncan and Voges, 1993). Even the administrative constraints that exist, such as the complexity of the British social security system which adds to the uncertainties faced by claimants, are not necessarily flaws intrinsic to state welfare but matters of system design.

The rigorous grasp that poor people have on autonomy and agency, illustrated in this volume by the pertinacious way in which claimants continue to look for work, is best demonstrated by qualitative studies some of which have adopted an explicitly dynamic approach. Dobson et al (1994) have shown how families newly afflicted by unemployment hold on to their dietary aspirations, inserting cheaper imitations into the core of their meals. Domestic managers (typically women) seek to ringfence money for specific expenditures and use food as an economic regulator because they can adjust both quantity and quality to make space for more urgent financial demands. The demands and needs of family members have to be negotiated, negotiations that frequently leave women worse off than either their partners or children, sometimes forcing them to smoke in order to suppress their hunger (Kempson, 1996).

However, it has to be recognised that some people do not cope and fall into debt, crime or worse (Kempson, 1996). Qualitative research in Britain has drawn up a list of financial coping strategies ranked in order of acceptability (Figure 15.1) that are used by people as they slip from 'keeping their heads above water' through 'sinking' to 'drowning'. During this process, agency moves into the hands of others – creditors seek to repossess and landlords to evict, employers receive questionable references and social welfare agencies move to coercion. Exclusion becomes a reality – jobs are unobtainable, social reciprocity is impossible and social workers withdraw: file notes, once replete with details of support measures, become 'a matter of shifting names on paper' (Walker, 1995a, p 119). While the evidence, limited though it yet is, suggests that it is easier to slip down through the coping strategies than to climb back up, some people do manage to work their way back up again. Of 26 British families defined as drowning, eight were not so a year later; of 16 who were struggling, 10 were keeping their heads above water (Kempson et al, 1994).

Figure 15.1: Hierarchy of options facing families with inadequate resources

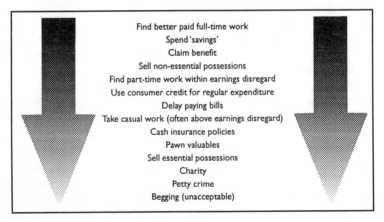

Find better paid full-time work
Spend 'savings'
Claim benefit
Sell non-essential possessions
Find part-time work within earnings disregard
Use consumer credit for regular expenditure
Delay paying bills
Take casual work (often above earnings disregard)
Cash insurance policies
Pawn valuables
Sell essential possessions
Charity
Petty crime
Begging (unacceptable)

Source: Kempson et al (1994)

However, agency for the poor means more than coping with financial hardship. Ludwig (1996) has shown that in Germany many social assistance claimants pursue wider biographical aims than just making ends meet. Their efforts are directed, for example, to raising a child as a lone parent, settling after marital break-up, recovering from an illness, preparing a vocational reorientation or finding a job.

More than three fourths of the claimants in Ludwig's qualitative study pursued such aims which in their view outweighed the material hardships they suffered. Ludwig found that people used social assistance in five different ways, ranked in order of degree and scope of coping (Figure 15.2). These findings help to explain why being on social assistance is not necessarily demoralising and why most new claimants manage to leave, even after long periods of claiming. In fact, most claimants are 'subjective bridgers' (Buhr, 1995), that is, they use social assistance to bridge critical phases in their lives – phases that may be short as in the case of most unemployed claimants, or they may be long as in the case of many lone mothers. In Germany, hopeless situations in which claimants seem to have little prospect of ever leaving benefit, often associated with low-coping capacities ('no coping' or 'financial coping only', see Figure 15.2), are mostly found among the male long-term unemployed (Ludwig, 1996).

Figure 15.2: A hierarchy of coping strategies – degree and scope of coping among social assistance claimants in Germany

- No coping ('victims')
- Financial coping only ('mere survivors')
- Pursuing wider biographical aims in a pragmatic way ('pragmatic copers')
- Pursuing wider biographical aims in a systematic way ('active copers')

- Using social assistance strategically (eligibility self-induced – 'strategic users')

Source: Ludwig (1996)

Fluidity and rigidity

If dynamic research lends itself to a principled support of the welfare state against its critics, the new picture of modern society and the modern individual that emerges is thoroughly ambivalent. At least two perspectives are apparent in the chapters of this book that may initially seem contradictory.

One perspective, employed by students of class and occupational mobility in particular, emphasises the *determination* of social processes. The German analyst Karl Ulrich Mayer, for example, refers to the life course as an 'endogenous causal nexus', noting the strong statistical correlation between family of origin, education, employment and income (Mayer, 1987a; cf Mayer, 1986). Jonathan Gershuny's notion of a 'recursive determination of activity patterns' is in many ways similar (Chapter Three). There is evidence from the USA which lends some support to the thesis of intergenerational transfer of poverty (Chapter Six), although the effects are not overwhelming and appear to be particularly sensitive to the precise nature of the trajectories of the individuals involved. Similarly, in Chapter Seven, McKay argues that increasing numbers of lone parents in Britain are at least as much a reflection of the lengthy periods of lone parenthood experienced by young unwed women from poor socioeconomic background as of divorce or separation among middle-class women.

The opposite perspective emphasises individual agency, change, choice and dynamics. For the vast majority of people thrown into poverty or forced on to benefit the experience is short-lived.

Income dynamics are vigorous with just as many people floating up the income distribution as down, albeit with some rather greater stability at the extremes (Chapters Nine and Ten). While the deterministic view reminds us of the rigidities of class and gender that act as barriers or constraints to people's life trajectories, the alternative view emphasises the fluidity of social life, opening up chances for individual self-expression and life plans, for changing the direction of your life after periods of disruption.[2]

These two conceptions of society, the former prominently proposed by Mayer and others, the latter by Giddens (1991) and Beck (1992; see also Beck et al, 1995) may appear to be diametrically opposed. Mayer (1991) maintains that some scholars mistakenly use the concept of the life course to undermine that of social inequality. However, there is a middle way that recognises the value of both perspectives and denies that they are mutually exclusive (see also Chapter Three).

The two approaches focus on different aspects of social reality and rely on different levels of analysis. The deterministic approach rests on statistical correlations of aggregate variables with a low temporal resolution, whereas the opponent approach typically employs high resolution measures of time and makes fine distinctions between different social states. Crossing the poverty line, increasing equivalent income from, say, 45% of the mean to 70%, need not impact significantly on a person's class position nor set them on a trajectory to the top half-decile. (In Germany, most movers do not seem to make it much beyond average incomes in the medium term, Chapter Ten.) Nevertheless, such changes usually have great personal significance for the individuals concerned and may well have major consequences for the roles that they play within other social domains. Moves off social assistance also clearly mark significant biographical changes as people break free from the associated stigma and attain self-sufficiency. From a policy perspective, moves of both types can be counted as significant successes.

Deterministic studies neglect changes of this order; the sociological microscope that is used is simply not powerful enough or else is not turned on to full power. To continue the analogy, cellular immunology – analysis at the level of cells – still has useful things to say even when the underlying biochemistry is ignored. Bridging this gap is an important goal in the applied medical sciences. Likewise, it is necessary to link the multiple levels of dynamic analysis in the way that Allmendinger and Hinz (Chapter Five) have begun to do. Using data from Karl Ulrich Mayer's new Eurocareers project they are able to contrast class and job mobility and to begin to link the differences to varying institutional structures in different countries.

It is easy to forget that the dynamic science of society is still in its infancy. Data sets, methods and analyses all need further elaboration. While household panel studies have been established in most European countries and comprehensive data sets like the Berlin Life Course Study (Mayer and Brückner, 1988) have been exploited at length, longitudinal data is expensive to generate and many fields of study are not yet adequately covered. Cross-national comparative datasets, such as the Europanel and Eurocareers, have only just been started and hence their potential has yet to be unleashed. Much more work of both a technical and substantive nature is required to investigate properly the sequences of transitions between varied states that typically define a person's life course. Likewise, we need to be able to investigate more comprehensively the intersections between trajectories in different domains and to explore the joint impact of different institutions (as in Chapter Twelve). There is also a great need better to integrate quantitative and qualitative approaches to dynamic analysis. As Gershuny (Chapter Three) notes, qualitative analysis can make sense of what appears as chaotic in the light of quantitative data. What appears as uniform in the light of quantitative socioeconomic variables may turn out to be highly variegated when looked at qualitatively through the eyes of the social actors themselves.

A new agenda for politics

The dynamic science of society calls for a new agenda of policy making, for 'dynamic policy-making' as David Ellwood terms it (Chapter Four). The agenda includes policies that are more sensitive to the life trajectories of the people concerned, that seek to identify the potential for change, and that recognise the crucial transitions in individual lives that indicate points where support could make a difference; policies that build on the agency of people in need and aim at restoring capabilities, and policies that secure self-esteem and dignity for those with limited capacities for self-help.

Impact of dynamics on policy

Policy makers are already moving in this direction driven by pressures on public expenditure and with the aim of making state welfare cheaper and, perhaps, more cost effective. Dynamic research and researchers have already made an impact on policies in several countries. In Chapter Four, David Ellwood recounts his experiences as Assistant Secretary in the US Department of Health and Human Services, and draws attention to the potential, intricacies and dangers of exploiting dynamic analyses at the heart of public policies. While the results show that public concern for long-term claiming and dependency had been grossly exaggerated, welfare state critics took up the theme 'duration' only to rehearse the old lament of 'welfare mothers' and 'scroungers'. While Ellwood established a link between what society can demand of claimants and what it has to do to enable them to meet these demands, the Republicans cut that link by calling for demands, but dropping support.[3]

The 1996 reform of social assistance in Germany also drew on dynamic concepts but moved in the opposite direction to those being introduced in the USA in the same year. The new measures sought to enable unemployed claimants to move off assistance more easily (by introducing wage subsidies to employers and taking increased disregard of earned income) without substantially reducing benefits. Provisions designed to help claimants cope better financially were actually improved: by strengthening immediate help in case of impending homelessness due to rent arrears and in case of over-indebtedness. Discretionary payments for clothing and other items of everyday living were transformed into standardised, lump sum cash benefits, which, it might be argued, increase claimants' autonomy and control over their own finances.

While leading social policy makers of the ruling Christian parties such as Ulf Fink and minister Horst Seehofer, made constructive use of the dynamic analysis of poverty,[4] some colleagues within the parties used the same results to play down the severity of poverty in Germany, drawing on the Bremen evidence of social assistance dynamics (Deutscher Bundestag, 1996, Chapters 11 and 14). Dynamic ideas have also been influential in local government, the level at which social assistance is implemented. Several municipalities, including Hamburg or Osnabrück, have successfully implemented measures to facilitate people to move off benefit, most notably by the appointment of 'exit advisors'.

Elsewhere within the German political spectrum, the justification for the basic income plan of the Green Party published in October 1996, which amounts to a wholesale modernisation of social assistance and the large-scale abolition of discretion, was derived from the Bremen longitudinal study of social assistance. To date, the Social Democrats have been little moved by the new analyses, while the trade unions and, above all, welfare associations first tended to reject the new ideas since they saw them as a challenge to their traditional role as advocates of the poor.

In Britain, too, dynamic analysis has accompanied political change and stimulated new thinking about welfare policies. The introduction of Jobseeker's Allowance by the outgoing Conservative government in 1996 was explicitly designed to shorten the time claimants spent unemployed both to reduce expenditure, and to increase the outflows into work so as to exert a downward pressure on wage rates through extra competition. It aims to achieve this by making more explicit the obligation on claimants to seek work as a condition of receiving benefit. If Jobseeker's Allowance was the stick, Earnings Top-Up, an in-work benefit for people without children which is being piloted, was to be the carrot. Several other reforms were introduced between 1994 and 1996 to smooth the transition between benefit and work and the research reported in Chapter Thirteen is officially credited to have informed the introduction of six separate reforms. Broadly, the same approach was adopted in the 1997 Labour Party Manifesto although, at the time of writing (May 1997), there are rumours of a range of views within the new Labour Government between those who emphasise the obligations which should be placed on jobseekers, and those that believe in the importance of support systems.

Interpretation of the results of scientific research appears to cut across party lines. It may be that the new dynamic science touches on newly emerging aspects of society that transcend the ideological models of society: conservative, liberal and social-democratic. Perhaps ideas relevant to the 21st century are about to replace those which originated in the 19th century.

The shape of dynamic policies

The new agenda points towards a differentiated policy targeted on specific events, transitions and episodes in people's lives rather than a policy designed with regard to static and aggregate problem groups such as 'the' unemployed, lone parents or 'the' elderly. It is a policy strategy that builds on the agency of those in need, a pro-active policy aiming to identify critical points of intervention early in problem careers.

Figure 15.3 provides a map of transitions to and from the labour market that provide points of intervention for policy. Whereas in the past a person might have expected to pass through each transition only once, milestones on a life time journey from education to retirement, such transitions today serve as gates to new opportunities that need to be opened several times. Figure 15.3 tells only half of the story. Men and women have to coordinate interdependent trajectories that unfold simultaneously, such as their employment and family careers. The aim of dynamic policy making is to speed the passages through these gates and to equip people with the skills and resources needed to exploit opportunities that are available and to cope with set-backs if necessary.

Pro-active policy may initially be more expensive since it generally requires investment in people to provide them with professional and technical support. In the middle and longer term it should pay dividends, reducing the time that people spend unproductively or even destructively, and enabling them to cope better with the uncertainty and change that is so much a feature of modernity.

Dynamic analyses may also point to new policies in response to newly identified realities. For example, it has been suggested that the notions of post-industrial poverty, discussed in Chapter One, call for new and newly differentiated responses. Transient spells of poverty might best be tackled by schemes that facilitate a person to spread their income across a longer period through saving or borrowing. Chronic or permanent poverty necessitates measures that redistribute resources between different people and sections of society, either in the form of cash transfers or through the provision of services to enhance the quality of life. Equally, though, it should not be assumed that the circumstances of all the long-term unemployed are homogeneous: the different narratives of their life trajectories will reveal much about their ability to respond to policy initiatives. Policy has to be increasingly flexible and differentiated to adapt to the variegated and rapidly changing realities created by the new economic order.

Dynamic policies also lead back to old ideas of *preventive* social protection. Many claimants of social assistance would be best helped by improved social security benefits which prevent them from falling on to the last safety net. The potential here for

Figure 15.3: Labour market transitions

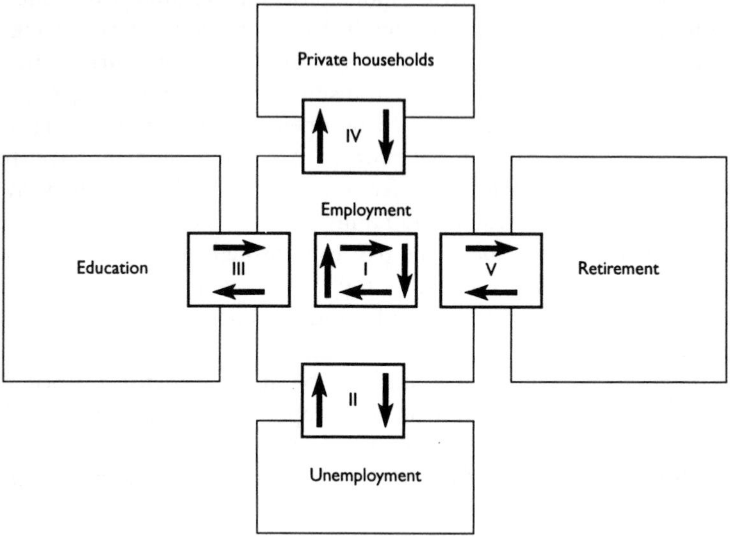

Notes:

I   Transitional arrangements between short-time working and full-time
employment or between dependent work and self-employment

II   Transitional arrangements between unemployment and employment

III   Transitional arrangements between education and employment

IV   Transitional arrangements between private domestic activities and
employment

V   Transitional arrangements between employment and retirement

Source: Adapted from Günther Schmid, cited in Reissert (1996)

unemployment benefits is obvious but changes need to be made to allow these benefits to operate better in a flexible labour market. Likewise, insurance-based pension provisions have almost extinguished poverty in old age in many countries but the restructuring of old age pensions currently debated has the potential to reintroduce destitution among the elderly in the middle years of the 21st century. The de-indexing of state pensions in Britain has already increased poverty in old age, putting into reverse the progress of half a century. However, preventive policies are not easily designed or implemented. This applies, in particular, to labour market policies designed to reduce unemployment.

Dynamic policies are policies for the 'life course' (Chapter One) and involve decisions about what we want life courses to look like. These include:

- Which life trajectories are desirable or acceptable, what life plans deserve support and which ones do not?

- For how long should lone parents be entitled to state benefits without being forced to earn a wage? Should the time be linked to the number and age of their children?

- For how long should unemployed people or casualties of accidents be supported by state benefits, at which level and with what degree of pro-active support?

- What standard of living should people be entitled to when they will never be able to earn an income because of chronic illness or disability?

There are other conundrums of a more strategic nature to be addressed:

- Which groups of people should be entitled to how much time out of the labour market?

- Should social policies aim to support similar life course patterns for men and women, as in Sweden, or should labour market policies and social security favour the traditional male breadwinner model (Chapters Five and Fourteen).

- Should people in old age have a right to the same living standard as people of working age?

- Should children have a right not to live in poverty irrespective of their parents' income?

- What type of transitional help should be available to help immigrants to integrate socially, for how long should it last and should it depend upon the type of immigration?

Social justice has to be redefined and specified with reference to the dimension of time.

Future perspectives

In a time when unprecedented change spans global forces and individual lives, the dynamic science of society helps to identify and define the challenges which society confronts and offers portfolios of possible policy responses. While no one can predict the future, contributions to this volume have shed light on political responses to recent dynamics and have commented on future scenarios.

During the British economic recession of the early 1990s, while the conventional instruments of social security, Unemployment Benefit, Income Support and Housing Benefit, were stretched to their limits, they nevertheless protected the state from the social unrest and political crises that occurred at a time of a similar recession during the 1930s (Chapter Twelve). However, concerns about high expenditure and about the time that people were spending on benefits led to the battery of reforms described above. While there is consensus on the need for pro-active policies, the appropriate balance between encouragement and deterrence is still contested.

At the same time Germany was facing the even greater problem of the economic transformation and incorporation of the former GDR command economy, initially facilitated by an unification boom in both parts of the country. However, the colossal size of the problems – 40% of the labour force made redundant in one stroke – was met by an equally colossal political response. With the social budget soaring to 73% of the East German gross domestic product in 1992, welfare spending reached an unprecedented scale. Active labour market policies, largely unheard of before unification, and comprehensive systems of early retirement offered routes out of unemployment and poverty. In this way the growth of poverty was kept to manageable proportions, eventually to converge to West German levels. For many East Germans it was a difficult, but transitory, experience (Chapter Ten).[5]

The other challenge for German social policy, namely the immigration of national Germans from Eastern Europe and the former Soviet Union, also ensued from the collapse of communism and was similarly met by social security systems. For most immigrants social assistance acted as a transitory bridge of integration into German society (Chapter Eleven). However, as in

Britain, escalating expenditure became the engine of restrictive reform: refugees seeking asylum became the first group to be excluded from the right to social assistance when a separate scheme with lower benefits was introduced in November 1993. This scheme was designed as a barrier to integration into German society and as a deterrent not to come to Germany in the first place.

The new challenges that confront societies at the end of the 20th century may require more thoroughgoing and imaginative solutions. Some argue that economic globalisation exerts a uniform pressure towards deregulation on all nation states, although Pierson (1996), for one, refutes this notion as a new and mistaken version of the old convergence thesis. There may still be different paths of development with, as Allmendinger and Hinz (Chapter Five) note, different institutions creating distinct opportunities and risks for individuals.

Whatever scenario will materialise, the new society to emerge is likely to involve an increasing variety of forms of self-expression and life chances as well as increased insecurities.[6] This is part of the ambivalence of modern society. As the contributions to this volume testify, social risks not only trap some people into social exclusion but expose many to the uncertainties typical of modern life courses. What will come out of this? Are we going to adapt to these new ways of living? Will we be able to develop a 'culture of discontinuity'?[7]

Prospects are not as bleak as some would make us believe. New ways of thinking, new forms of social life are already emerging. Dahrendorf (1997, p 123), for example, has noted that:

> Former and present-day lives of women are more characteristic of the world to come than present-day lives of men.... In women's lives there has always been part-time work or interruptions of careers, always much work not counted in statistics of gross national product though it was not less hard. It was always necessary to react to new demands of private or occupational life in a more flexible way than men do who kept climbing the steps upward'.[8]

Beck (1992) and Giddens (1991) emphasise that the current stage of modern society involves not only dissolution of old structures and divisions but also the emergence of new forms of integration.

The dynamics of modern society are neither heading towards a deregulated world where everything is possible nor, so we hope, towards social entropy and the immobility of social exclusion or, for that matter, to the iron cage of bureaucratisation that Weber envisaged. A dynamic society requires more, not less institutions, ones that exhibit flexibility in their ability to enable and assist individuals to pursue their life goals. A reformed welfare state is one such institution,[9] the shape of which is a key choice to be made through the democratic process. In fighting poverty, illness and other contingencies of modern life by way of institutional control, 'existential questions become institutionally repressed at the same time as new fields of opportunity are created for social activity and for personal development' (Giddens, 1991, p 164f). We cannot escape the ambivalence of modern society.

Notes

[1] See the classic article by Ryder (1965) and the elaboration of the cohort approach in the light of event history analysis by Mayer and Huinink (1990).

[2] For examples of this type of work in the field of family studies see Furstenberg et al (1987) for a longitudinal study of adolescent mothers in later life, and Wallerstein and Blakeslee (1989) for a longitudinal study of the consequences of divorce. Anthony Giddens (1991) makes a more general point on the ambivalence of modern institutions and illuminates the idea of his book by starting with a depiction of the optimistic results of the latter study in his first chapter.

[3] See DeParle's fascinating account (1996) of the rise and fall of Ellwood as a major force of welfare reform.

[4] See Fink's (1997) moving account of the political impact of dynamic research.

[5] Against all expectation, claiming social assistance equally became only a transitory experience for most applicants, just like in West Germany (Rentzsch and Buhr 1996).

[6] Berger (1996) sees these two sides as joint facets of Beck's notion of 'individualisation'.

[7] We owe this term to Heinz Bude.

[8] Translated by Lutz Leisering/Robert Walker.

[9] See also Leibfried and Rieger (1995) who argue that the nations newly participating in the global economy need to build welfare states and are actually already starting to do so. Similarly, the old welfare states are calling for restructuring, not for dismantling social protection altogether.

Bibliography

Aguilar, R. and Gustafsson, B. (1994) 'Immigrants in Sweden's labour market during the 1980s', *Scandinavian Journal of Social Welfare*, vol 3, pp 139-47.

Allmendinger, J. (1989) 'Educational systems and labour market outcomes', *European Sociological Review*, vol 5, pp 231-50.

Allmendinger, J. (1994) *Lebenslauf und Sozialpolitik. Die Ungleichheit von Mann und Frau und ihr öffentlicher Ertrag*, Frankfurt am Main/New York, NY: Campus.

Allmendinger, J. and Brückner, E. (1991) 'Arbeitsleben und Lebensarbeitsentlohnung: Zur Entstehung von finanzieller Ungleichheit im Alter', in K.U. Mayer, J. Allmendinger and J. Huinink (eds) *Vom Regen in die Traufe: Frauen zwischen Beruf und Familie*, Frankfurt am Main: Campus, pp 423-59.

Allmendinger, J. and Hinz, Th. (1997) 'Mobilität und Lebensverlauf', in S. Hradil and S. Immerfall (eds) *Die westeuropäischen Gesellschaften im Vergleich*, Opladen: Leske und Budrich, pp 247-85.

An, C., Haveman, R. and Wolfe, B. (1992) *The 'window problem' in studies of children's attainment*, Cambridge: National Bureau of Economic Research, Technical Working Paper 125.

Andreß, H.-J. (1994) 'Steigende Sozialhilfezahlen. Wer bleibt, wer geht und wie sollte die Sozialverwaltung darauf reagieren? Eine Analyse der Bezugsdauer von Sozialhilfe mit Hilfe der Bielefelder Datenbank Sozialhilfe-Statistik', in M. Zwick (ed) *Finmal arm, immer arm? Neue Befunde Zur Armut in Deutschland*, Frankfurt am Main/New York, NY: Campus, pp 75-105.

Ashworth, K. and Walker, R. (1995) 'Measuring claimant populations', in N. Buck, J. Gershuny, D. Rose and J. Scott (eds) *Changing households*, Colchester: ESRC Research Centre on Micro-Social Change.

Ashworth, K., Hill, M. and Walker, R. (1993) 'A new approach to poverty dynamics', *Bulletin de Methodologie Sociologique*, vol 38, pp 14-37.

Ashworth, K., Hill, M. and Walker, R. (1994) 'Patterns of childhood poverty: New challenges for policy', *Journal of Policy Analysis and Management*, vol 13, no 4, pp 658-80.

Ashworth, K., Walker, R. and Trinder, P. (1997a) *The dynamics of Income Support and Unemployment Benefit*, Working Paper 242S, Loughborough: CRSP.

Ashworth, K., Walker, R. and Trinder, P. (1997b) *Benefit dynamics in Britain: Routes on and off Income Support*, Working Paper 253S, Loughborough: CRSP.

Atkinson, A.B. (1983) *The economics of inequality*, 2nd edn, Oxford: Clarendon Press.

Atkinson, A.B. (1989) *Poverty and social security*, London: Harvester Wheatsheaf.

Bäcker, G. (1995) 'Altersarmut – Frauenarmut: Dimensionen eines sozialen Problems und sozialpolitische Reformoptionen', in W. Hanesch (ed) *Sozialpolitische Strategien gegen Armut*, Opladen: Westdeutscher Verlag, pp 275-403.

Backes, G.M. (1994). 'Armut im Alter – (k)ein Thema mehr (?)!', *Neue Praxis*, vol 24, no 2, pp 119-31.

Balsen, W., Nakielski, H., Rössel, K. and Winkel, R. (1984) *Die Neue Armut – Ausgrenzung von Arbeitslosen aus der Arbeitslosenunterstützung*, Köln: Bund Verlag.

Baltes, P.B., Mayer, K.U., Helmchen, H. and Steinhagen-Thiessen, E. (1993) 'The Berlin Aging Study (BASE): Overview and design', *Ageing and Society* (Special Issue 'The Berlin Aging Study'), vol 13, pp 483-515.

Baltes, P.B., Mayer, K.U., Helmchen, H. and Steinhagen-Thiessen, E. (1996) 'Die Berliner Altersstudie (BASE): Überblick und Einführung', in K.U. Mayer and P.B. Baltes (eds) *Die Berliner Altersstudie* , Berlin: Akademie Verlag, pp 21-54.

Bane, M.J. and Ellwood, D.T. (1986) 'Slipping in and out of poverty: the dynamics of spells', *Journal of Human Resources*, vol 21, no 1, pp 1-23.

Bane, M. and Ellwood, D. (1994) *Welfare realities: From rhetoric to reform*, Cambridge, MA: Harvard University Press.

Barnes, M., Ashworth, K. and Walker, R. (1997) *Predicting the length of spells on Income Support using administrative and survey data*, Working Paper 259aS, Loughborough: CRSP.

Beck, U. (1983) 'Jenseits von Klasse und Stand? Soziale Ungleichheit, gesellschaftliche Individualisierungsprozesse und die Entstehung neuer sozialer Formationen und Identitäten', in R. Kreckel (ed) *Soziale Ungleichheiten*, Göttingen: Schwartz, pp 35-74.

Beck, U. (1986) *Risikogesellschaft: Auf dem Weg in eine andere Moderne*, Frankfurt am Main: Suhrkamp.

Beck, U. (1992) *Risk society. Towards a new modernity*, London: Sage (German 1986: *Risikogesellschaft. Auf dem Weg in eine andere Moderne*, Frankfurt am Main: Suhrkamp).

Beck, U., Giddens, A. and Lash, S. (1995) *Reflexive modernisation. Politics, tradition and aesthetics in the modern social order*, Cambridge: Polity Press.

Becker, G.S. (1964) *Human capital: A theoretical and empirical analysis, with special reference to education*, New York, NY: Columbia University Press for National Bureau of Economic Research.

Becker, G.S. (1976) *Economic approach to human behaviour*, Chicago, IL: University of Chicago Press.

Becker, G.S. (1981) *A treatise on the family*, Cambridge, MA: Harvard University Press.

Becker, W.E. and Lewis, D.R. (1993) 'Preview of higher education and economic growth', in W.E. Becker and D.R. Lewis (eds) *Higher education and economic growth*, Boston, MA: Kluwer Academic Publishers, pp 1-20.

Benjamin, O. (1995) *The marital conversation and the domestic division of labour*, unpublished D Phil thesis, Oxford University.

Berger, P.A. (1996) *Individualisierung. Statusunsicherheit und Erfahrungsvielfalt*, Opladen: Westdeutscher Verlag.

Biernacki, R. (1995) *The fabrication of labour. Germany and Britain, 1650-1914*, Berkeley, CA: University of California Press.

Bingley, P. and Walker, I. (1997) *Household unemployment and the labour supply of married women*, Working Paper W97/1, London: Institute for Fiscal Studies.

Blossfeld, H.P. and Rohwer, G. (1995) *Techniques of event history modelling: New approaches to causal analysis*, Mahwak, NJ: Erlbaum.

Bolderson, H. and Mabbett, D. (1995) 'Mongrels or thoroughbreds: a cross-national look at social security systems', *European Journal of Political Research*, vol 28, pp 119-39.

Bolte, K.M. (1983) 'Anmerkungen zu Aspekten und Problemen der Erforschung sozialer Ungleichheit', in R. Kreckel (ed) *Soziale Ungleichheiten*, Göttingen: Schwartz, pp 391-407.

Bottomley, D., McKay, S. and Walker, R. (1997) *Unemployment and jobseeking*, DSS Research Report 62, London: Stationary Office.

Bourdieu, P. (1984) *Distinction: A social critique of the judgement of taste*, London: Routledge and Kegan Paul.

Bradshaw, J. and Millar, J. (1991) *Lone parent families in the UK*, London: HMSO.

Brandon, P. (1993) 'Trends over time in the educational attainment of single mothers', *Focus*, vol 15, no 2, pp 26-34.

Brose, H.-G. and Hildenbrand, B. (1988) 'Biographisierung von Erleben und Handeln', in H.-G. Brose and B. Hildenbrand (eds) *Vom Ende des Individuums zur Individualität ohne Ende*, Opladen: Leske und Budrich.

Brückner, H. (1995) 'Poverty in transition? Life course, social policy, and changing images of poverty', in Dan A. Chekki (ed) *Urban poverty in affluent nations*, Greenwich, CT und London: JAI Press (Research in Community Sociology no 5).

Büchel, F. and Hauser, R. (1998) 'Dynamic approaches to comparative social policy analyses. A methodological framework', in W. Voges and G. Duncan (eds) *Dynamic approaches to comparative social research. Recent developments and application*, Aldershot: Avebury (forthcoming).

Buck, N., Gershuny, J., Rose, D., and Scott, J. (eds) (1994) *Changing households: The British Household Panel Survey 1990-1992*, Colchester: ESRC Research Centre on Micro-Social Change, University of Essex.

Buhr, P. (1991) 'Plädoyer für eine dynamische Armutsforschung – das Modell der USA', *Zeitschrift für Sozialreform*, vol 37, pp 415-33.

Buhr, P. (1995) *Dynamik von Armut. Dauer und biographische Bedeutung des Sozialhilfebezugs*, Opladen: Westdeutscher Verlag.

Buhr, P. and Voges, W. (1998) 'Akten als Datenquelle Die Bremer Längschnitts-Stichprobe von Sozialhilfeakten (LSA)', in W. Voges (ed) *Kommunale Sozialberichterstattung*, Opladen: Leske und Budrich (forthcoming).

Bundesministerium für Arbeit und Sozialordnung (ed) (1992a) *Alterssicherung in Deutschland 1986* (vol IV: Haushalte und Ehepaare), Bonn.

Bundesministerium für Arbeit und Sozialordnung (ed) (1992b) *Alterssicherung in Deutschland 1986. Zusammenfassender Bericht: Einkommenssituation der Bevölkerung ab 55 Jahren*, Bonn.

Bundesministerium für Arbeit und Sozialordnung (ed) (1994) *Übersicht über das Sozialrecht*, Bonn.

Bundesministerium für Arbeit und Sozialordnung (ed) (1995) *Sozialgesetzbuch*, Bonn.

Bundesministerium für Wirtschaft (BMWI) (1994) *Wirtschaft in Zahlen*, Bonn.

Burkhauser, R.V. and Duncan, G.J. (1989) 'Economic risks of gender roles: Income loss and life events over the life course', *Social Science Quarterly*, vol 70, no 1, pp 3-23.

Burkhauser, R.V., Holden, F. and Feaster, D. (1988) 'Incidence timing and events associated with poverty: A dynamic view of poverty in retirement', *Journal of Gerontology*, vol 43, pp 846-52.

Centre for Research in Social Policy (CRSP) (1993) *Barriers to people moving off Income Support*, Project Proposal 70, Loughborough: CRSP.

Cherlin, A. (1992) *Marriage, divorce, remarriage*, London: Harvard University Press.

Corcoran, M. (1995) 'Rags to rags: The intergenerational transmission of poverty', *Annual Review of Sociology*, vol 21, pp 237-67.

Corcoran, M. and Boggess, S. (1994) *The intergenerational transmission of poverty and inequality: A review of the literature*, Report to the New Zealand Department of the Treasury, Wellington, New Zealand.

Cox, D. (1972), 'Regression models and life tables', *Journal of the Royal Statistical Society B*, vol 34, pp 187-203.

Dahrendorf, R. (1988) *The modern social conflict. An essay on the politics of liberty*, London: Weidenfeld and Nicolson (rev German edn 1992: *Der moderne soziale Konflikt. Essay zur Politik der Freiheit*, Stuttgart: Deutsche Verlags-Anstalt).

Dahrendorf, R. (1997) '*Die wahre Revolution*', Interview with Ralf Dahrendorf, *Der Spiegel*, special issue 1947-97, pp 112-23.

DaVanzo, J. and Goldscheider, F.K. (1990) 'Coming home again', *Population Studies*, vol 44, pp 241-55.

Davies, M. (1995) 'Household incomes and living standards: The interpretation of data on very low incomes', Analytical Notes Number 4, London: DSS Analytical Services Division.

Dawes, L. (1993) *Long-term unemployment and labour market flexibility*, Leicester: Centre for Labour Market Studies.

Deacon, A. (1996) 'Welfare and character', in F. Field, *Stakeholder welfare*, London: Institute for Economic Affairs.

Dean, H. and Taylor-Gooby, P. (1992) *Dependency culture: The explosion of a myth*, London: Harvester Wheatsheaf.

DeParle, J. (1996) 'Mugged by reality', *The New York Times Magazine*, December 8, pp 64-100.

Department of Social Security (DSS) (1993) *The growth of social security*, London: HMSO.

Department of Social Security (DSS) (1995) *Households below average income 1979-1992/93*, London: HMSO.

Department of Social Security (DSS) (1996) *Department of Social Security Press Release 96/177*, London: DSS.

Deutscher Bundestag (1996) *Stenographischer Bericht*, 126, Sitzung, Bonn, 27/9/1996 (Parliamentary Papers).

Dex, S. (1984) *Women's work histories: An analysis of the women and employment survey*, London: Department of Employment Research Paper 46.

Dieck, M., and Naegele, G. (1993) '"Neue Alte" und alte soziale Ungleichheiten – vernachlässigte Dimensionen in der Diskussion des Altersstrukturwandels', in G. Naegele and H.P. Tews (eds) *Lebenslagen im Strukturwandel des Alters. Alternde Gesellschaft – Folgen für die Politik*, Opladen: Westdeutscher Verlag, pp 43-60.

Dobson, B., Walker, R., Middleton, S., Beardsworth, A. and Keil, T. (1994) *Diet, choice and poverty*, London: Family Policy Studies Centre.

Duncan, G.J. (ed) (1984) *Years of poverty, years of plenty. The changing econonic fortunes of American workers and families*, Ann Arbor: Institute for Social Research.

Duncan, G.J. (1988) 'The volatility of family income over the life course', in P. Baltes, D.L. Featherman and R.M. Lerner (eds) *Life-span development and behavior*, Hillsdale, NJ: Lawrence Erlbaum Associates, pp 317-57.

Duncan, G.J. and Voges, W. (1993) *Do generous social assistance programs lead to dependence? A comparative study of lone-parent families in Germany and the United States*, Working Paper No 11/93, Centre for Social Policy Research, University of Bremen.

Duncan, G.J., Gustafsson, B., Hauser, R., Schmaus, G., Jenkins, S., Messinger, H., Muffels, R., Nolan, B., Ray, J.-C. and Voges, W. (1991) 'Poverty and social assistance dynamics in the United States, Canada and Europe', shortened in K. Fate, R. Lawson and W.J. Wilson (eds) *Poverty, inequality and the future of social policy: Western states in the new world order*, New York, NY: Russell Sage, pp 65-108.

Eardley, T., Bradshaw, J., Ditch, J., Gough, I. and Whiteford, P. (1996) *Social assistance in OECD countries*, DSS Research Report 46, London: HMSO.

Ehmer, J. (1990) *Sozialgeschichte des Alters*, Frankfurt am Main: Suhrkamp.

Erikson, R. and Goldthorpe, J.H. (1992) *The constant flux. A study of class mobility in industrial societies*, Oxford: Clarendon Press.

Ermisch, J. (1991) *The economics of lone parenthood*, London: National Institute for Economic and Social Research.

Ermisch, J. (1995) 'Pre-marital cohabitation, childbearing and the creation of one parent families', *Working Papers of the ESRC Research Centre on Micro-Social Change*, Paper 95-17 Colchester: University of Essex.

Ermisch, J. and Francesconi, M. (1996) *Partnership formation and dissolution in Great Britain*, Working Paper 96-10, Colchester: ESRC Research Centre on Micro-Social Change.

Esping-Andersen, G. (1990) *The three worlds of welfare capitalism*, Oxford: Polity Press.

Esping-Andersen, G. (1993) *Changing classes. Stratification and mobility in post-industrial societies*, London: Sage.

Esping-Andersen, G. (ed) (1996) *Welfare states in transition*, London, Thousand Oaks and New Delhi: Sage.

Eurostat (ed) (1995) *Poverty statistics in the late 1980s*, Study by J. Aldi, M. Hagenaars, Klaas de Vos and M. Asghar Zaidi, Luxembourg: Theme 3 Population and Social Conditions, Series C.

Falkingham, J. and Hills, J. (eds) (1995) *The dynamic of welfare. The welfare state and the life cycle*, London: Harvester Wheatsheaf.

Field, F. (1995) *Making welfare work: Reconstructing welfare for the millennium*, London: Institute of Community Studies.

Fink, U. (1997) 'Zeit der Armut – Zeit für Politik', *Zeitschrift für Sozialreform*, vol 43, pp 156-64.

Ford, R., Marsh, A. and McKay, S. (1995) *Changes in lone parenthood 1989-93*, London: HMSO.

Fukuyama, F. (1996) *Trust. The social virtues and the creation of prosperity*, New York, NY: Free Press.

Furstenberg, F.F., Brooks-Gunn, J. and Morgan, P.S. (1987) *Adolescent mothers in later life*, Cambridge: Cambridge University Press.

Furstenberg, F.F., Levine, J. and Brooks-Gunn, J. (1990) 'The children of teenage mothers', *Family Planning Perspectives*, vol 22, pp 54-61.

Gallie, D., Marsh, C. and Vogler, C. (eds) (1994) *Social change and the experience of unemployment*, Oxford: Oxford University Press.

Gallon, T.-P., Bank, H.-P. and Kreikebohm, R. (1994) 'Flexibles System eigenständiger und leistungsbezogener Alterssicherung (FleSelAs) – Konzeption einer Weiterentwicklung der Gesetzlichen Rentenversicherung (Teile-1-111)', *Neue Zeitschrift für Sozialrecht*, vol 3, pp 385-444, 444-50, 489-96.

Garfinkel, I. and McLanahan, S. (1986) *Single mothers and their children: A new American dilemma*, Washington: Urban Institute Press.

Gauthier, A.H. (1996) 'The measured and unmeasured effects of welfare benefits on families: Implications for Europe's demographic trends' in D. Coleman (ed) *Europe's population in the 1990s*, Oxford: Oxford University Press.

Gershuny, J. and Marsh, C. (1994) 'Unemployment in work histories', in D. Gallie, C. Marsh and C. Vogler (eds) *The sociology of unemployment*, Oxford: Oxford University Press.

Giddens, A. (1984) *The constitution of society: Outline of the theory of structuration*, Cambridge: Polity Press.

Giddens, A. (1991) *Modernity and self-identity. Self and society in the late modern age*, Cambridge: Polity Press.

Giddens, A. (1994) *Beyond left and right. The future of radical politics*, Cambridge: Polity Press.

Glennerster, H. (1995) 'The life cycle: Public or private concern?', in J. Falkingham and J. Hills (eds) (1995) *The dynamic of welfare. The welfare state and the life cycle*, London: Harvester Wheatsheaf.

Glotz, P. (1985) *Manifest für eine Neue Europäische Linke*, Berlin: Siedler.

Goldscheider, F.K. and DaVanzo, J. (1989) 'Pathways to independent living in early adulthood', *Social Forces*, vol 65, pp 187-201.

Goodman, A. and Webb, S. (1994) 'For richer, for poorer: The changing distribution of income in the UK, 1961-1991', *IFS Commentary No 42*, London: Institute for Fiscal Studies.

Goodman, A. and Webb, S. (1995) 'The distribution of UK household expenditure', *IFS Commentary No 49*, London: Institute for Fiscal Studies.

Gottschalk, P. (1994) 'Is the correlation in welfare participation across generations spurious?', *Journal of Boston Economics*, vol 63, no 1, pp 1-5.

Granovetter, M. (1985) 'Economic action and social structure: The problem of embeddedness', *American Journal of Sociology*, vol 91, pp 481-510.

Gustafsson, B. (1984) 'Macroeconomic performance, old age security and the rate of social assistance recipients in Sweden', *European Economic Review*, vol 26, pp 319-38.

Gustafsson, B. and Tasiran, A. (1993) 'Social assistance in Sweden: What do microdata tell us?', Paper presented at the annual meeting of European Society of Population Economics, Budapest, June.

Gustafsson, S. (1992) 'Separate taxation and married women's labour supply. A comparison of West Germany and Sweden', *Journal of Population Economics*, vol 5, pp 61-85.

Gustafsson, S., Vlasblom, J.-D. and Wetzels, C. (1995) 'Women's labour force transitions in connection with child birth. A comparison between Germany and Sweden', Paper presented at the *15th Arne Ryde Symposium*, Rungstedgaard, Denmark.

Habich, R. and Krause, P. (1992) 'Niedrigeinkommen und Armut', in Statistisches Bundesamt (ed) *Datenreport 1992*, Bonn, pp 482-95.

Hagenaars, A.J.M. (1986) *The perception of poverty*, Amsterdam, New York, NY and Oxford: North-Holland.

Hansen, H. (1995) 'Net replacement rates and reservation wages for low income earners', Paper presented at the annual meeting of European Society for Population Economics, Lisbon, June.

Hauser, R. and Berntsen, R. (1992) 'Einkommensarmut – Determinanten von Aufstiegen und Abstiegen', in R. Hujer, H.

Schneider and W. Zapf (eds) *Herausforderungen an den Wohlfahrtsstaat im strukturellen Wandel*, Frankfurt am Main/New York, NY: Campus, pp 73-97.

Hauser, R. and Wagner, G. (1992) 'Altern und soziale Sicherung', in P.B. Baltes and J. Mittelstraß (eds) *Zukunft des Alterns und gesellschaftliche Entwicklung*, Berlin/New York, NY: de Gruyter, pp 581-613.

Haveman, R. and Wolfe, B.L. (1994) *Succeeding generations*, New York, NY: Russell Sage Foundation.

Haveman, R., Wolfe, B. and Spalding, J. (1991) 'Childhood events and circumstances influencing high school completion', *Demography*, vol 28, pp 133-57.

Headey, B., Habich, R. and Krause, P. (1990) *The duration and extent of poverty – Is Germany a two-thirds-society?*, Berlin, Social Science Research Centre, no P 90-103.

Helmchen, H., Baltes, M.M., Geiselmann, B., Kanowski, S., Linden, M., Reischies, F.M., Wagner, M. and Wilms, H.-U. (1996) 'Psychische Erkrankungen im Altern', in K.U. Mayer and P.B. Baltes (eds) *Die Berliner Altersstudie*, Berlin: Akademie Verlag, pp 185-219.

Hill, D., Axinn, W.G. and Thornton, A. (1993) 'Competing hazards with shared unmeasured risk factors', *Sociological Methodology*, vol 23, pp 245-78.

Hill, M.S. (with assistance of the staff of the PSID) (1992) *The panel study of income dynamics: A user's guide*, Newbury Park, London, New Delhi: Sage Publications.

Hill, M.S. (1992) *The panel study of income dynamics*, Newbury Park, London, New Delhi: Sage Publications.

Hill, M.S., Yeung, W.J. and Duncan, G.J. (1996) *Parental family structure across childhood and young adulthood behaviors*, mimeo, University of Michigan, Ann Arbor.

Hirsch, F. (1977) *Social limits to growth*, London and Henley: Routledge & Kegan Paul.

Hirvonen, P. (1993) *Alterssicherung und Alterseinkommens-verteilung. Eine empirische Analyse der Einkommenslage der älteren Bevölkerung in der Bundesrepublik Deutschland*, Frankfurt/New York, NY: Campus.

Hochschild, A. (1990) *The second shift*, London: Piatkus.

Hoffman, S.D., Foster, E.M. and Furstenberg, F.F. (1993) 'Reevaluating the costs of teenage childbearing', *Demography*, vol 30, no 1, pp 1-13.

Hoffmann, T. (1995) *Strukturen und Einstellungen: Sozialpolitische Regimes und Geschlechterkulturen im europäischen Vergleich*, unpublished dissertation, University of Munich.

Hope, K. and Goldthorpe, J.H. (1974) *The social grading of occupations*, Cambridge: Cambridge University Press.

Hoskins, H. (1971) *The Hindu religious tradition*, Encino: Dickenson.

Howe, W. (1993) 'The effects of higher education on unemployment rates', in W. Becker and D. Lewis (eds) *Higher education and economic growth*, Boston, MA: Kluwer Academic Publishers, pp 129-44.

Hradil, S. (1990) 'Postmoderne Sozialstruktur? Zur empirischen Relevanz einer "modernen" Theorie sozialen Wandels', in P.A. Berger and S. Hradil (eds) *Lebenslagen, Lebensläufe, Lebensstile*, Göttingen: Schwartz, pp 125-50.

Huinink, J., Mayer, K.U., Diewald, M., Solga, H., Sørensen, A. and Trappe, H. (1995) *Kollektiv und Eigensinn, Lebensverläufe in der DDR und danach*, Berlin: Akademie, Verlag.

Hutton, W. (1995) *The state we're in*, London: Vintage.

Jahoda, M., Lazarsfeld, P. and Zeisel, H. (1971) *Marienthal. The sociography of an unemployed community*, Aldine: Atherton (German 1980: *Die Arbeitslosen von Marienthal. Ein soziographischer Versuch*, Frankfurt am Main: Suhrkamp, first edn 1933).

Janowitz, M. (1976) *Social control of the welfare state*, New York, NY, Oxford, Amsterdam: Elsevier.

Jarvis, S. and Jenkins, S.P. (1995) *Do the poor stay poor? New evidence about income dynamics from the British Household Panel Survey*, Occasional Paper No 95-2, Colchester: ESRC Research Centre on Micro-Social Change, University of Essex.

Jenkins, S.P. (1991) 'Poverty measurement and the within-household distribution: Agenda for action', *Journal of Social Policy*, vol 20, no 4, pp 457-83.

Jenkins, S.P. (1996) 'Recent trends in the UK income distribution: What happened and why', *Oxford Review of Economic Policy*, vol 12, pp 29-46.

Jenkins, S.P. and Millar, J. (1989) 'Income risk and income maintenance: Implications for incentives to work', in A. Dilnot and I. Walker (eds) *The economics of social security*, Oxford: Oxford University Press, pp 137-52.

Kaufmann, F.-X. (1975) 'Makro-soziologische Überlegungen zu den Folgen des Geburtenrückgangs in industriellen Gesellschaften', in F.-X. Kaufmann (ed) *Bevölkerungsbewegung zwischen Quantität und Qualität*, Stuttgart: Enke.

Kaufmann, F.-X. and Leisering, L. (1984) 'Demographic changes as a problem for social security systems', *International social security review*, vol 37, pp 388-409.

Kempson, E. (1996) *Life on a low income*, York: York Publishing Service.

Kempson, E., Bryson, A. and Rowlingson, K. (1994) *Hard times? How poor people make ends meet*, London: Policy Studies Institute.

Kohli, M. (1986) 'The world we forgot: An historical review of the life course', in V.M. Marshall (ed) *Later life: The social psychology of aging*, Beverly Hills, CA: Sage.

Kohli, M. (1989) 'Moralökonomie und "Generationenvertrag"', in M. Haller (ed) *Kultur und Gesellschaft. Verhandlungen des 24. Deutschen Soziologentags*, Frankfurt/New York, NY: Campus. pp 532-55.

Kohli, M. and Künemund, H. (1997) *Nachberufliche Tätigkeitsfelder – Konzepte, Forschungslage, Empirie*, Stuttgart: Kohlhammer.

Kohli, M., Guillemard. A.-M. and Gunsteren, H. van (eds) (1992) *Time for retirement: Comparative studies of early exit from the labour force*, Cambridge: Cambridge University Press.

Krause, P. (1994) 'Zur zeitlichen Dimension von Einkommensarmut', in W. Hanesch, W. Adamy, R. Martens, D. Rentzsch, U. Schneider, U. Schubert and M. Wißkirchen, *Armut in Deutschland. Der Armutsbereicht des DGB und das Paritätischen Wohlfahrtsverbands*, Reinbek: Rowohlt, pp 189-206.

Leibfried, S. (1987) 'Projektantrag: Sozialhilfekarrieren – Wege aus der und durch die Sozialhilfe und ihre sozialstaatliche Rahmung', in W. Heinz (ed) *Statuspassagen und Risikolagen im Lebensverlauf*, University of Bremen, mimeo, pp 801-61.

Leibfried, S. and Pierson, P. (eds) (1995) *European social policy between fragmentation and integration*, Washington, DC: Brookings.

Leibfried, S. and Rieger, E. (1995) *Conflicts over Germany's competitiveness ('Standort Deutschland'): Exiting from the global economy?*, Occasional Paper, University of California at Berkeley: Center for German and European Studies.

Leibfried, S. and Tennstedt, F. (1985) *Politik der Armut und die Spaltung des Sozialstaats*, Frankfurt am Main: Suhrkamp.

Leibfried, S., Leisering, L., Buhr, P., Ludwig, M., Mädje, E., Olk, T., Voges, W. and Zwick, M. (1995) *Zeit der Armut. Lebensläufe im Sozialstaat*, Frankfurt am Main: Suhrkamp (revised and updated English edition forthcoming with Cambridge University Press, 1998).

Leisering, L. (1992) *Sozialstaat und demographischer Wandel. Wechselwirkungen, Generationenverhältnisse, politisch-institutionelle Steuerung*, Frankfurt/New York, NY: Campus.

Leisering, L. (1995a) *Lebenslauf als Politik*, University of Bremen, mimeo.

Leisering, L. (1995b) 'Zweidrittelgesellschaft oder Risiko-gesellschaft? Zur gesellschaftlichen Verortung der "Neuen Armut" in der Bundesrepublik', in K.-J. Bieback. and H. Milz (eds) *Neue Armut*, Frankfurt am Main/New York, NY: Campus.

Leisering, L. (1997) 'Individualisierung und "sekundäre Institutionen" – der Sozialstaat als Voraussetzung des modernen Individuums', in U. Beck and P. Sopp (eds) *Individualisierung und Integration. Neue Konfliktlinien und neuer Integrationsmodus?*, Opladen: Leske und Budrich, pp 143-59.

Leisering, L. and Voges, W. (1992) 'Erzeugt der Wohlfahrtsstaat seine eigene Klientel? Eine theoretische und empirische Analyse von Armutsprozessen', in S. Leibfried and W. Voges (eds) *Armut im modernen Wohlfahrtsstaat, Kölner Zeitschrift für Soziologie und Sozial-psychologie*, Special Issue 32, Opladen: Westdeutscher Verlag, pp 475-95.

Leisering, L. and Voges, W. (1996) 'Secondary poverty in the welfare state. Do social security institutions create their own clients?', in H. Bojer, N. Keilman, J. Lyngstad and I. Tomsen (eds) *Poverty and distribution*, Oslo: Scandinavian University Press.

Leisering, L., Buhr, P. and Gangl, M. (1997) 'Kleine Revolution', *Die Mitbestimmung*, vol 43, no 10, pp 39-42.

Lewis, O. (1959) *Five families. Mexican case studies in the culture of poverty*, New York, NY: Science Editions.

Lindenberger, U., Gilberg, R., Pötter, U., Little, T.D., and Baltes, P.B. (1996) 'Stichprobenselektivität und Generalisierbarkeit der Ergebnisse in der Berliner Altersstudie', in K.U. Mayer and P.B. Baltes (eds) *Die Berliner Altersstudie*, Berlin: Akademie Verlag, pp 85-108.

Lister, R., Middleton, S. and Vincent, V. (1997) *Negotiating transitions to citizenship*, Project Proposal 218, Loughborough: CRSP.

Ludwig, M. (1996) *Armutskarrieren. Zwischen Abstieg und Aufstieg im Sozialstaat*, Opladen: Westdeutscher Verlag.

Luhmann, N. (1977) 'Differentiation of society', *Canadian Journal of Sociology*, vol 2, pp 29-53.

Luhmann, N. (1990) 'Meaning as sociology's basic concept', in N. Luhmann, *Essays on self-reference*, New York, NY: Columbia University Press, pp 21-79.

Maas, I. and Staudinger, U.M. (1996) 'Lebensverlauf und Altern: Kontinuität und Diskontinuität der gesellschaftlichen Beteiligung, des Lebensinvestments und ökonomischer Ressourcen', in K.U. Mayer and P.B. Baltes (eds) *Die Berliner Altersstudie*, Berlin: Akademie Verlag, pp 543-72.

Maas, I., Borchelt, M. and Mayer, K.U. (1996) 'Kohortenschicksale der Berliner Alten', in K.U. Mayer and P.B. Baltes (eds) *Die Berliner Altersstudie*, Berlin: Akademie Verlag, pp 109-34.

Mannheim, K. (1952) 'The problem of generations', in K. Mannheim, *Essays on the sociology of knowledge*, New York, NY: Oxford University Press (German 1928: 'Das Problem der Generationen', *Kölner Vierteljahreshefte für Soziologie*, vol 7, no 2, pp 157-85, no 3, pp 309-30).

Marini, M. (1984) 'Age and sequencing norms in the transition to adulthood', *Social Forces*, vol 63, no 1, pp 229-44.

Marsh, A., Ford, R. and Finlayson, L. (1997) 'Lone parents', *Work and Benefits*, London: Stationary Office.

Marshall, T.H. (1950) 'Citizenship and social class', in T.H. Marshall (1964) *Class, citizenship and social development*, Chicago, IL and London: University of Chicago Press, pp 71-134.

Marshall, T.H. (1972) 'Value problems of welfare capitalism', in T.H. Marshall (1981) *The right to welfare*, London: Heinemann, pp 104-37.

Massey, D.S. (1996) 'The age of extremes: Concentrated affluence and poverty in the twenty-first century', *Demography*, vol 33, no 4, pp 395-412.

Maurice, M. and Sellier, F. (1979) 'A societal analysis of industrial relations: A comparison between France and West Germany', *British Journal of Industrial Relations*, vol 17, pp 322-36.

Mayer, K.U. (1986) 'Structural constraints on the life course', *Human Development*, vol 29, pp 163-71.

Mayer, K.U. (1987a) 'Lebenslaufforschung', in W. Voges (ed) *Methoden der Biographie- und Lebenslaufforschung*, Opladen: Leske und Budrich, pp 51-73.

Mayer, K.U. (1987b) 'Zum Verhältnis von Theorie und empirischer Forschung zur sozialen Ungleichheit', in B. Giesen and H. Haferkamp (eds) *Soziologie der sozialen Ungleichheit*, Opladen: Westdeutscher Verlag, pp 370-92.

Mayer, K.U. (1991) 'Soziale Ungleichheit und die Differenzierung von Lebensverläufen', in W. Zapf (ed) *Die Modernisierung moderner Gesellschaften. Verhandlungen des Deutschen Soziologentages in Frankfurt am Main, 1990*, Frankfurt am Main/New York, NY: Campus, pp 667-87.

Mayer, K.U. and Blossfeld, H.P. (1990) 'Die gesellschaftliche Konstruktion sozialer Ungleichheit im Lebebsverlauf', in P.A. Berger and S. Hradil (eds) *Lebenslagen, Lebensläufe, Lebensstile*, Göttingen: Schwartz, pp 297-318.

Mayer, K.U. and Brückner, E. (1988) *Lebensverläufe und Wohlfahrtsentwicklung. Konzeption, Design und Methodik der Erhebung von Lebensverläufen der Geburtsjahrgänge 1921-1931, 1939-1941, 1949-1951*, Materialien aus der Bildungsforschung Nr 35, Max-Planck-Institute for Human Development and Education, Berlin.

Mayer, K.U. and Carroll, G.R. (1987) 'Jobs and classes: Structural constraints on career mobility', *European Sociological Review*, vol 3, pp 14-38.

Mayer, K.U. and Huinink, J. (1990) 'Age, period and cohort in the study of the life course: A comparison of classical A-P-C-analysis with event history analysis or farewell to Lexis?', in S. Magnusson and L.R. Bergman (eds) *Data quality in longitudinal research*, Cambridge: Cambridge University Press, pp 211-32

Mayer, K.U. and Müller, W. (1986) 'The state and the structure of the life-course', in A.B. Sørensen, F.E. Weinert and L.R. Sherrod (eds) *Human development and the life-course*, Hillsdale, NJ: Erlbaum, pp 217-45.

Mayer, K.U. and Müller, W. (1989) 'Individualisierung und Standardisierung im Strukturwandel der Moderne. Lebensverläufe im Wohlfahrtsstaat', in A. Weymann (ed) *Handlungsspielräume*, Stuttgart: Enke, pp 41-60.

Mayer, K.U. and Schoepflin, U. (1989) 'The state and the life course', *Annual Review of Sociology*, vol 15, pp 187-209.

Mayer, K.U. and Wagner, M. (1993) 'Socio-economic resources and differential ageing', *Ageing and Society* (Special Issue 'The Berlin Aging Study'), vol 13, no 4, pp 517-50.

Mayer, K.U. and Wagner, M. (1996) 'Lebenslagen und soziale Ungleichheit im hohen Altern', in K.U. Mayer and P.B. Baltes (eds) *Die Berliner Altersstudie*, Berlin: Akademie Verlag, pp 251-75.

McKay, S. and Marsh, A. (1994) *Lone parents and work: The effects of benefits and maintenance*, London: HMSO.

McLanahan, S.S. and Sandefur, G.D. (1994a) *Uncertain childhood, uncertain future*, Cambridge, MA: Harvard University Press.

McLanahan, S.S. and Sandefur, G.D. (1994b) *Growing up with a single parent: What hurts, what helps*, London: Harvard University Press.

Meissner, M., Humphries, E.W., Meis, S.M., and Scheu, W.J. (1975) 'No exit for wives: Sexual division of labour and the cumulation of household demands', *Canadian Review of Sociology and Anthropology*, vol 12, pp 424-39.

Meyer, J.W. (1986a) 'Myths of socialization and of personality', in T.C. Heller, M. Sosna and D.E. Wellbery (eds) *Reconstructing individualism*, Stanford, CA: Stanford University Press.

Meyer, J.W. (1986b) 'The self and the life course: Institutionalization and its effects', in A.B. Sørensen, F. Weinert and L.R. Sherrod (eds) *Human development and the lifecourse*, Hillsday NJ: Erlbaum, pp 199-216.

Middleton, S., Ashworth, K. and Braithwaite, I. (1997) *Small fortunes: Spending on children, childhood poverty and parental sacrifice*, Working Paper No 274A, Loughborough: CRSP.

Motel, A. and Wagner, M. (1993) 'Armut im Alter? Ergebnisse der Berliner Altersstudie zur Einkommenslage alter und sehr alter Menschen', *Zeitschrift für Soziologie*, vol 22, no 6, pp 433-48.

Mückenberger, U. (1985) 'Die Krise des Normalarbeitsverhältnisses – Hat das Arbeitsrecht noch eine Zukunft?', *Zeitschrift für Sozialreform*, vol 31, no 7, pp 415-34 (part 1); no 8, pp 457-75 (part 2).

Müller, W., Shavit, Y. and Ucen, P. (1996) 'The institutional embeddedness of the stratification process: A comparative study of qualifications and occupations in 13 countries', Paper presented at the 1996 meetings of the American Sociological Association, New York City.

Murray, C. (1984) *Losing ground: American Social Policy 1950-1980*, New York, NY: Basic Books.

Myles, J. (1995) *After the golden age: Labour market polarisation and the Canadian public policy*, Tallahassee, FL: Florida State University.

Nuthmann, R. and Wahl, H.-W. (1996) 'Methodische Aspekte der Erhebungen der Berliner Altersstudie', in K.U. Mayer and P.B. Baltes (eds) *Die Berliner Altersstudie*, Berlin: Akademie Verlag, pp 55-83.

O'Higgins, M., Bradshaw, J. and Walker, R. (1988) 'Income distribution over the life cycle', in R. Walker and G. Parker (eds) *Money matters: Income, wealth and financial welfare*, London: Sage, pp 227-53.

Oberender, P. and Streit, M.E. (eds) (1995) *Europas Arbeitsmärkte im Integrationsprozess*, Baden-Baden: Nomos.

Office for Population Consensus and Surveys (OPCS) (1994) *General Household Survey*, London: HMSO.

Organization for Economic Co-operation and Development (OECD) (1992a)*OECD Economic Outlook 52*, December, Paris: OECD.

OECD (1992b) *OECD Employment Outlook*, July, Paris: OECD.

OECD (1994) *OECD – Revenue Statistics 1965-93*, Paris: OECD.

OECD (1995a) *OECD Economic Outlook*, July, Paris: OECD.

OECD (1995b) *OECD Employment Outlook*, July, Paris: OECD.

OECD (1995c) *Labour Force Statistics*, July, Paris: OECD.

Ostner, I. and Voges, W. (1995) 'Verschwindet der Ernährer-Ehemann?', in K.-J. Bieback and H. Milz (eds) *Neue Armut*, Frankfurt am Main/New York, NY: Campus, pp 93-106.

Parsons, T. (1966) *Societies: Evolutionary and comparative perspectives*, Englewood Cliffs, NJ: Prentice Hall, Inc.

Parsons, T. and Platt, G.M. (1974) *The American university*, Cambridge, MA: Harvard University Press.

Pencavel, J. (1993) 'Higher education, economic growth and earnings', in W.E. Becker and D.R. Lewis (eds) *Higher education and economic growth*, Boston, MA: Kluwer Academic Publishers, pp 51-85.

Pfaff, A. (1992) 'Feminisierung der Armut durch den Sozialstaat?', in S. Leibfried and W. Voges (eds) *Armut im modernen Wohlfahrtsstaat*, Opladen: Westdeutscher Verlag, pp 421-45.

Piachaud, D. (1992) 'Wie mißt man Armut', in S. Leibfried and W. Voges (eds) *Armut im modernen Wohlfahrtsstaat*, Opladen: Westdeutscher Verlag, pp 63-87.

Pierson, P. (1996) 'The new politics of the welfare state', *World Politics*, vol 48, pp 147-79.

Pirog-Good, M.A. (1993) *The education and labor market outcomes of adolescent fathers*, Discussion Paper 1014, Madison: Institute for Research on Poverty.

Reif, H. (1982) 'Soziale Lage und Erfahrungen des alternden Fabrikarbeiters in der Schwerindustrie', *Archiv für Sozialgeschichte*, vol 22, pp 1-94.

Reissert, (1996) 'How are social protections systems coping with change? A comparative approach', Paper presented at the 1996 Joint ETUC/ETUI Annual Conference, Brussels, 7-8 November.

Rendtel, U. (1990) 'Teilnahmebereitschaft in Panelstudien: Zwischen Beeinflussung, Vertrauen und Sozialer Selektion', in *Kölner Zeitschrift für Soziologie und Sozialpsychologie*, vol 42, pp 280-99.

Rendtel, U. and Wagner, G. (eds) (1991) *Lebenslagen im Wandel: Zur Einkommensdynamik in Deutschland seit 1984*, Frankfurt am Main/New York, NY: Campus.

Rendtel, U., Langeheine, R. and Berntsen, R. (1992) 'The estimation of poverty-dynamics using different Household Income Measures', *European Scientific Network on Household Panel Studies* (ESF), Working Paper No 50, Colchester: University of Essex.

Rendtel, U., Wagner, G. and Frick, J. (1995) 'Eine Strategie zur Kontrolle von Längsschnittgewichtungen in Panelerhebungen – Das Beispiel des Sozio-Oekonomischen Panels (SOEP)', *Allgemeines Statistisches Archiv*, vol 79, 3, S 252-77.

Rentzsch, D. and Buhr, P. (1996) *Im Osten nichts Neues? Sozialhilfeverläufe in Ost- und Westdeutschland im Vergleich*, Bremen: Special Research Programme 186 (Sfb 186, Working Paper no 41).

Room, G. (ed) (1995) *Beyond the threshold. The measurement and analysis of social exclusion*, Bristol: The Policy Press.

Rose, D., Dex, S., Taylor, M., Clark, A. and Perren, K. (1994) 'Changes in economic activity', in N. Buck, J. Gershuny, D. Rose and J. Scolt (eds) *Changing households*, Colchester: ESRC Research Centre on Micro-Social Change, pp 154-98.

Rowntree, B.S. (1901) *Poverty. A study of town life*, 2nd edn, London: Thomas Nelson & Sons.

Rutter, M. and Madge, N. (1976) *Cycles of disadvantage. A review of research*, London: Heinemann.

Ryder, N.B. (1965) 'The cohort as a concept in the study of social change', *American Sociological Review*, vol 30, pp 843-61.

Sainsbury, D. (1994) 'Women's and men's social rights', in D. Sainsbury (ed) *Gendering welfare states*, London: Sage.

Samson, R. (1992) 'Analyse der Bezugsdauer von Hilfe zum Lebensunterhalt anhand der Abrechnungsdaten der Stadt Bielefeld', in N. Johrendt, H.R. Schneider (eds) *Computergestützte Sozialbereichterstallung und Sozialplanung*, Bielefeld: Berufsverband Deutscher Soziologen, vol 11.

Schlomann, H. (1992) *Vermögensverteilung und private Altersvorsorge*, Frankfurt am Main/New York, NY: Campus.

Shaw, A. and Walker, R. (1996) 'Disjointed interaction: The labour market and the benefit system', in P. Meadows (ed) *Work out or work in?*, York: York Publishing Service/Joseph Rowntree Foundation, pp 87-115.

Shaw, A., Walker, R., Ashworth, K., Jenkins, S. and Middleton, S. (1996a) *Moving off Income Support: Barriers and bridges*, DSS Research Report 53, London: HMSO.

Shaw, A., Kellard, K. and Walker, R. (1996b) *Barriers, bridges and behaviour*, in-house report 18, London: DSS.

Simmel, G. (1908) 'Der Arme', *Soziologie*, Berlin: Duncker und Humblot, pp 345-74 (English 1965: 'The poor', *Social problems*, vol 13, pp 118-40).

Solon, G. (1992) 'Intergenerational mobility in the United States', *American Economic Review*, vol 82, pp 393-408.

Soskice, D. (1990) 'Reinterpreting corporatism and explaining unemployment: Coordinated and non-coordinated market economies', in R. Brunetta and C. Dell'Aringa (eds) *Labour relations and economic performance*, London: Macmillan, pp 170-211.

Soskice, D. (1994) 'Reconciling markets and institutions: The German apprenticeship system', in L.M. Lynch (ed) *Training and the private sector*, Chicago, IL: University of Chicago Press, pp 25-60.

Statistisches Bundesamt (ed) (1994) *Datenreport. Zahlen und Fakten über die Bundesrepublik Deutschland* (vol 6: 1993/94), München: Bonn Aktuell.

Strasser, H. (1987) 'Diesseits von Stand und Klasse: Prinzipien einer Theorie der sozialen Ungleichheit', in B. Giesen and H. Haferkamp (eds) *Soziologie der sozialen Ungleichheit*, Opladen: Westdeutscher Verlag, pp 50-92.

Taylor, A. (1994) 'Appendix: Sample characteristics, attrition and weighting' in N. Buck, J. Gershuny, D. Rose and J. Scolt (eds), *Changing households*, Colchester: ESRC Research Centre on Micro-Social Change, pp 291-311.

Taylor, M.F. (ed) (1994) *British Household Panel Survey user manual. Introduction, technical reports and appendices*, Colchester: ESRC Research Centre on Micro-Social Change, University of Essex.

Taylor, M.P., Keen, M., Buck, N. and Corti, L. (1994) 'Income, welfare and consumption', in N. Buck, J. Gershuny, D. Rose and J. Scolt (eds), *Changing households*, Colchester: ESRC Research Centre on Micro-Social Change, pp 88-113.

Unell, J., Leeming, A. and Walker, R. (1994) *Lone mothers*, DSS Research Report, London: HMSO.

van Oorschot, W. (1994) 'Take it or leave it', *TISSER Series on Work and Social Security*, Tilburg: Tilburg University Press.

Vermunt, J. (1996) *Log-linear event history analysis*, Tilburg: Tilburg University Press.

Voges, W. and Klein, P. (1994) '"Creaming the poor" in Beschäftigungsprogrammen als Ergebnis unsystematischer Ansprache von Adressaten', in M. Schulze-Böing and N. Johrendt (eds) *Wirkungen kommunaler Beschäftigungsprogramme*, Stuttgart: Birkhäuser.

Voges, W. and Rohwer, G. (1992) 'Receiving social assistance in Germany: Risk and duration', *Journal of European Social Policy*, vol 2, pp 175-92.

Voges, W. and Weber, A. (1998) 'Armut und Sozialhilfebezug von Ausländern und Zuwanderern', in W. Voges (ed) *Kommunale Sozialberichterstattung*, Opladen: Leske und Budrich (forthcoming).

Voges, W. and Zwick, M.M. (1991) 'Die Bremen Stichprobe von Sozialhilfeakten: Möglichkeiten für die empirische Sozialforschung', *Zeitschrift für Soziologie*, vol 20, pp 77-81.

Wagner, G., Motel, A., Spieß, K. and Wagner, M. (1996) 'Wirtschaftliche Lage und wirtschaftliches Handeln alter Menschen', in K.U. Mayer and P.B. Baltes (eds) *Die Berliner Altersstudie*, Berlin: Akademie Verlag, pp 277-99.

Wagner, M. and Kanowski, S. (1995) 'Socio-economic resources, life course, and dementia in old age', in M. Bergener, J.C. Brocklehurst and S.I. Finkel (eds) *Aging, health, and healing*, New York, NY: Springer, pp 475-85.

Wagner, M. and Motel, A. (1996) 'Die Qualität der Einkommensmessung bei alten Menschen', *Kölner Zeitschrift für Soziologie und Sozialpsychologie*, vol 48, no 3, pp 493-512.

Walker, R. (1988) 'The costs of household formation', in R. Walker and G. Parker (eds) *Money matters: Income, wealth and financial welfare*, London: Sage, pp 9-26.

Walker, R. (1994) 'Income Support and the dynamics of recession', *Benefits*, vol 10, pp 25-6.

Walker, R. with Ashworth, K. (1994) *Poverty dynamics: Issues and examples*, Aldershot: Avebury.

Walker, R. (1995a) 'The dynamics of social exclusion', in G. Room (ed) *Beyond the threshold*, Bristol: The Policy Press, pp 102-28.

Walker, R. (1995b) 'Benefit dynamics targeting and take-up', in W. van Oorschot (ed) *New perspectives on the non-take-up of social security benefits*, Tilburg: TISSER Series on Work on Social Security, pp 97-127.

Walker, R. (1997a) 'Poverty and social exclusion in Europe', in A. Walker and C. Walker (eds) *Britain divided*, London: CPAG.

Walker, R. (1997b) 'Rethinking poverty', in H.-J. Andreß (ed) *Empirical poverty research in a comparative perspective*, Aldershot: Avebury.

Walker, R. and Huby, M. (1989) 'Social security spending in the United Kingdom', *Government and Policy*, no 7, pp 321-40.

Walker, R. and Wiseman, M. (1997) *An earned income tax credit for Britain: Possibilities and alternatives*, Working Paper 303S, Loughborough: CRSP.

Walker, R., Hull, L. and Shaw, A. (1995) 'Responding to the risk of unemployment', in ABI *Risk, insurance and welfare*, London: Association of British Insurers, pp 37-52.

Wallerstein, J. and Blakeslee, S. (1989) *Second chances*, London: Bantam.

Webb, S. (1995) 'Poverty dynamics in Great Britain: Preliminary analysis from the British Household Panel Survey', *IFS Commentary No 48*, London: Institute for Fiscal Studies.

Weber, A. (1912) 'Das Berufsschicksal der Industriearbeiter', *Archiv für Sozialwissenschaft und Sozialpolitik*, vol 34, pp 377-405.

Wiseman, M. (1996) 'Welfare reform in the United States: A background paper', *Housing Policy Debate*, vol 7, pp 595-648.

Wrong, D. (1961) 'The oversocialised conception of man in modern sociology', *American Sociological Review*, vol 26, no 2, pp 183-93.

Yamaguchi, K. (1991) *Event history analysis*, Newbury Park: Sage, Applied Research Methods, 28.

Zacher, H. (1987) 'Grundtypen des Sozialrechts', in W. Fürst, R. Herzog and D.C. Umbach (eds) *Festschrift für Wolfgang Zeidler*, Berlin: de Gruyter, pp 571-95.

Ziegler, R., Brüderl, J. and Diekmann, A. (1989) 'Stellensuchdauer und Anfangseinkommen bei Hochschulabsolventen. Ein empirischer Beitrag zur Job-Search-Theorie', *Zeitschrift für Wirtschafts – und Sozialwissenschaften*, vol 108, pp 247-70.

Zimmermann, K. (1993) 'Labour response to taxes and benefits in Germany' in A.B. Atkinson and G.V. Mogensen (eds) *Welfare and work incentives*, Oxford: Oxford University Press.

Zwick, M.M. (ed) (1994) *Einmal arm, immer arm? Neue Befunde zur Armut in Deutschland*, Frankfurt am Main/New York, NY: Campus.

Index